**50% OFF!**

EMT Online Test Prep Course

We consider it an honor and a privilege that you chose our EMT Study Guide. As a way of showing our appreciation and to help us better serve you, we have partnered with Mometrix Test Preparation to offer you 50% off their online EMT Prep Course.

Mometrix has structured their online course to perfectly complement your printed study guide. Many EMT courses are needlessly expensive and don't deliver enough value. With their course, you get access to the best EMT prep material, and you only pay half price.

WHAT'S IN THE EMT TEST PREP COURSE?

- ✓ **EMT Study Guide**: Get access to content that complements your study guide.

- ✓ **Progress Tracker**: Their customized course allows you to check off content you have studied or feel confident with.

- ✓ **450+ Practice Questions**: With 450+ practice questions and lesson reviews, you can test yourself again and again to build confidence.

- ✓ **EMT Flashcards**: Their course includes a flashcard mode consisting of over 556 content cards to help you study.

TO RECEIVE THIS DISCOUNT, VISIT THE WEBSITE AT

link.mometrix.com/emt

USE THE DISCOUNT CODE:
STARTSTUDYING

IF YOU HAVE ANY QUESTIONS OR CONCERNS, PLEASE CONTACT MOMETRIX AT SUPPORT@MOMETRIX.COM

Free Video   Free Video

Essential Test Tips Video from Trivium Test Prep

Dear Customer,

Thank you for purchasing from Trivium Test Prep! We're honored to help you prepare for your EMT exam.

To show our appreciation, we're offering a **FREE EMT *Essential Test Tips* Video by Trivium Test Prep.*** Our video includes 35 test preparation strategies that will make you successful on the EMT. All we ask is that you email us your feedback and describe your experience with our product. Amazing, awful, or just so-so: we want to hear what you have to say!

To receive your **FREE *EMT Essential Test Tips* Video**, please email us at 5star@triviumtestprep.com. Include "Free 5 Star" in the subject line and the following information in your email:

1. The title of the product you purchased.

2. Your rating from 1 – 5 (with 5 being the best).

3. Your feedback about the product, including how our materials helped you meet your goals and ways in which we can improve our products.

4. Your full name and shipping address so we can send your **FREE *EMT Essential Test Tips* Video**.

If you have any questions or concerns please feel free to contact us directly at 5star@triviumtestprep.com.

Thank you!

– Trivium Test Prep Team

*To get access to the free video please email us at 5star@triviumtestprep.com, and please follow the instructions above.

NREMT STUDY GUIDE 2025-2026:

2 Practice Tests and EMT Exam Prep Book
[7th Edition]

Jeremy Downs

Copyright ©2025 by Ascencia Test Prep

ISBN: 9781637985199

ALL RIGHTS RESERVED. By purchase of this book, you have been licensed one copy for personal use only. No part of this work may be reproduced, redistributed, or used in any form or by any means without prior written permission of the publisher and copyright owner. Ascencia Test Prep, Trivium Test Prep, Accepted, and Cirrus Test Prep are all imprints of Trivium Test Prep, LLC.

The National Registry of Emergency Medical Technicians (NREMT) was not involved in the creation or production of this product, is not in any way affiliated with Ascencia Test Prep, and does not sponsor or endorse this product. All test names (and their acronyms) are trademarks of their respective owners. This study guide is for general information only and does not claim endorsement by any third party.

Image(s) used under license from Shutterstock.com

Table of Contents

Online Resources i
Introduction..............................iii

1 Human Anatomy and Physiology 1
THE BIOLOGICAL HIERARCHY 1
DIRECTIONAL TERMINOLOGY AND PLANES............................2
THE CARDIOVASCULAR SYSTEM...................3
THE RESPIRATORY SYSTEM.......................... 12
THE SKELETAL SYSTEM 14
THE MUSCULAR SYSTEM 17
THE NERVOUS SYSTEM 19
THE GASTROINTESTINAL SYSTEM 22
THE IMMUNE SYSTEM 24
THE ENDOCRINE SYSTEM 25
THE REPRODUCTIVE SYSTEM 27
THE URINARY SYSTEM............................... 31
THE INTEGUMENTARY SYSTEM 32
PHARMACOLOGY....................................... 33
ANSWER KEY... 37

2 Patient Assessment and Transfer...................... 39
ASSESSING THE SCENE 39
ASSESSING THE PATIENT 43
MOVING THE PATIENT 53
ANSWER KEY... 57

3 Respiratory Emergencies 59
AIRWAY, RESPIRATION, AND VENTILATION.................................. 59

ACUTE PULMONARY EDEMA 66
AIRWAY OBSTRUCTION.............................. 67
ASTHMA 68
CHRONIC OBSTRUCTIVE PULMONARY DISEASE (COPD).................... 70
PULMONARY ASPIRATION........................... 71
HYPERVENTILATION 72
PLEURAL EFFUSION 73
PNEUMOTHORAX...................................... 74
PULMONARY EMBOLISM 75
RESPIRATORY INFECTIONS 76
ANSWER KEY... 78

4 Cardiovascular Emergencies 79
THE ROLE OF EMTS IN CARDIOVASCULAR EMERGENCIES... 79
ACUTE CORONARY SYNDROME................... 85
CARDIAC ARREST 87
AORTIC ANEURYSM 88
HYPERTENSIVE CRISIS 89
SHOCK.. 90
ANSWER KEY... 93

5 Medical Emergencies 95
ABDOMINAL PAIN 95
ANAPHYLACTIC SHOCK 96
GASTROINTESTINAL BLEEDING................... 97
HEADACHE.. 98
HYPERGLYCEMIA 99
HYPOGLYCEMIA....................................... 100
SUDDEN INFANT DEATH SYNDROME (SIDS) 101

- Seizure 102
- Stroke 103
- Answer Key 105

6 Environmental Emergencies 107
- Bites 107
- Cold Exposure 108
- Heat Exposure 110
- High-Altitude Emergencies 112
- Electrical Injuries 113
- Submersion Injuries 114
- Answer Key 116

7 Psychiatric Emergencies 117
- Pathophysiology 117
- Psychiatric Conditions 118
- Approaching a Behavioral Crisis 119
- Using Restraints 120
- Answer Key 122

8 Trauma 123
- Amputation 123
- Blast Injuries 124
- Bleeding 125
- Burns 127
- Crush Injuries 129
- Facial Injuries 129
- Eye Injuries 131
- Falls 132
- Motor Vehicle Crash 132
- Neck Injuries 135
- Orthopedic Injuries 135
- Penetration Injuries and Impaled Objects 140
- Sexual Assault 141
- Soft Tissue Injuries 142
- Spine Injuries 143
- Traumatic Brain Injuries 144
- Answer Key 147

9 Obstetrical Emergencies 149
- Anatomy and Physiology of Pregnancy 149
- Labor and Delivery 150
- Pregnancy and Delivery Complications 152
- Care of the Neonate 154
- Answer Key 156

10 Pharmacology and Toxicology 157
- Pharmacology 157
- Drug Overdose 164
- Substance Withdrawal 169
- Carbon Monoxide and Cyanide Poisoning 170
- Answer Key 171

11 Special Populations 173
- Geriatric Patients 173
- Pediatric Patients 176
- Answer Key 180

12 EMS Operations 181
- EMT Scope of Practice 181
- Patient Communication 182
- Professional Communication and Documentation 183
- Maintaining the Truck 184
- Driving to the Scene and Receiving Facility 185
- Postrun 186
- Legal and Ethical Considerations 187
- Answer Key 192

13 The Psychomotor Exam 193
- What is the Psychomotor Exam? 193
- Patient Assessment/ Management – Trauma 194
- Patient Assessment/ Management – Medical 196
- BVM Ventilation of an Apneic Adult Patient 198

Oxygen Administration
by Non-Rebreather Mask 198
Cardiac Arrest
Management/AED 199
Spinal Immobilization
(Supine Patient) 200
Spinal Immobilization
(Seated Patient) 202
Bleeding Control/
Shock Management 203
Long Bone Immobilization 204
Joint Immobilization 205

14 Practice Test 207
Answer Key 223

INTRODUCTION

Congratulations on choosing to take the National Registry of Emergency Medical Technicians (NREMT) exam! Passing the EMT exam is an important step forward in your health care career. In the following pages, you will find information about the exam, what to expect on test day, how to use this book, and the content covered on the exam.

The Certification Process

The **National Registry of Emergency Medical Technicians (NREMT)** provides certifications for prehospital emergency providers. To become certified, the **Emergency Medical Technician (EMT)** candidate must:

- complete a state-approved EMT course within the two years prior to certification
- possess a current Basic Life Support (BLS) for health care provider card (or equivalent)
- pass the NREMT cognitive exam (a written multiple-choice test)
- pass the NREMT psychomotor exams (a practical skills test)

Candidates must have completed or be currently enrolled in an EMT course before they are approved to take the NREMT exams. If the candidate does not pass both exams within two years of completing the course, they must repeat the EMT course.

To apply for the exams, the EMT candidate should create an account at www.NREMT.org and submit an application. Approved candidates will receive an **Authorization to Test (ATT)** that is valid for 90 days. Candidates who successfully complete their EMT certification will then need to obtain the necessary state licensure to practice as an EMT.

Most states do not require the EMT to maintain their NREMT certification after receiving a state license. However, some EMTs may need to go through the recertification every two years to maintain their NREMT certification. These EMTs can recertify in one of two ways:

1. Complete 40 hours of continuing education.
2. Take the written exam (only one attempt is allowed).

The Cognitive Exam

QUESTIONS AND TIMING

The NREMT **cognitive exam** includes 70 to 120 multiple-choice questions. Ten of these questions are not scored and are instead used by NREMT to test new questions. Candidates have two hours to complete the exam.

The exam covers five content areas (see table below). In all content areas except EMS Operations, 85 percent of the questions are related to adults and 15 percent are related to pediatrics.

EMT Cognitive Exam Content Outline

Content Area	Percentage of Exam
Airway, Respiration, and Ventilation	18 – 22%
Cardiology and Resuscitation	20 – 24%
Trauma	14 – 18%
Medical; Obstetrics and Gynecology	27 – 31%
EMS Operations	10 – 14%

The cognitive exam is a computer-adaptive test (CAT). In a CAT, the computer adapts to the examinee's abilities, selecting questions based on the examinee's responses. When the examinee answers a question correctly, the next question the computer presents is more difficult than the last. If the examinee answers a question incorrectly, the computer offers a question of lesser difficulty.

Remember: because CAT adapts to your abilities, once you submit an answer, you CANNOT go back to change your answer to a previous question.

ADMINISTRATION

The EMT cognitive exam is administered by Pearson VUE at testing centers around the nation. Arrive at least 30 minutes before the exam. Bring proper ID and a printed copy of your ATT (found in your online NREMT account). Expect the testing center to use biometric scanning (a fingerprint or palm print) and to take your picture.

You must bring two forms of ID to the testing center. The primary ID must be government issued and include a recent photograph and signature. The secondary ID must have your name and signature. The names on both IDs must match the name on your ATT. If you do not have proper ID, you will not be allowed to take the test.

You will not be allowed to bring any personal items, such as calculators or phones, into the testing room. You may not bring pens, pencils, or scratch paper. Prohibited items also include hats, scarves, and coats. You may wear religious garments, however. Most testing centers provide lockers for valuables.

An untimed tutorial will be provided before the exam. You will also have time to read and sign a nondisclosure agreement before the exam begins.

RESULTS

Cognitive exam results are posted within five business day to the candidate's NREMT account. The results for each test category will be denoted as follows:

- Above Passing: The candidate displayed enough knowledge to pass.
- Near Passing: The candidate may or may not have displayed enough knowledge to pass.
- Below Passing: The candidate has not displayed enough knowledge to pass.

Candidates who pass each category can apply to a state for an EMT license. Candidates who do not pass the exam can apply to take the exam again after 15 days. If the candidate fails three times, they must complete remedial training before they can take the test again. If the candidate fails the test six times, they must retake an initial EMT course.

The Psychomotor Exam

SKILLS

The **psychomotor exam** is a standardized, hands-on test in which the EMT candidate must perform specific emergency medical skills. Skills are demonstrated on simulated patients using real equipment. The EMT candidate is graded using standard NREMT performance checklists. Each skill has **critical criteria**, which is a list of items that if performed incorrectly will lead to automatic failure.

The psychomotor exam consists of seven skills:

- Patient Assessment/Management – Trauma
- Patient Assessment/Management – Medical
- Bag-Valve Mask (BVM) Ventilation of an Apneic Adult Patient
- Oxygen Administration by Non-Rebreather Mask
- Cardiac Arrest Management/AED
- Spinal Immobilization (Supine Patient)
- Random EMT Skill (one)
    - Spinal Immobilization (Seated Patient)
    - Bleeding Control/Shock Management
    - Long Bone Immobilization
    - Joint Immobilization

ADMINISTRATION

The psychomotor exam is administered by state EMS officials or other agents approved by the state EMS. Candidates should schedule the exam either through their EMT training course or through the state EMS office.

On the day of the exam, candidates will gather at the testing site. You should bring a government-issued ID and plan to leave your phone or other communication devices locked in a secure location. When it is your turn to test, you will be called into the testing room where a skill examiner will guide you through the scenarios and grade your performance. (See chapter twelve, "The Psychomotor Exam," for more details on how the exam is conducted.)

RESULTS

Availability of exam results will vary depending on state EMS guidelines. They may be communicated to candidates on testing day, or candidates may have to wait longer. All results will be available in the candidate's NREMT account.

Candidates must pass all seven skills to earn their certification.

- If a candidate fails three or fewer skills, they are eligible to retake those skills twice. If the candidate fails those skills twice, they must take remedial education courses before retaking the full exam.
- If a candidate fails four or more skills, they must take remedial education courses before retaking the full exam.
- Candidates who fail the exam twice must take another complete EMT training course before retesting.

Using This Book

This book is divided into two sections. In the content area review, you will find a summary of the knowledge and skills included in the exam content outline. Throughout the chapter you'll also see practice questions that will reinforce important concepts and skills.

The book also includes two full-length practice tests (one in the book and one online) with answer rationales. You can use these tests to gauge your readiness for the test and determine which content areas you may need to review more thoroughly.

Ascencia Test Prep

With health care fields such as nursing, pharmacy, emergency care, and physical therapy becoming the fastest-growing industries in the United States, individuals looking to enter the health care industry or rise in their field need high-quality, reliable resources. Ascencia Test Prep's study guides and test preparation materials are developed by credentialed industry professionals with years of experience in their respective fields. Ascencia recognizes that health care professionals nurture bodies and spirits, and save lives. Ascencia Test Prep's mission is to help health care workers grow.

ONE: HUMAN ANATOMY and PHYSIOLOGY

The Biological Hierarchy

- The biological hierarchy is a systematic breakdown of the structures of the human body organized from smallest to largest (or largest to smallest).
- The smallest unit of the human body is the **cell**, a microscopic, self-replicating structure that performs many different jobs.
- **Tissues** comprise the next largest group of structures in the body; they are a collection of cells that all perform a similar function. The human body has four basic types of tissue:
  - **Connective** tissues—which include bones, ligaments, and cartilage—support, separate, or connect the body's various organs and tissues.
  - **Epithelial** tissues are found in the skin, blood vessels, and many organs.
  - **Muscular** tissues contain contractile units that pull on connective tissues to create movement.
  - **Nervous** tissue makes up the peripheral nervous systems that transmit impulses throughout the body.
- **Organs** are a collection of tissues within the body that share a similar function (e.g., the esophagus or heart).

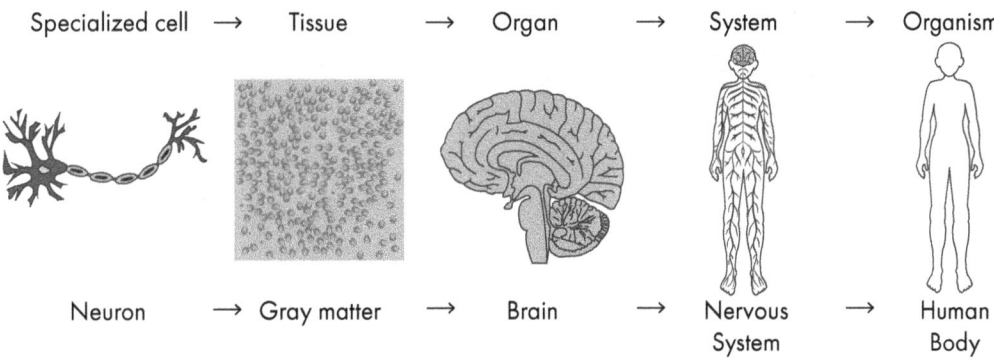

Figure 1.1. Biological Hierarchy and Levels of Organization

- **Organ systems** are a group of organs that work together to perform a similar function (e.g., the digestive system).
- Finally, an **organism** is the total collection of all the parts of the biological hierarchy working together to form a living being; it is the largest structure in the biological hierarchy.

PRACTICE QUESTION

1. The meninges are membranes that surround and protect the brain and spinal cord. What type of tissue would the meninges be classified as?

Directional Terminology and Planes

HELPFUL HINT

In anatomy, the terms *right* and *left* are used with respect to the subject, not the observer.

- When discussing anatomy and physiology, specific terms are used to refer to directions.
- Directional terms include the following:
    - **inferior**: away from the head
    - **superior**: closer to the head
    - **anterior**: toward the front
    - **posterior**: toward the back
    - **dorsal**: toward the back
    - **ventral**: toward the front
    - **medial**: toward the midline of the body
    - **lateral**: farther from the midline of the body
    - **proximal**: closer to the trunk
    - **distal**: away from the trunk

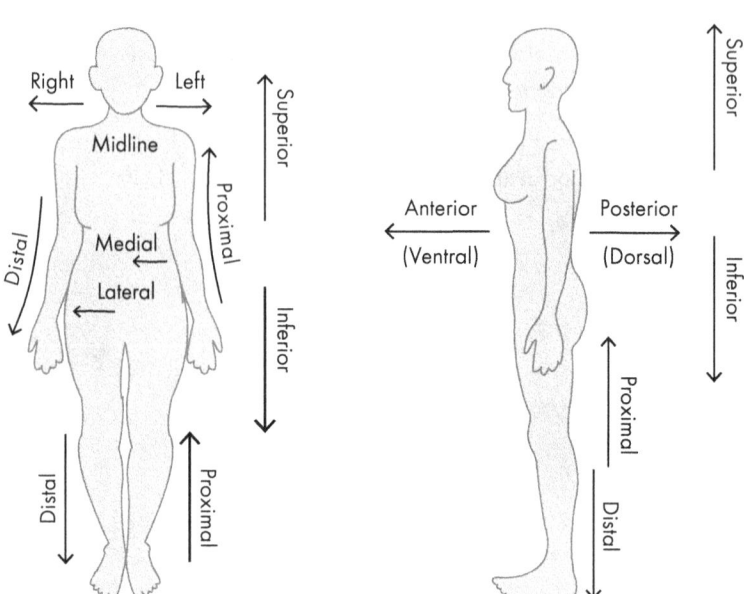

Figure 1.2. Directional Terminology

2 **EMT Study Guide**

- The human body is divided by three imaginary planes.
  - The transverse plane divides the body into a top and bottom half.
  - The coronal (frontal) plane divides the body into a front and back half.
  - The sagittal plane divides the body into a right and left half.

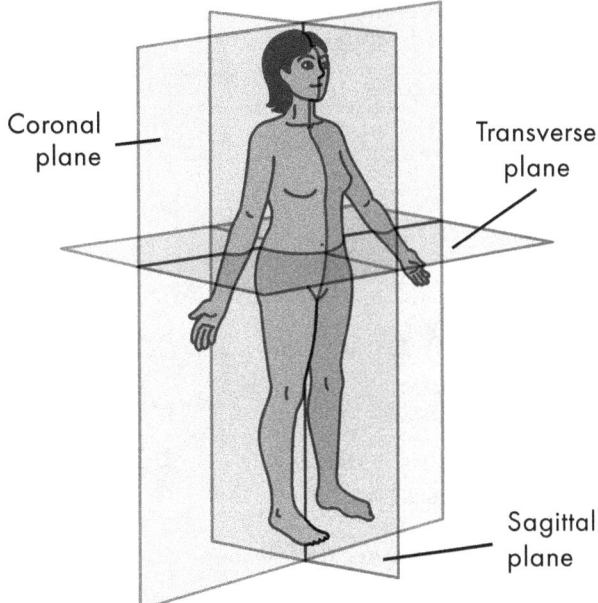

Figure 1.3. Planes of the Human Body

PRACTICE QUESTION
2. Which directional term describes the neck relative to the head?

The Cardiovascular System
STRUCTURE AND FUNCTION OF THE CARDIOVASCULAR SYSTEM

- The cardiovascular system circulates **blood**, which carries nutrients, waste products, hormones, and other important substances dissolved or suspended in liquid **plasma**.
  - **Red blood cells (RBCs)** transport oxygen throughout the body. RBCs contain **hemoglobin**, a large molecule with iron atoms that bind to oxygen.
  - **White blood cells (WBCs)** fight infection.
- The circulatory system is a closed double loop.
  - In the **pulmonary loop**, deoxygenated blood leaves the heart and travels to the lungs, where it loses carbon dioxide and becomes rich in oxygen. The oxygenated blood then returns to the heart.
  - The heart then pumps blood through the **systemic loop**, which delivers oxygenated blood to the rest of the body and returns deoxygenated blood to the heart.

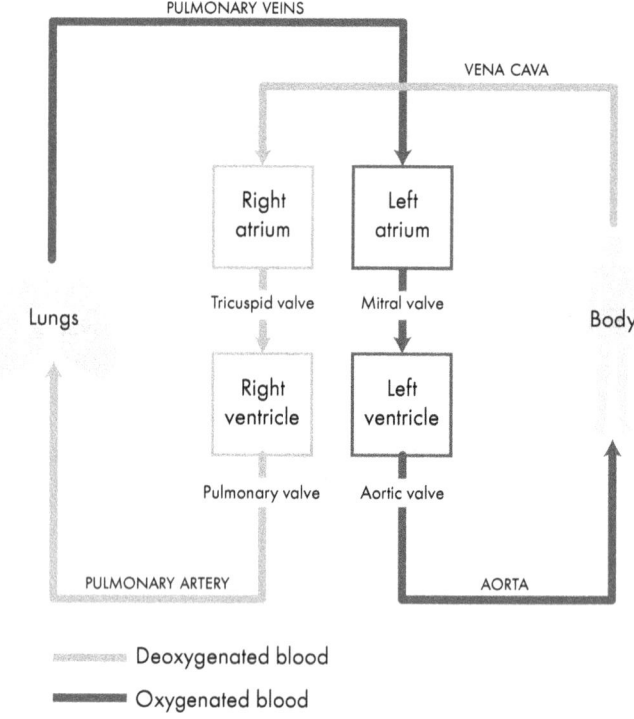

Figure 1.4. The Pulmonary and Systemic Loops

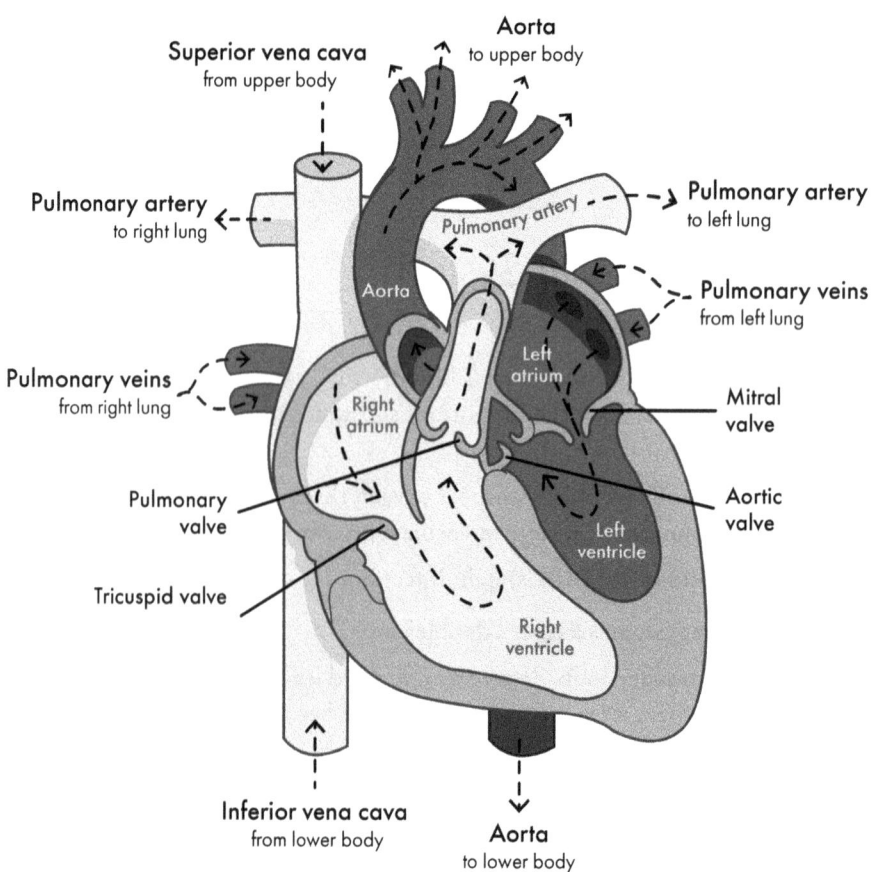

Figure 1.5. Anatomy of the Heart

- The heart has four chambers: the left atrium, right atrium, left ventricle, and right ventricle.
  - The **right atrium** collects blood from the body.
  - The **right ventricle** pumps blood to the lungs.
  - The **left atrium** collects blood from the lungs.
  - The **left ventricle** pumps blood to the body.
  - The atria are separated by the **atrial septum**, and the ventricles by the **ventricular septum**.
- The **atrioventricular valves** are located between the atria and ventricles and cause the first heart sounds (S1) when they close.
  - The **tricuspid valve** separates the right atrium and right ventricle.
  - The **mitral valve** separates the left atrium and left ventricle.
- The two **semilunar valves** are located between the ventricles and great vessels and cause the second heart sound (S2) when they close.
  - The **pulmonic valve** separates the right ventricle and pulmonary artery.
  - The **aortic valve** separates the left ventricle and aorta.
- The heart includes several layers of tissue:
  - **pericardium**: the outermost protective layer of the heart, which contains a lubricative liquid
  - **epicardium**: the deepest layer of the pericardium, which envelops the heart muscle
  - **myocardium**: the heart muscle
  - **endocardium**: the innermost, smooth layer of the heart walls
- Blood leaves the heart and travels throughout the body in **blood vessels**, which decrease in diameter as they move away from the heart and toward the tissues and organs.
- Blood exits the heart through **arteries**.
- The arteries branch into **arterioles** and then **capillaries**, where gas exchange between blood and tissue takes place.
- Deoxygenated blood travels back to the heart through **veins**.
- Some veins have valves that prevent deoxygenated blood from flowing back to the extremities.
- Blood is supplied to the heart by coronary arteries: the **right coronary artery (RCA)**, **left anterior descending (LAD) artery**, and **left circumflex artery**.

HELPFUL HINT

The movement of blood to tissues through the capillaries is called **perfusion**.

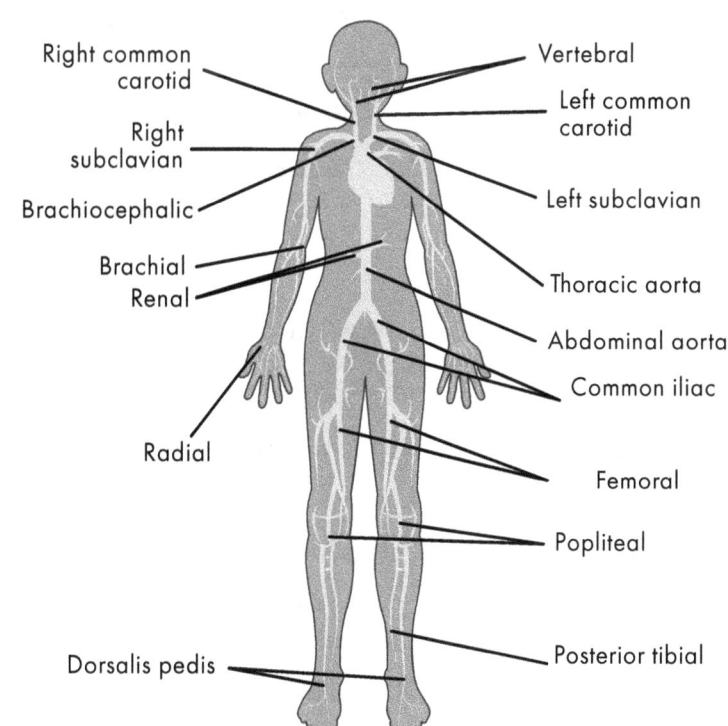

Figure 1.6. Major Arteries

HUMAN ANATOMY AND PHYSIOLOGY

- The heart's pumping action is regulated by the **cardiac conduction system**, which produces and conducts electrical signals in the heart.
    - The **sinoatrial (SA) node** sets the heart's pace by sending out electrical signals that cause the atria to contract. It is located in the anterior wall of the right atrium.
    - The **atrioventricular (AV)** node relays the electrical impulse of the sinoatrial node to the ventricles. The impulse is delayed to allow the atria to fully contract and fill the ventricles. The node is located at the base of the right atrial wall.
- **Stroke volume (SV)**, the volume of blood pumped from the left ventricle during one contraction, depends on several conditions:
    - **preload**: how much the ventricles stretch at the end of diastole
    - **afterload**: the amount of resistance needed for the heart to open the aortic valve and force blood into circulation
    - **contractility**: the force of the heart, independent of preload and afterload
- Normal SV is 60 – 130 mL per contraction.
- **Heart rate (HR)** is how many times the ventricles contract each minute.

Table 1.1. Normal Heart Rates

Age	Normal Heart Rate: Awake (bpm)	Normal Heart Rate: Sleeping (bpm)
Newborn to 3 months	85 – 205	80 – 160
3 months to 2 years	100 – 180	75 – 160
2 – 10 years	60 – 140	60 – 90
10 years	60 – 100	50 – 90

- **Cardiac output (CO)** is the volume of blood that the heart pumps every minute.
    - To calculate CO, multiply SV by HR.
    - Normal CO is 4 – 8 L per minute.

PRACTICE QUESTION

3. Left-sided heart failure can cause pulmonary edema, while right-sided heart failure is more likely to cause edema in the abdomen and extremities. How does the anatomy of the heart produce this difference?

CARDIAC MONITORING

- An **electrocardiogram (ECG)** is a noninvasive diagnostic tool that records the heart's cardiac rhythm and rate.
- An ECG can help diagnose myocardial infarctions (MI), electrolyte imbalances, and other damage to the heart.

- The readout from the ECG, often called an **ECG strip**, is a continuous waveform whose shape corresponds to each stage in the cardiac cycle.
  - **P wave**: right and left atrial contraction
  - **QRS complex**: contraction of the ventricles
  - **T wave**: relaxation of the ventricles
- A normal heart rhythm and rate is called **normal sinus rhythm**.

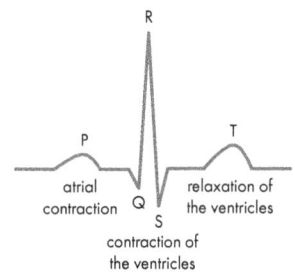

Figure 1.7. Waveforms and Intervals on an ECG

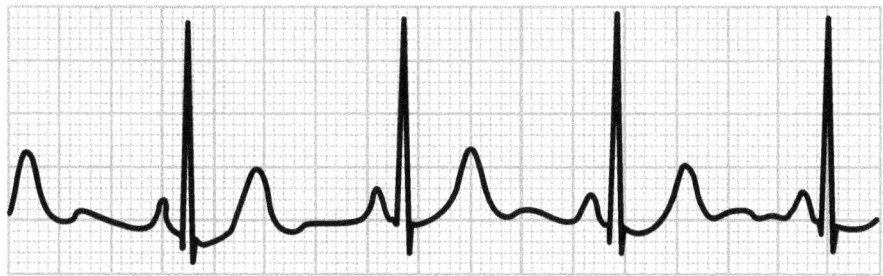

Figure 1.8. ECG: Normal Sinus Rhythm

- A **12-Lead ECG** is performed by placing 10 electrodes in specific locations on the patient's chest, arms, and legs.
  - In order for the leads to stick to the skin, the patient's skin has to be clean and dry.
  - If there is excess chest hair, it is sometimes necessary to shave the area to keep the lead on the skin.
  - Patients, especially those with breasts, should be offered a cover for the chest once electrode lead placement is done.

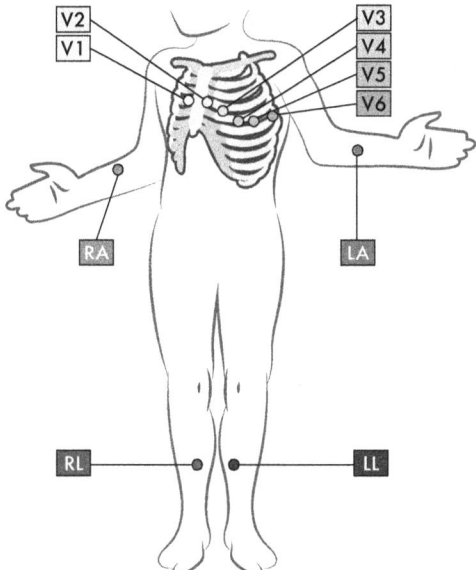

Figure 1.9. 12-Lead ECG Electrode Placement Diagram

HUMAN ANATOMY AND PHYSIOLOGY

Table 1.2. 12-Lead ECG Electrode Placement

Electrode	Placement
V1	fourth intercostal space to the right of the sternum
V2	fourth intercostal space to the left of the sternum
V3	midway between V2 and V4
V4	fifth intercostal space at the midclavicular line
V5	anterior axillary line at the same level as V4
V6	midaxillary line at the same level as V4 and V5
RA	between right shoulder and right wrist
LA	between left shoulder and left wrist
RL	above right ankle and below the torso
LL	above left ankle and below the torso

PRACTICE QUESTION

4. If a rhythm is missing P waves or has an excessive number of P waves, which area of the heart is having difficulty conducting?

CARDIAC DEVICES

- A **pacemaker** is a device that uses electrical stimulation to regulate the heart's electrical conduction system and maintain a normal heart rhythm.
    - **Permanent pacemakers** are implanted subcutaneously, and the leads are then run through the subclavian vein into the heart. The device is battery operated and allows the physician to continuously monitor the patient's rhythm.
    - **Temporary pacemakers** can include transvenous leads or transcutaneous adhesive pads attached to the chest. Temporary pacemakers are controlled by an external pulse generator and are used to maintain normal heart rhythm in critical care settings.
    - Signs of pacemaker malfunction include chest pain, palpitations, dizziness, syncope, and weakness.
    - If the patient has an implanted pacemaker, ensure that automated external defibrillator (AED) pads are placed at a distance from the pacemaker to avoid interference with the shock (about 1 inch is recommended).
- An **implantable cardioverter defibrillator (ICD)** continuously monitors heart rhythms and emits an electric shock that terminates emergent dysrhythmias such as V-tach and V-fib, preventing cardiac arrest.
- **Left ventricular assist devices (LVADs)** provide support for weakened left ventricles in patients with end-stage heart failure.

DID YOU KNOW?
Strong magnets can reset the settings on pacemakers and ICDs, causing them to malfunction.

- A mechanical pump is placed in the left ventricle. The pump moves blood from the left ventricle to the ascending aortic branch, from which it can be further circulated to the rest of the body.
- The LVAD is battery operated, and patients can remain on the device for months to years.
- EMTs should check with medical control before beginning CPR or administering nitroglycerin to patients with LVADs.

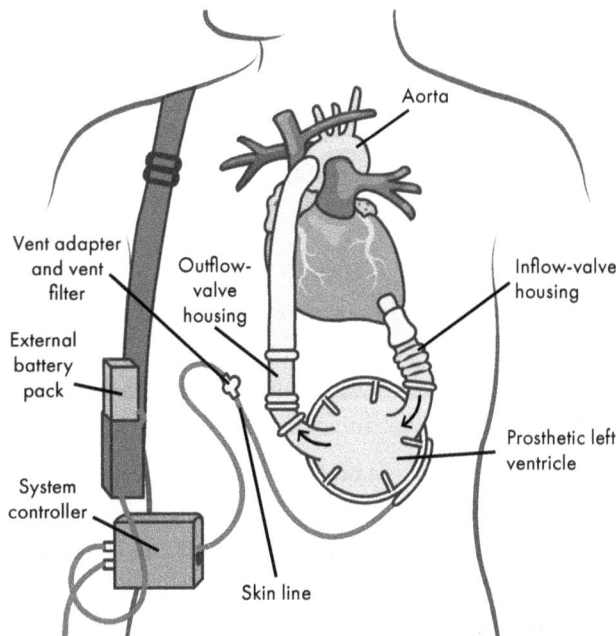

Figure 1.10. Left Ventricular Assist Device

PATHOLOGIES OF THE CARDIOVASCULAR SYSTEM

- **Ischemia** is reduced or restricted blood flow to tissues caused by:
  - occlusion of blood vessels by an **embolus** (a mass made of fat, bacteria, or other materials) or **thrombus** (blood clot; also called a thromboembolism)
  - narrowed blood vessel (e.g., aneurysm or atherosclerosis)
  - trauma
- **Infarction** is the death of tissue caused by restricted blood flow and the subsequent lack of oxygen.
- **Atherosclerosis**, also called atherosclerotic cardiovascular disease (ASCVD), is a progressive condition in which **plaque** (composed of fat, white blood cells, and other waste) builds up in the arteries.
  - Atherosclerosis can occur in any artery and is categorized according to the location of the plaque buildup.
    - **coronary artery disease (CAD)**: narrowing of the coronary arteries
    - **peripheral artery disease (PAD)**: narrowing of the peripheral arteries

- The presence of advanced atherosclerosis places patients at a high risk for several cardiovascular conditions.
    - Arteries may become **stenotic**, or narrowed, limiting blood flow to specific areas of the body (e.g., carotid stenosis).
    - When a plaque **ruptures**, the plaque and the clot that forms around it (superimposed thrombus) can quickly lead to complete occlusion of the artery (e.g., MI).
    - The clots or loosened plaque released by a rupture may also move through the bloodstream and occlude smaller vessels (e.g., ischemic stroke).
    - Atherosclerosis is also a cause of **aneurysms** (widened arteries), which weaken arterial walls, increasing the risk of arterial dissection or rupture (e.g., abdominal aortic aneurysm [AAA]).
- **Dysrhythmias** are abnormal heart rhythms.
    - **Bradycardia** is a heart rate < 60 bpm.
        - Bradycardia is normal in certain individuals and does not require an intervention if the patient is stable.
        - Symptomatic patients, however, need immediate treatment to address the cause of bradycardia and to correct the dysrhythmia.
    - **Atrial fibrillation (A-fib)** is a rapid, irregular contraction of the atria.
        - During A-fib, the heart cannot adequately empty, causing blood to pool and clots to form. These clots can break off and travel to the heart or brain, causing a heart attack or stroke.
        - The irregular atrial contractions also decrease cardiac output.
    - **Atrioventricular (AV)** block is the disruption of electrical signals between the atria and ventricles. The electrical impulse may be delayed (first degree), intermittent (second degree), or completely blocked (third degree).
    - During **ventricular fibrillation (V-fib)** the ventricles contract rapidly (300 – 400 bpm) with no organized rhythm. There is no cardiac output.

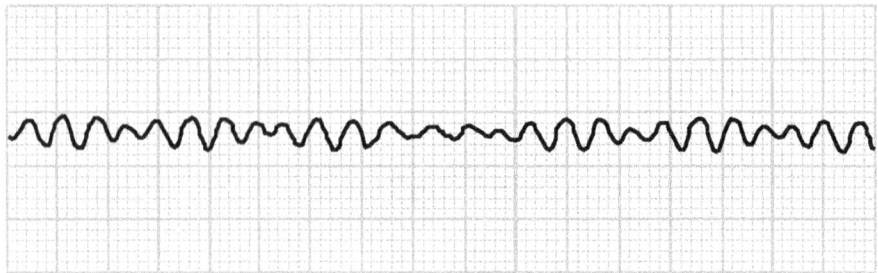

Figure 1.11. Ventricular Fibrillation

- **V**entricular tachycardia (**V-tach**) is tachycardia originating in the ventricles with > 3 consecutive ventricular beats occurring at a rate > 100 bpm.
    - Because the ventricles cannot refill before contracting, patients in this rhythm may have reduced cardiac output, resulting in hypotension.

- - V-tach may be short and asymptomatic, or it may precede V-fib and cardiac arrest.
  - **Pulseless electrical activity (PEA)** is an organized rhythm in which the heart does not contract with enough force to create a pulse. PEA is a nonshockable rhythm with a poor survival rate.
  - **Asystole**, also called a "flat line," occurs when there is no electrical or mechanical activity within the heart. Like PEA, asystole is a nonshockable rhythm with a poor survival rate.

> **DID YOU KNOW?**
> V-fib and V-tach are the two *shockable rhythms*, meaning they can be corrected using an automatic external defibrillator.

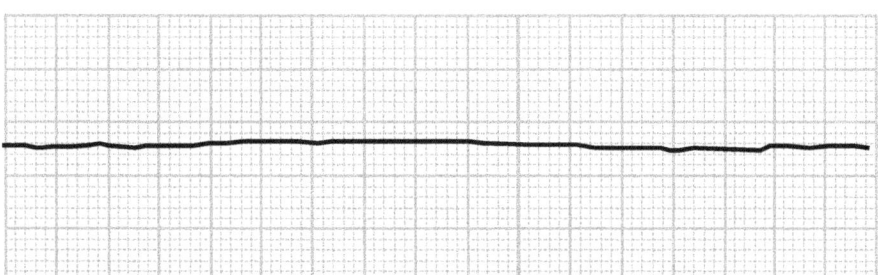

Figure 1.12. Asystole

- **Heart failure** occurs when either one or both of the ventricles in the heart cannot efficiently pump blood.
  - The condition is typically due to another disease or illness, most commonly CAD.
  - Because the heart is unable to pump effectively, blood and fluid back up into the lungs (causing pulmonary congestion), or the fluid builds up peripherally (causing edema of the lower extremities).
  - Heart failure is most commonly categorized into **left-sided heart failure** or **right-sided heart failure**, although both sides of the heart can fail at the same time.
- **Hemophilia** is a recessive, X-chromosome-linked bleeding disorder characterized by the lack of coagulation factors.
  - Generally, the condition is seen in males. Females usually only act as carriers, but female carriers can develop symptoms.
  - The deficiency in coagulation factors causes abnormal bleeding after an injury or medical procedure, and spontaneous bleeding can occur in patients with severe hemophilia.
- **Sickle cell disease** is an inherited form of hemolytic anemia that causes deformities in the shape of the RBCs.
  - When oxygen levels in the venous circulation are low, the RBCs dehydrate and form a sickle shape. This process can be exacerbated by exposure to cold temperatures or high altitudes.
  - Sickle cell disease is a chronic disease that can lead to complications that require emergency care:

HELPFUL HINT
See chapter 4, "Cardiovascular Emergencies," for a more detailed discussion of cardiac conditions commonly seen by EMTs.

- **Vaso-occlusive pain** (previously called sickle cell crisis): sickle-shaped cells clump together and restrict blood flow, causing localized ischemia, inflammation, and severe pain.
- **Acute chest syndrome (ACS)**: vaso-occlusion in the lungs (often after an infection) that exacerbates the sickle formation of RBCs.
- Infection: the leading cause of death for children with sickle cell disease; common infections include bacteremia, pneumonia, and osteomyelitis.
- Priapism: a common complication for men with sickle cell disease.

PRACTICE QUESTION

5. An EMT has attached an AED to a patient, and the AED advised a shock is necessary. What possible cardiac rhythms has the AED identified in the patient?

The Respiratory System
STRUCTURE AND FUNCTION OF THE RESPIRATORY SYSTEM

- The **respiratory system** is responsible for the exchange of gases between the human body and the environment.
- **Oxygen** is brought into the body for use in glucose metabolism, and the **carbon dioxide** created by glucose metabolism is expelled.
- Gas exchange takes place in the **lungs**.
  - Humans have a **right lung** and **left lung**. The right lung is slightly larger than the left.
  - The right lung has three **lobes**, and the left has two.
  - The lungs are surrounded by a thick membrane called the **pleura**.
- Respiration begins with pulmonary ventilation, or **breathing**.

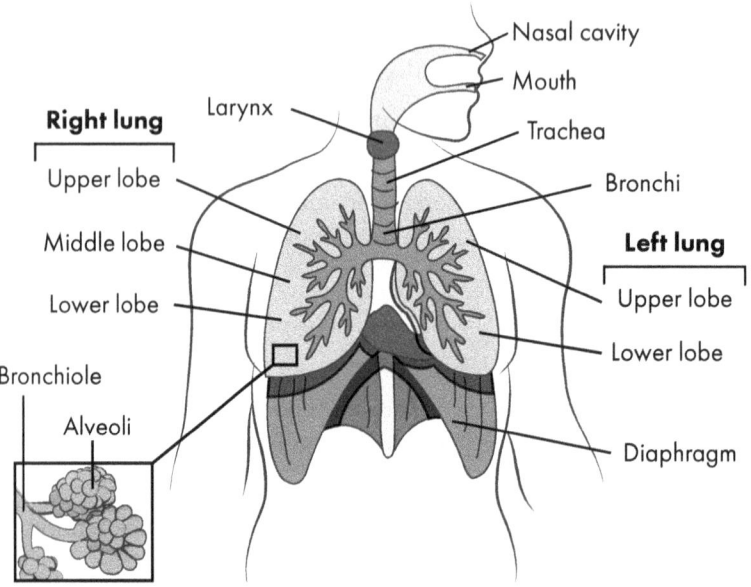

Figure 1.13. The Respiratory System

- The first stage of breathing is **inhalation**. During this process, the thoracic cavity expands and the diaphragm muscle contracts, which decreases the pressure in the lungs, pulling in air from the atmosphere.
- Air is drawn in through the **nose** and **mouth**, then into the throat, where cilia and mucus filter out particles before the air enters the **trachea**.
- The **epiglottis** prevents food or other materials from entering the trachea.
- Once it passes through the trachea, the air passes through either the left or right **bronchi**, which are divisions of the trachea that direct air into the left or right lung.
- These bronchi are further divided into smaller **bronchioles**, which branch throughout the lungs and become increasingly smaller.
- Eventually, air enters the **alveoli**—tiny air sacs located at the ends of the smallest bronchioles. The alveoli have very thin membranes, only one cell thick, and are the location of gas exchange with the blood.
- Carbon dioxide is then expelled from the lungs during **exhalation**, the second stage of breathing. During exhalation, the diaphragm relaxes and the thoracic cavity contracts, causing air to leave the body because the lung pressure is now greater than the atmospheric pressure.
- Lung function can be gauged by measuring the volume of air moved by the lungs. Important values include:
  - **total lung capacity**: amount of air in the lungs when full
  - **tidal volume**: amount of air inhaled or exhaled during normal breathing
  - **residual volume**: amount of air left in the lungs after a large exhalation

PRACTICE QUESTION

6. Describe the pathway air follows once it has been inhaled through the nostrils.

PATHOLOGIES OF THE RESPIRATORY SYSTEM

- Disruptions to the respiratory system can result in abnormal breathing patterns.
  - **eupnea**: normal breathing
  - **tachypnea**: rapid breathing
  - **bradypnea**: slow breathing
  - **dyspnea**: difficulty breathing
  - **apnea**: not breathing
  - **hyperventilation**: increase in rate or volume of breaths, which causes excessive elimination of CO_2
  - **agonal breathing**: irregular gasping breaths accompanied by involuntary twitching or jerking. Agonal breathing is associated with severe hypoxia and is a sign the patient requires immediate medical treatment.

- - Biot's breathing: alternating rapid respirations and apnea. Causes include stroke, trauma, and opioid use.
  - Cheyne-Stokes breathing: deep breathing alternating with apnea or a faster rate of breathing; associated with left heart failure or sleep apnea
  - Kussmaul breathing: type of hyperventilation characterized by deep, labored breathing that is associated with metabolic acidosis
- The lungs and kidneys work together to maintain a blood pH between 7.35 and 7.45.
  - Acidosis is abnormally low (acidic) blood pH.
  - Alkalosis is abnormally high (alkaline or basic) blood pH.
  - Disruption in blood pH can be caused by respiratory or metabolic factors (see Table 1.3).

HELPFUL HINT
See chapter 3, "Respiratory Emergencies," for a more detailed discussion of respiratory conditions EMTs commonly see.

Table 1.3. Causes and Symptoms of Acidosis and Alkalosis

Abnormality	pH	Common Causes	Symptoms
Respiratory acidosis	decreased	asthma, COPD	anxiety, dyspnea, lethargy, confusion, delirium
Respiratory alkalosis	increased	hyperventilation	dyspnea, dizziness, numbness or tingling in extremities, spasms of hands and feet
Metabolic acidosis	decreased	diabetic disorders, diarrhea or vomiting, kidney dysfunction	Kussmaul breathing; non-specific symptoms such as chest pain, altered mental status, and nausea
Metabolic alkalosis	increased	kidney dysfunction or diabetic disorders	usually asymptomatic; patient may have symptoms related to underlying condition

PRACTICE QUESTION

7. Kussmaul breathing is a symptom associated with what disorder?

The Skeletal System
STRUCTURE AND FUNCTION OF THE SKELETAL SYSTEM

- The skeletal system is made up of over 200 different bones, a stiff connective tissue in the human body.
- The bones have many functions, including:
  - protecting internal organs
  - synthesizing blood cells
  - storing necessary minerals
  - providing the muscular system with leverage to create movement

- Bones are covered with a thin layer of vascular connective tissue called the periosteum, which serves as a point of muscle attachment, supplies blood to the bone, and contains nerve endings.
- **Osseous tissue** is the primary tissue that makes up bone. There are two types of osseous tissue: cortical (compact) bone and cancellous (spongy) bone.
    - **Cortical bone** is the dense, solid material that surrounds the bone and gives it hardness and strength. It is usually concentrated in the middle part of the bone.
    - **Cancellous bone** is less dense, more porous, and softer. It is located at the ends of long bones, where it does not bear a structural load.

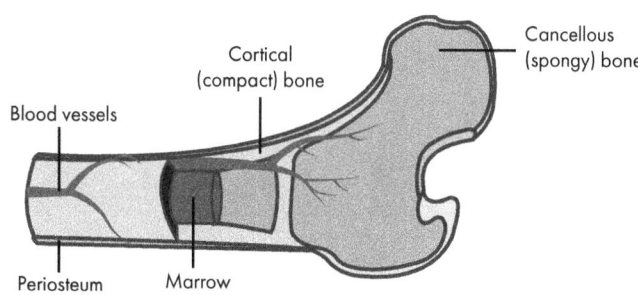

Figure 1.14. Structure of Bone

HELPFUL HINT

Long bones are longer than they are wide. The term is usually used to refer to the long bones of the arm and leg, such as the femur and humerus.

- Bone marrow is stored in cancellous bone.
    - **Red bone marrow** is responsible for producing red blood cells, platelets, and white blood cells.
    - **Yellow bone marrow** is composed mostly of fat tissue and can be converted to red bone marrow in response to extreme blood loss in the body.
- The hundreds of bones in the body make up the human **skeleton**.
- The **axial skeleton** contains 80 bones that support and protect many of the body's vital organs. It has 3 major subdivisions:
    - the skull, which contains the cranium and facial bones
    - the thorax, which includes the sternum and 12 pairs of ribs
    - the vertebral column, which contains the body's vertebrae
- The **vertebral column**, or the **spine**, is made up of 24 vertebrae, plus the sacrum and the coccyx (the tailbone). These 24 vertebrae are divided into three groups:
    - the cervical, or the neck vertebrae (7 bones)
    - the thoracic, or the chest vertebrae (12 bones)
    - the lumbar, or the lower back vertebrae (5 bones)
- The **appendicular skeleton's** 126 bones make up the body's appendages. The main function of the appendicular skeleton is locomotion.

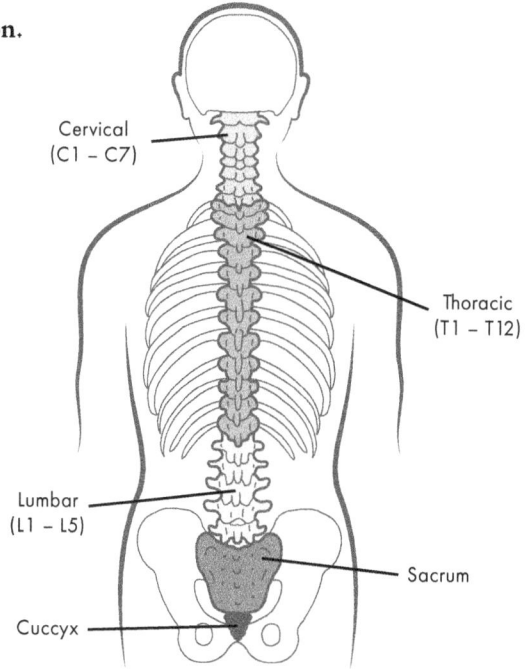

Figure 1.15. The Vertebral Column

HUMAN ANATOMY AND PHYSIOLOGY

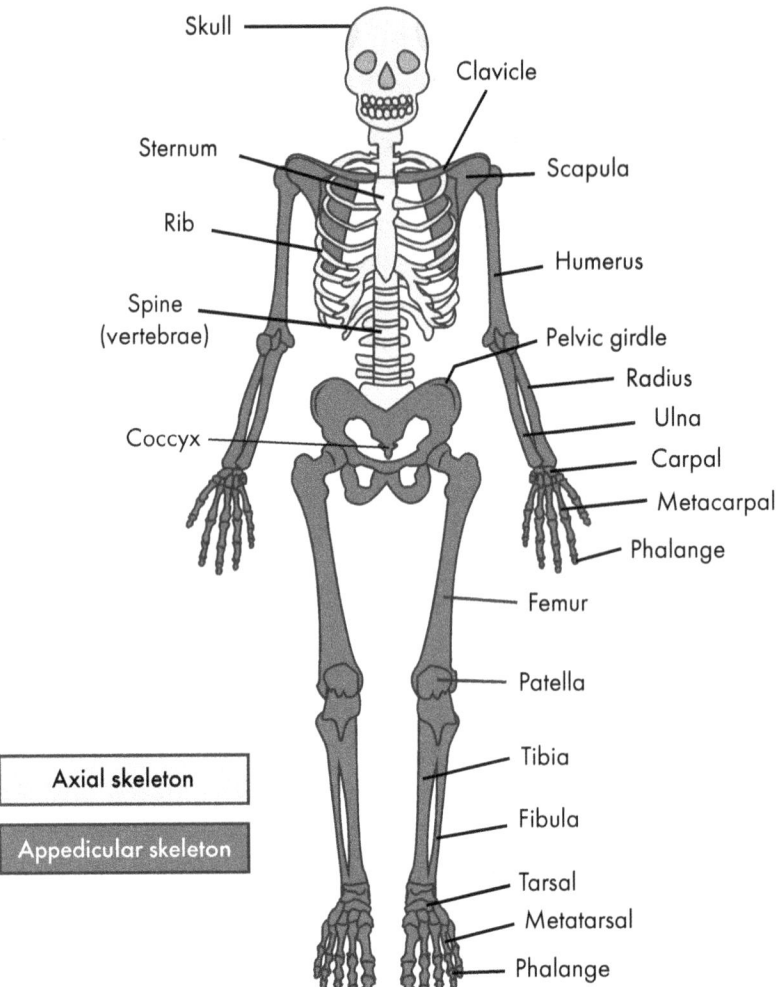

Figure 1.16. The Axial and Appendicular Skeletons

- Various connective tissues join the parts of the skeleton together to other systems.
  - **Ligaments** join bone to bone.
  - **Tendons** join bones to muscles.
  - **Cartilage** cushions the bones in joints, provides structural integrity for many body parts (e.g., the ear and nose), and maintains open pathways (e.g., the trachea and bronchi).
- The point at which a bone is attached to another bone is called a joint. There are three basic types of joints:
  - **Fibrous joints** connect bones that do not move.
  - **Cartilaginous joints** connect bones with cartilage and allow limited movement.
  - **Synovial joints** allow for a range of motion and are covered by articular cartilage that protects the bones.

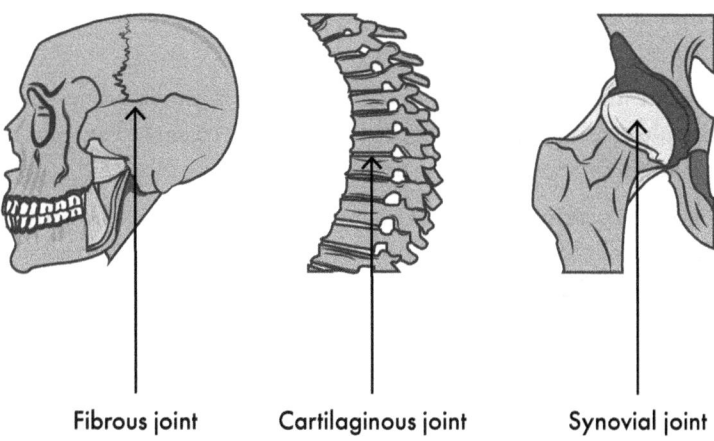

Fibrous joint   Cartilaginous joint   Synovial joint

Figure 1.17. Types of Joints

PRACTICE QUESTION

8. A patient is complaining of severe lower back pain after a fall. Which vertebrae has the patient possibly injured?

PATHOLOGIES OF THE SKELETAL SYSTEM

- **Rheumatoid arthritis** is a type of inflammation at the joint caused by chronic autoimmune disorder, which can lead to excessive joint degradation. The immune system attacks healthy joint tissue, making the joints stiff and causing the cartilage and bone to deteriorate.
- **Osteoporosis** is poor bone mineral density due to the loss or lack of the production of calcium content and bone cells, which makes bones more likely to fracture.
- **Osteomyelitis** is an infection in the bone that can occur directly (after a traumatic bone injury) or indirectly (via the vascular system or other infected tissues).

PRACTICE QUESTION

9. An EMT is doing a head-to-toe assessment of a 75-year-old patient who fell in the bathtub. The patient states she has severe pain in both hands. She states the pain has increased recently, and she is progressively losing function of her hands. The EMT notes that the joints in both hands are reddened, swollen, and disfigured. What condition should the EMT suspect is causing her pain?

The Muscular System

STRUCTURE AND FUNCTION OF THE MUSCULAR SYSTEM

- The primary function of the muscular system is movement: muscles contract and relax, resulting in motion.

- The muscular system consists of three types of muscle: cardiac, visceral, and skeletal.
    - **Cardiac muscle** is only found in the heart. It is a **striated** muscle, with alternating segments of thick and thin filaments, that contracts involuntarily, creating the heartbeat and pumping blood.
    - **Visceral**, or **smooth**, **muscle** tissue is found in many of the body's essential organs, including the stomach and intestines. It slowly contracts and relaxes to move nutrients, blood, and other substances throughout the body. Visceral muscle movement is involuntary.
    - **Skeletal muscle** is responsible for voluntary movement and, as the name suggests, is linked to the skeletal system.

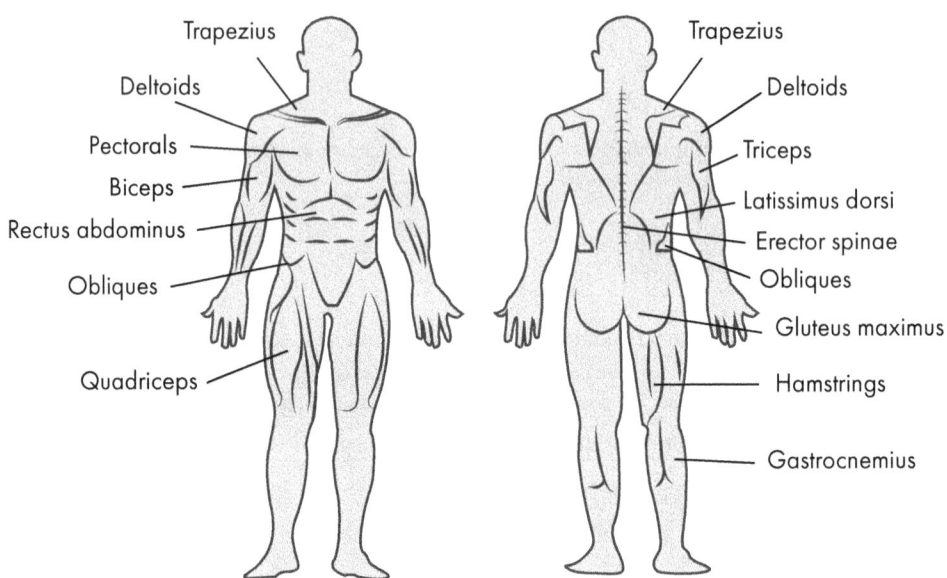

Figure 1.18. Major Muscles of the Body

PRACTICE QUESTION

10. During assessment of a patient with possible heat cramps, the patient complains of severe pain in his lower right leg. What muscle is most likely causing the patient's pain?

PATHOLOGIES OF THE MUSCULAR SYSTEM

- **Muscular dystrophy (MD)** is a genetically inherited condition that results in progressive muscle wasting, which limits movement and can cause respiratory and cardiovascular difficulties.
- **Rhabdomyolysis** is the rapid breakdown of dead muscle tissue.
    - Common symptoms of rhabdomyolysis include dark urine, muscle pain, and muscle weakness.

- Rhabdomyolysis can be caused by crush injuries, overexertion (particularly in extreme heat), and a variety of drugs and toxins (particularly statins, which are prescribed to lower cholesterol levels).
- Muscle cramps are involuntary muscle contractions (or **spasms**) that cause intense pain.

PRACTICE QUESTION

11. What symptoms should an EMT expect to see in an adult patient with muscular dystrophy?

The Nervous System
STRUCTURE AND FORM OF THE NERVOUS SYSTEM

- The **nervous system** coordinates the processes and action of the human body.
- **Nerve cells**, or **neurons**, communicate through electrical impulses and allow the body to process and respond to stimuli.
  - Neurons have a nucleus and transmit electrical impulses through their axons and dendrites.
  - The **axon** is the stem-like structure, often covered in a fatty insulating substance called **myelin**, that carries information to other neurons throughout the body.
  - **Dendrites** receive information from other neurons.
- The nervous system is broken down into two parts: the **central nervous system (CNS)** and the **peripheral nervous system (PNS)**.
  - The CNS is made up of the brain and spinal cord.
    - The **brain** acts as the control center for the body and is responsible for nearly all the body's processes and actions.
    - The **spinal cord** relays information between the brain and the peripheral nervous system; it also coordinates many reflexes.
    - The spinal cord is protected by the vertebral column, a structure of bones that enclose the delicate nervous tissue.
  - The PNS is the collection of nerves that connect the central nervous system to the rest of the body.
- The brain is composed of myelinated **white matter** and unmyelinated **gray matter**.

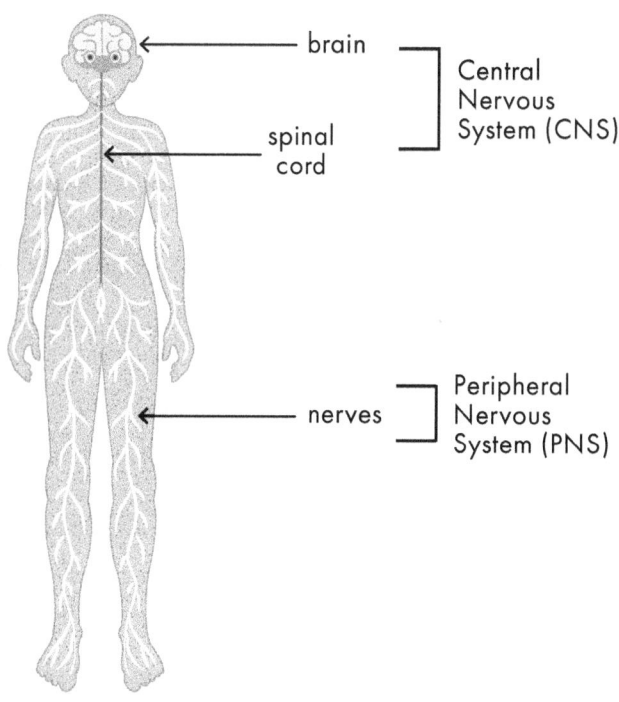

Figure 1.19. The Nervous System

- The **meninges** form a protective coating over the brain and spinal cord. They consist of three layers:
  - The outermost layer is the **dura mater**. The epidural space (above the dura) and the subdural space (below the dura) contain vasculature that can bleed following injury to the brain.

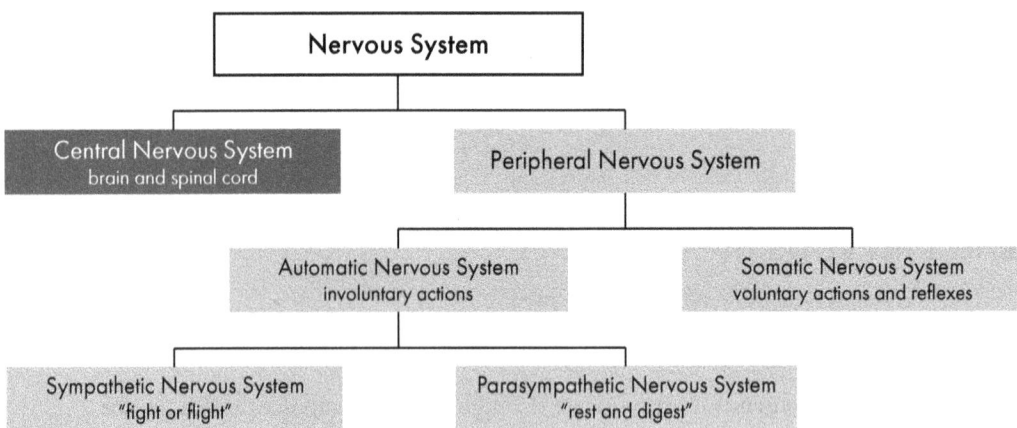

Figure 1.20. Divisions of the Nervous System

  - The **arachnoid mater** is below the dura mater.
  - The **pia mater** is the innermost layer that is attached to the CNS.
- The functions of the nervous system are broken down into the somatic nervous system and the autonomic nervous system.
  - The **somatic nervous system** is responsible for the body's ability to control skeletal muscles and voluntary movement as well as the involuntary reflexes associated with skeletal muscles.
  - The **autonomic nervous system** controls involuntary actions that occur in the body, such as respiration, heartbeat, digestive processes, and more.
- The autonomic nervous system is further broken down into the sympathetic nervous system and parasympathetic nervous system.
  - The **sympathetic nervous system** is responsible for the body's reaction to stress and induces a "fight or flight" response to stimuli. The "fight or flight" reaction includes accelerated breathing and heart rate, dilation of blood vessels in muscles, release of energy molecules for use by muscles, relaxation of the bladder, and slowed or stopped movement in the upper digestive tract.
  - The **parasympathetic nervous system** is stimulated by the body's need for rest or recovery. The parasympathetic nervous system responds by decreasing the heart rate, blood pressure, and muscular activation when a person is getting ready for activities such as sleeping or digesting food.

PRACTICE QUESTION

12. Many neurological disorders are the result of demyelination, the loss of myelin from neurons. Why would the lack of a myelin sheath impact the functions of the nervous system?

DID YOU KNOW?
A **contrecoup** injury is when an injury occurs after a blow to the head, and the injury to the brain is opposite to where the head is struck. A **coup** injury is when the injury is on the side where the blow to the head occurs.

PATHOLOGIES OF THE NERVOUS SYSTEM

- **Syncope** (fainting) is the temporary loss of consciousness caused by the brief decrease of blood flow to the brain brought on by hypotension.
  - Syncope typically causes muscle weakness and collapse, which may lead to fall injuries.
  - The causes of syncope are generally grouped into three categories:
    - Syncope can also be caused by underlying cardiac conditions, such as dysrhythmias or coronary artery disease.
    - **Reflex syncope** is neurologically mediated and occurs as a result of stress, pain, or specific triggers such as coughing.
    - **Orthostatic syncope** is caused by a drop in blood pressure after standing.
- **Alzheimer's disease** is characterized by the loss of memory and deteriorating cognitive function, usually later in life, due to the degeneration of neurons in the brain.
  - The disease is a form of dementia that progresses gradually and has no known cure.
  - Onset usually occurs past age 60 but can also occur as early as age 40.
- **Multiple sclerosis (MS)** involves the gradual breakdown and scarring of the myelin sheaths on axons, causing disruption of nervous transmission of impulses.
  - The nerve damage associated with MS causes vision trouble, difficulty walking, fatigue, pain, involuntary spasms, and numerous other symptoms.
  - This disease is thought to be genetic, and there is no known cure. However, treatments are available to slow the disease's progression.
- **Amyotrophic lateral sclerosis (ALS)**, sometimes called Lou Gehrig's disease, is a neurodegenerative disorder that affects the neurons in the brain stem and spinal cord.
  - ALS presents with progressive, asymmetrical weakness.
  - Symptoms progressively worsen until the respiratory system is affected; ALS is ultimately fatal.
- **Peripheral neuropathy** is impairment of the peripheral nerves.
  - Common causes include diabetes (diabetic neuropathy), autoimmune conditions, and infections.
  - Peripheral neuropathy can cause pain and impair motor or sensory function.

PRACTICE QUESTION

13. An EMT responds to a call for an unconscious 56-year-old male. When she arrives at the scene, the EMT finds the patient alert and oriented. What details in the patient's history should lead an EMT to suspect orthostatic syncope?

The Gastrointestinal System
STRUCTURE AND FORM OF THE GASTROINTESTINAL SYSTEM

- The gastrointestinal system is responsible for the breakdown and absorption of food necessary to power the body.
- The gastrointestinal system starts at the **mouth**, which allows for the consumption and mastication of nutrients via an opening in the face.
  - The mouth contains the muscular **tongue** to move food and uses the liquid **saliva** to assist in the breakdown of food.
- The chewed and lubricated food travels from the mouth through the **esophagus** via **peristalsis**, the contraction of smooth muscles.
- The esophagus leads to the **stomach**, the organ of the digestive tract found in the abdominal cavity that mixes food with powerful acidic liquid for further digestion.
  - The stomach creates an acidic bolus of digested food known as **chyme**.

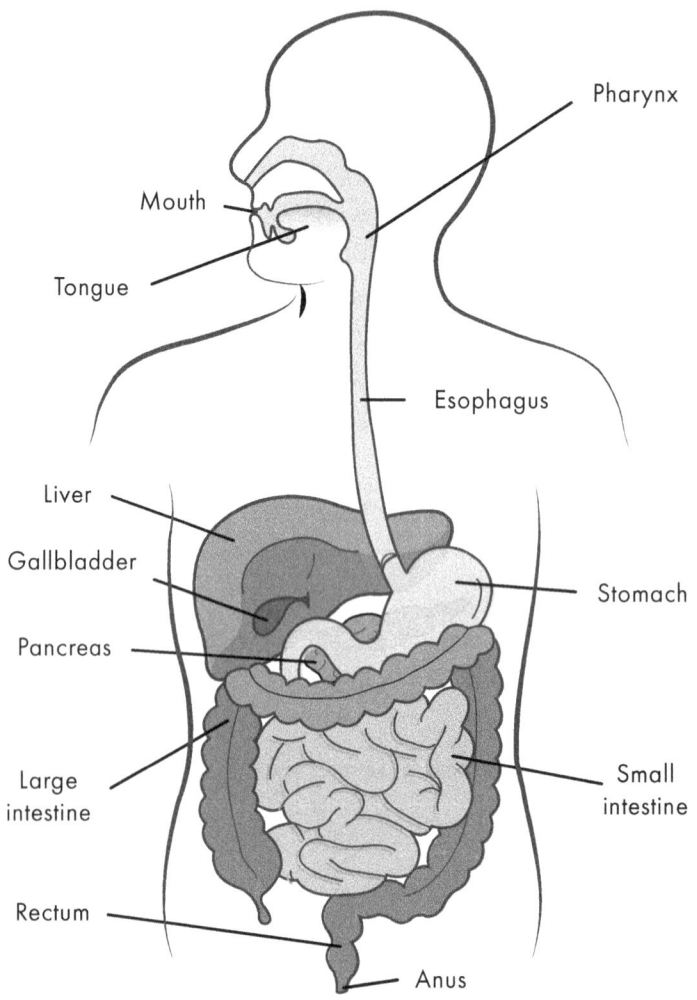

Figure 1.21. The Gastrointestinal System

- Chyme travels to the **small intestine,** where a significant amount of nutrient absorption takes place.
  - The tube-like small intestine contains millions of finger-like projections known as **villi** and microvilli to increase the surface area available for the absorption of nutrients found in food.
- The small intestine then transports food to the **large intestine.**
  - The large intestine is similarly tube-like but larger in diameter than the small intestine.
  - The large intestine assists in water absorption, further nutrient absorption, waste collection, and the production of feces for excretion.
- At the end of the large intestine is the **rectum**, which stores feces.
- Feces are expelled through the **anus**.
- Along the digestive tract are several muscular rings, known as **sphincters**, which regulate the movement of food through the tract and prevent reflux of material into the previous cavity.
- The digestive system also includes accessory organs that aid in digestion:
  - **salivary glands**: produce saliva, which begins the process of breaking down starches and fats
  - **liver**: produces bile, which helps break down fat in the small intestine
  - **gallbladder**: stores bile
  - **pancreas**: produces pancreatic juice, which neutralizes the acidity of chyme, and digestive enzymes

PRACTICE QUESTION

14. What role does the liver play in digestion?

PATHOLOGIES OF THE DIGESTIVE SYSTEM

- **Food poisoning** occurs when an acute infection (bacterial or viral) affects the lining of the digestive system and the resulting immune response triggers the body to void the contents of the digestive system.
- **Irritable bowel syndrome (IBS)** refers to recurrent abdominal pain, bloating, diarrhea, or constipation.
- **Crohn's disease** is an inflammatory bowel disorder that occurs when the immune system attacks the digestive system.
- **Cirrhosis** is a chronic disease in which the liver has permanent scarring and loses cells, impairing normal functioning.
  - Symptoms of cirrhosis include jaundice, bruising easily, ascites, and asterixis.
  - Cirrhosis can also decrease blood flow to the liver; the resulting hypertension in the portal vein can lead to related conditions, including an enlarged spleen and esophageal varices.

> **DID YOU KNOW?**
> About half of patients with cirrhosis will develop esophageal varices, which are dilated veins in the esophagus that can cause severe bleeding.

- ○ Common causes of liver cirrhosis include hepatitis, chronic alcohol abuse, and hemochromatosis (excess iron).
- **Heartburn** occurs when the lower esophageal sphincter does not close completely, allowing stomach acid to move into the esophagus.
- **Peritonitis** is inflammation of the peritoneum (the lining of the abdominal cavity). It can cause **ileus**, paralysis of the digestive tract, resulting in severe pain, nausea, and vomiting.

PRACTICE QUESTION

15. Why do patients with cirrhosis often experience bleeding in their esophagus?

The Immune System
STRUCTURE AND FUNCTION OF THE IMMUNE SYSTEM

- The human **immune system** protects the body against bacteria and viruses that cause disease.
  - ○ The **innate immune system** includes nonspecific defenses (physical barriers and immune cells) that work against a wide range of infectious agents.
  - ○ The **adaptive immune system** "learns" to respond only to specific invaders.
- The body has a number of innate defense systems against pathogens that enter the body.
  - ○ **Barriers to entry** (e.g., skin, mucus) prevent pathogens from entering the body.
  - ○ **Inflammation** increases blood flow to the infected area, bringing large numbers of **white blood cells** (WBCs, also called **leukocytes**) to fight the infection.
- The adaptive immune system relies on molecules called antigens that appear on the surface of pathogens to which the system has previously been exposed.
  - ○ In the cell-mediated response, **T cells** destroy any cell that displays an antigen.
  - ○ In the antibody-mediated response, **B cells** are activated by antigens and release antibodies that destroy the targeted cells.
- During an infection, **memory B cells** specific to an antigen are created, allowing the immune system to respond more quickly if the infection appears again.

> **HELPFUL HINT**
> Memory B cells are the underlying mechanisms behind vaccines, which introduce a harmless version of a pathogen into the body to activate the body's adaptive immune response.

PRACTICE QUESTION

16. Breastmilk contains antibodies from the mother's immune system. How do these antibodies protect breastfeeding infants from infection?

PATHOLOGIES OF THE IMMUNE SYSTEM

- The immune system of individuals with an **autoimmune disease** will attack healthy tissues. Autoimmune diseases (and the tissues they attack) include:
  - psoriasis (skin)
  - rheumatoid arthritis (joints)
  - multiple sclerosis (nerve cells)
  - lupus (kidneys, lungs, and skin)
- **Leukemia** is cancer of the WBCs. It occurs in the bone marrow, disrupting the production of WBCs and platelets.
- **Human immunodeficiency virus (HIV)** attacks T cells, eventually causing **acquired immunodeficiency syndrome (AIDS)**, which allows opportunistic infections to overrun the body.

PRACTICE QUESTION

17. What signs and symptoms should an EMT expect to see in a patient diagnosed with leukemia?

DID YOU KNOW?
Cachexia, also called wasting syndrome, is a state of weight loss, muscle weakness, and fatigue seen in people with advanced cancer, AIDS, and heart failure.

The Endocrine System
STRUCTURE AND FORM OF THE ENDOCRINE SYSTEM

- The endocrine system is made up of **glands** that regulate numerous processes throughout the body by secreting chemical messengers called **hormones**.
- Hormones regulate a wide variety of bodily processes, including metabolism, growth and development, sexual reproduction, the sleep-wake cycle, and hunger.

Table 1.4. Endocrine Glands and Their Functions

Gland	Regulates	Hormones Produced
Adrenal glands	"fight or flight" response and regulation of salt and blood volume	epinephrine, norepinephrine, cortisol, androgens
Hypothalamus	pituitary function and metabolic processes including body temperature, hunger, thirst, and circadian rhythms	thyrotropin-releasing hormone (TRH), dopamine, growth-hormone-releasing hormone (GHRH), gonadotropin-releasing hormone (GnRH), oxytocin, vasopressin
Ovaries	maturation of sex organs, secondary sex characteristics, pregnancy, childbirth, and lactation	progesterone, estrogens
Pancreas	blood glucose levels and metabolism	insulin, glucagon, somatostatin

Table 1.4. Endocrine Glands and Their Functions (continued)

Gland	Regulates	Hormones Produced
Parathyroid	calcium and phosphate levels	parathyroid hormone (PTH)
Pineal gland	circadian rhythms (the sleep-wake cycle)	melatonin
Pituitary gland	growth, blood pressure, reabsorption of water by the kidneys, temperature, pain relief, and some reproductive functions related to pregnancy and childbirth	human growth hormone (HGH), thyroid-stimulating hormone (TSH), prolactin (PRL), luteinizing hormone (LH), follicle-stimulating hormone (FSH), oxytocin, antidiuretic hormone (ADH)
Placenta	gestation and childbirth	progesterone, estrogens, human chorionic gonadotropin, human placental lactogen (hPL)
Testes	maturation of sex organs and secondary sex characteristics	androgens (e.g., testosterone)
Thyroid gland	energy use and protein synthesis	thyroxine (T_4), triiodothyronine (T_3), calcitonin

PRACTICE QUESTION

18. Which endocrine gland regulates blood glucose levels?

PATHOLOGIES OF THE ENDOCRINE SYSTEM

- Hormone production in endocrine glands can be disrupted by disease, tumors, or congenital conditions.
- **Diabetes mellitus** is a metabolic disorder that affects the body's ability to produce and use **insulin**, a hormone that regulates cellular uptake of glucose (sugar).
  - Uncontrolled diabetes can lead to high blood glucose levels (**hyperglycemia**) or low blood glucose levels (**hypoglycemia**).
  - Diabetes mellitus is classified as type 1 or type 2.
    - **Type 1 diabetes** is an acute-onset autoimmune disease predominant in children, teens, and adults < 30 years. Beta cells in the pancreas are destroyed and are unable to produce sufficient amounts of insulin, causing blood glucose to rise.
    - **Type 2 diabetes** is a gradual-onset disease predominant in adults 40 years, but it can develop in individuals of all ages. The person develops insulin resistance, which prevents the cellular uptake of glucose and causes blood glucose to rise. Type 2 diabetes accounts for 90 percent of all diabetes diagnoses in the United States.
  - Diabetes requires long-term management with insulin or oral hypoglycemic drugs.

DID YOU KNOW?
Over 30 million Americans have been diagnosed with diabetes. In the US, more money is spent on health care related to diabetes than on any other single medical condition.

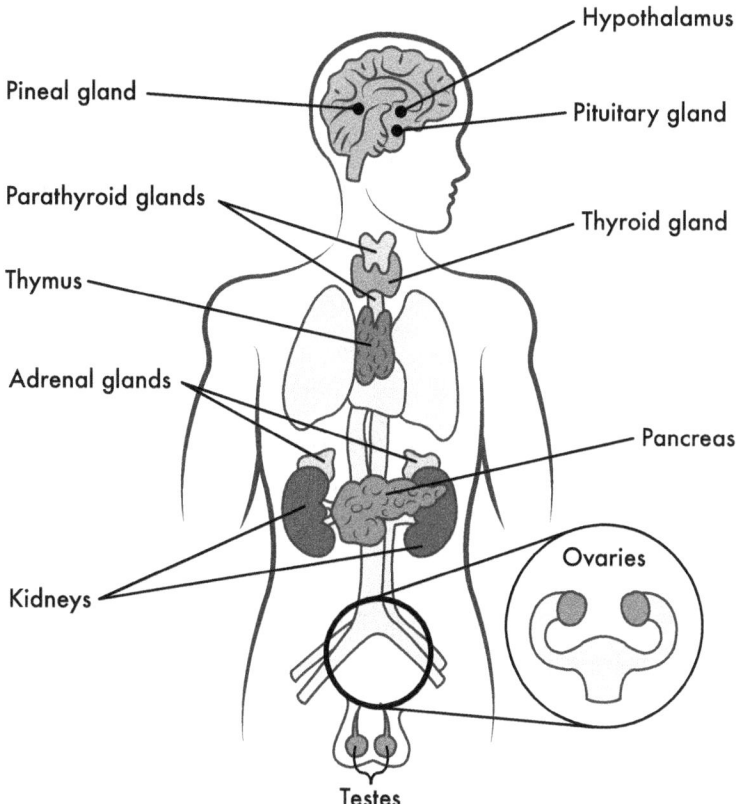

Figure 1.22. The Location of Endocrine Glands

- **Hypothyroidism** occurs when insufficient thyroxine is produced and can result in fatigue, weight gain, and cold intolerance.
- **Hyperthyroidism** occurs when too much thyroxine is produced and can cause anxiety, mood swings, weight loss, and palpitations.
- **Adrenal insufficiency** (Addison's disease) is the chronic underproduction of steroids.
  - Signs and symptoms of adrenal insufficiency include fatigue, nausea, hypotension, and darkening of the skin.
  - Adrenal insufficiency can cause shock.

PRACTICE QUESTION

19. How is insulin production and use affected by type 1 and type 2 diabetes?

The Reproductive System
THE MALE REPRODUCTIVE SYSTEM

- The male reproductive system produces **sperm**, or male gametes, and passes them to the female reproductive system.

- Sperm are produced during **spermatogenesis** in the **testes** (also called testicles), which are housed in a sac-like external structure called the **scrotum**.
- Mature sperm are stored in the **epididymis**.
- During sexual stimulation, sperm travel from the epididymis through a long, thin tube called the **vas deferens**. Along the way, the sperm are joined by fluids from three glands:
  - The **seminal vesicles** secrete a fluid composed of various proteins, sugars, and enzymes.
  - The **prostate** contributes an alkaline fluid that counteracts the acidity of the vaginal tract.
  - The **Cowper's gland** secretes a protein-rich fluid that acts as a lubricant.
- The mix of fluids and sperm, called **semen**, travels through the **urethra** and exits the body through the **penis**, which becomes rigid during sexual arousal.
- The main hormone associated with the male reproductive system is **testosterone**, which is released mainly by the testes.
  - Testosterone is responsible for the development of the male reproductive system and male secondary sexual characteristics, including muscle development and facial hair growth.

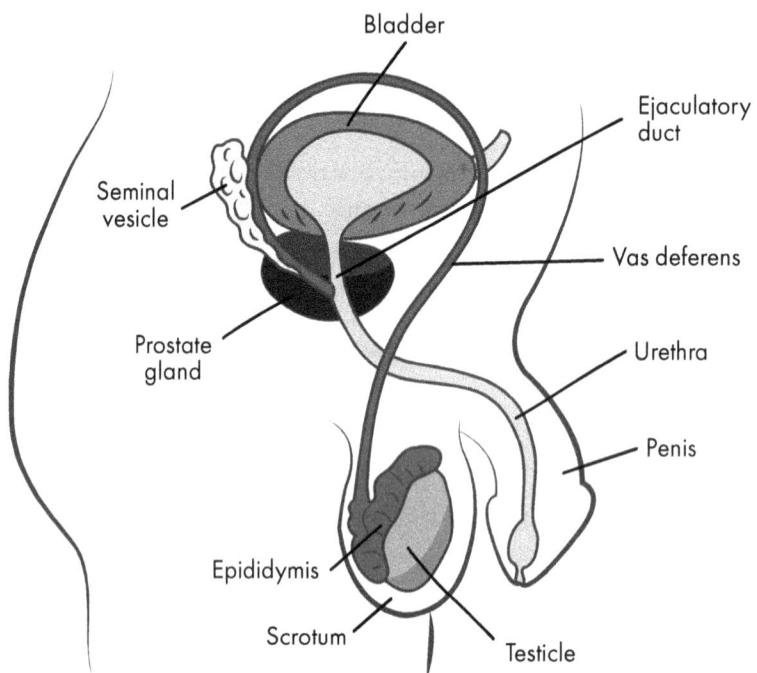

Figure 1.23. The Male Reproductive System

PRACTICE QUESTION

20. What role does the urethra play in the male reproductive system?

THE FEMALE REPRODUCTIVE SYSTEM

- The female reproductive system produces **eggs**, or female gametes, and gestates the fetus during pregnancy.
- Eggs are produced in the **ovaries** and travel through the **fallopian tubes** to the **uterus**, which is a muscular organ that houses the fetus during pregnancy.
- The uterine cavity is lined with a layer of blood-rich tissue called the **endometrium**.
  - If no pregnancy occurs, the endometrium is shed monthly during **menstruation**.
- An opening in the uterus called the **cervix** leads to the **vagina**.
- **Fertilization** occurs when the egg absorbs the sperm; it usually takes place in the fallopian tubes but may happen in the uterus itself. (See chapter 9, "Obstetrical Emergencies" for anatomy and physiology of pregnancy.)
- The female reproductive cycle is controlled by several different hormones, including **estrogen** and **progesterone**.

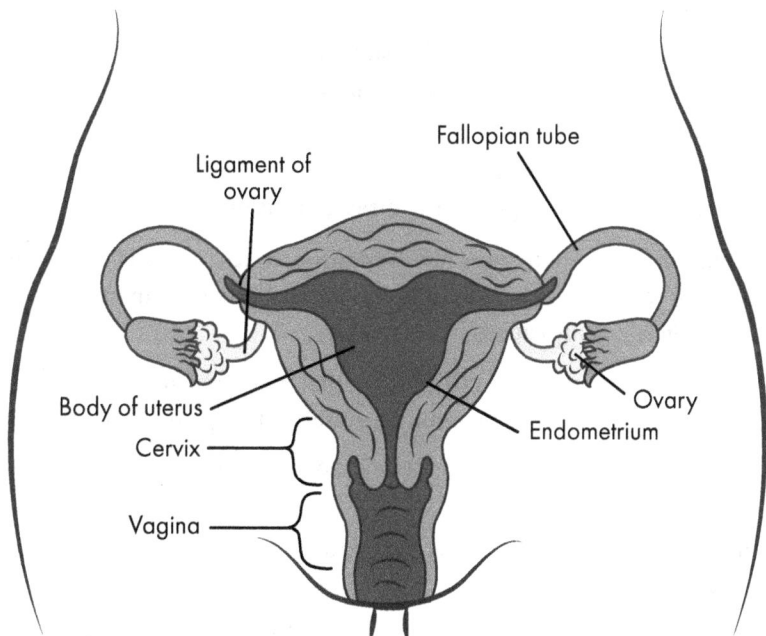

Figure 1.24. The Female Reproductive System

PRACTICE QUESTION

21. What is the role of the fallopian tubes in the female reproductive system?

PATHOLOGIES OF THE REPRODUCTIVE SYSTEM

- **Sexually transmitted infections (STIs)** occur in both males and females.
  - **Chlamydia** is caused by the bacteria *Chlamydia trachomatis*; it is the most commonly reported STI in the United States.

- The infection can be found in the cervix, urethra, rectum, or pharynx.
- Symptoms include vaginal, penile, or rectal discharge; vaginal bleeding; and lower abdominal pain.
- Chlamydia infections may be asymptomatic for long periods.
○ **Gonorrhea** is caused by the gram-negative diplococcus *Neisseria gonorrhoeae*; it is the second highest reported STI in the United States.
- Common infection sites include the cervix, vagina, rectum, and pharynx.
- Symptoms include painful urination; itching and burning; and vaginal, penile, or rectal discharge.
- Gonorrhea infections may be asymptomatic, especially in women.
○ **Genital herpes** is an STI caused by the two strains of the herpes simplex virus (HSV-1 and HSV-2).
- Both strains cause blisters on the mouth, anus, or genital area.
- The first outbreak after the initial infection is the most severe; recurrent outbreaks, which vary in frequency and duration, will generally be less severe.
○ **Syphilis** is an STI caused by the bacteria *Treponema pallidum*.
- The first sign of infection is **chancres** (sores) that appear 3 to 6 weeks after infection.
- Syphilis is a progressive disease: severe cardiovascular and neurological symptoms may appear if the disease is left untreated for years.
- Inflammation of the epididymis (**epididymitis**), testes (**orchitis**), and prostate (**prostatitis**) can cause pain, swelling, and painful urination in males. The inflammation is usually caused by infection.
- **Pelvic inflammatory disease (PID)** is an infection of the upper organs of the female reproductive system, including the uterus, fallopian tubes, and ovaries.
  ○ The infection, usually chlamydia or gonorrhea, ascends from the cervix or vagina.
  ○ PID is often asymptomatic; left untreated, it can lead to infertility and increased risk of cancer.
- **Ovarian cysts** form in the ovaries and are usually asymptomatic. However, the cysts can burst, causing sudden, intense pelvic pain.
- **Priapism** is an unintentional, prolonged erection that is unrelated to sexual stimulation and is unrelieved by ejaculation.
  ○ **Ischemic (low-flow) priapism** occurs when blood becomes trapped in the erect penis.
  ○ Ischemic priapism is considered a medical emergency requiring immediate intervention to preserve function of the penis.
- **Penile fractures** occur when there is a rupture of the penis's internal membranes; they are medical emergencies that require immediate treatment.

- **Testicular torsion** occurs when the spermatic cord, which supplies blood to the testicles, becomes twisted, leading to an ischemic testicle. The condition is considered a medical emergency that requires immediate treatment to preserve the function of the testicle.

PRACTICE QUESTION

22. Why is it important for patients diagnosed with an STI to be treated even if they have no symptoms?

The Urinary System

STRUCTURE AND FUNCTION OF THE URINARY SYSTEM

- The **urinary system** excretes water and waste from the body and is crucial for maintaining the balance of water and salt in the blood (also called electrolyte balance).
- The main organs of the urinary system are the **kidneys**, which perform several important functions:
    - filter waste from the blood
    - maintain the electrolyte balance in the blood
    - regulate blood volume, pressure, and pH
- **Nephrons** in the kidneys filter the blood and excrete the waste products as **urine**.
- Urine passes out of the kidneys through the **renal pelvis** and then through two long tubes called **ureters**.
- The two ureters drain into the **urinary bladder**, which holds up to one liter of liquid.
- Urine exits the bladder through the **urethra**.
    - In males, the urethra goes through the penis and also carries semen.
    - In females, the much shorter urethra ends just above the vaginal opening.

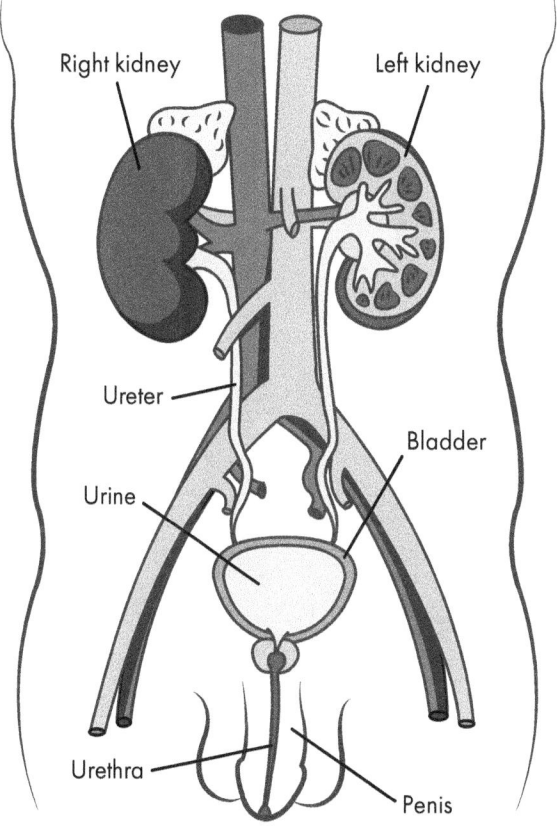

Figure 1.25. The Urinary System (Male)

PRACTICE QUESTION

23. What structure drains the urine into the bladder?

PATHOLOGIES OF THE URINARY SYSTEM

- **Renal calculi** (kidney stones) are hardened mineral deposits that form in the kidneys. They are usually asymptomatic but will cause debilitating pain and urinary symptoms once they pass into the urinary tract.

HUMAN ANATOMY AND PHYSIOLOGY

- **Urinary tract infections (UTIs)** can occur in the lower urinary tract (bladder and urethra) or in the upper urinary tract (kidneys and ureters). Symptoms include frequent, painful urination; cloudy, foul-smelling urine; and pelvic or lower abdominal pain.
- **Pyelonephritis**, infection of the kidneys, occurs when bacteria reach the kidney via the lower urinary tract or the bloodstream.
    - The clinical triad for kidney infections is fever, nausea or vomiting, and costovertebral pain.
    - Pyelonephritis can damage organs, can be a life-threatening infection, and will lead to renal scarring without prompt diagnosis and treatment.
- **Renal failure** is the loss of kidney function that leads to buildup of waste in the bloodstream. It can be acute or chronic.
    - **Acute renal failure** (also called acute kidney injury) occurs quickly as a result of hypovolemia, shock, infection, or obstruction of the urinary tract.
    - **Chronic kidney disease** is the progressive and irreversible loss of kidney function over months or years. The most common causes of chronic kidney disease are diabetes mellitus and hypertension.

PRACTICE QUESTION

24. An EMT is assessing a patient with complaints of bloody urine and severe side and back pain. The patient is alert and oriented with no abnormal vital signs. What condition should the EMT suspect?

The Integumentary System

- The **integumentary system** refers to the skin (the largest organ in the body) and related structures, including the hair and nails.
- **Skin** is composed of three layers.
    - The **epidermis** is the outermost layer of the skin. This waterproof layer contains no blood vessels and acts mainly to protect the body.
    - Under the epidermis lies the **dermis**, which consists of dense connective tissue that allows skin to stretch and flex. The dermis is home to blood vessels, glands, and **hair follicles**.
    - The **hypodermis** is a layer of fat below the dermis that stores energy (in the form of fat) and acts as a cushion for the body. The hypodermis is sometimes called the **subcutaneous layer**.
- The skin has several important roles.
    - It acts as a barrier to protect the body from injury, the intrusion of foreign particles, and the loss of water and nutrients.
    - Skin helps **thermoregulation**: blood vessels near the surface of the skin can dilate to release heat and contract to conserve heat.
    - The skin houses nerve endings that sense temperature, pressure, and pain.

- ○ Skin produces vitamin D when exposed to sunlight.
- **Sweat glands** release the water and salt mixture (sodium chloride, NaCl) called **sweat**.
  - ○ Sweat helps the body maintain the appropriate salt-water balance.
  - ○ Sweat can also contain small amounts of other substances the body needs to expel, including alcohol, lactic acid, and urea.

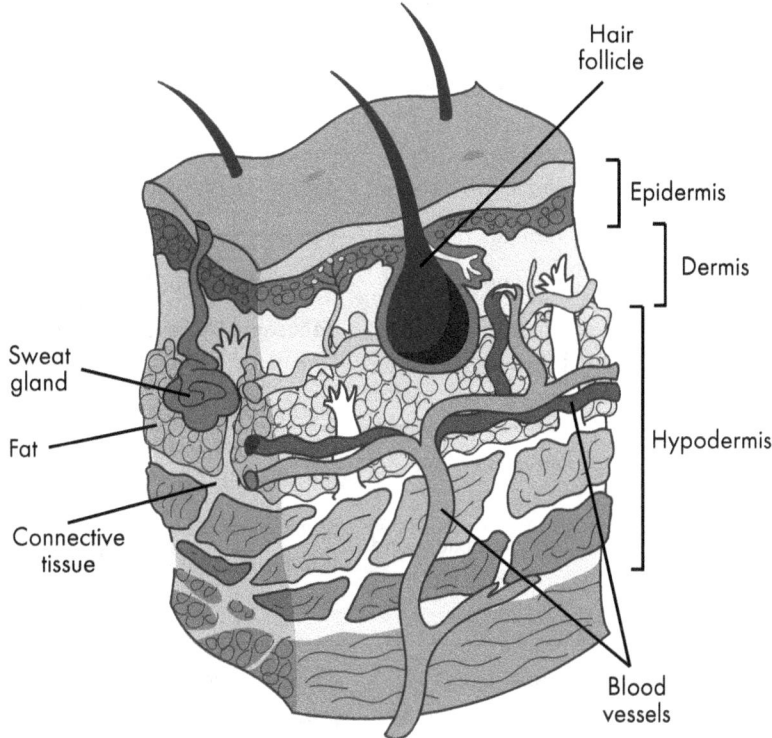

Figure 1.26. The Skin

PRACTICE QUESTION

25. What is the outermost layer of the skin called?

Pharmacology

- **Pharmacology** is the science of drugs and their effects on the human body.
  - ○ Medications work by bonding to receptors on cells in the body and either amplifying or inhibiting the activity of those cells.
  - ○ **Agonists** bond to receptors to amplify activity.
  - ○ **Antagonists** (blockers) bond to receptors to block the receptor sites, inhibiting the cell's normal functioning.
- Drugs are grouped into classes based on their chemical structures and the conditions they treat. The major drug classes, their general purpose, and examples of each are given in Table 1.5.

Table 1.5. Common Medications

Drug Class	Purpose	Example(s) generic name (brand name)
Antibiotics	inhibit growth of or kill bacteria	penicillin; amoxicillin; ciprofloxacin
Anticoagulants (blood thinners)	prevent blood clots	rivaroxaban (Xarelto); warfarin (Coumadin)
Anticonvulsants	prevent seizures	carbamazepine (Tegretol); topiramate (Topamax)
Antidepressants	treat depression and mood disorders	fluoxetine (Prozac); sertraline (Zoloft); bupropion (Wellbutrin, Zyban)
Antihistamines	treat allergies	diphenhydramine (Benadryl)
Antipsychotics	manage psychosis	aripiprazole (Abilify); lithium carbonate
Antivirals	inhibit growth of or kill viruses	docosanol (Abreva); oseltamivir (Tamiflu)
Barbiturates	depress the central nervous system	amobarbital (Amytal Sodium); butabarbital (Butisol Sodium); phenobarbital (Nembutal)
Benzodiazepines	reduce anxiety and relax muscles	alprazolam (Xanax); clonazepam (Klonopin); diazepam (Valium); lorazepam (Ativan)
Beta blockers	reduce blood pressure and improve blood flow	acebutolol (Sectral); atenolol (Tenormin); metoprolol (Lopressor); propranolol (Inderal)
Calcium channel blockers	relax and widen blood vessels	amlodipine (Norvasc); diltiazem (Cardizem); felodipine (Plendil); nifedipine (Procardia)
Corticosteroids	reduce inflammation	dexamethasone (Decadron); prednisone (Sterapred)
Diuretics	increase the output of urine	furosemide (Lasix); valsartan (Diovan)
Histamine-2 blockers	reduce stomach acid	famotidine (Pepcid); ranitidine (Zantac)
Hypnotics	reduce anxiety and induce sleep	eszopiclone (Lunesta); zolpidem (Ambien)
Immunosuppressants	suppress the immune system	adalimumab (Humira); methotrexate (Trexall)
Local anesthetics	block sensation in a small area	benzocaine; lidocaine (Xylocaine, Lidoderm)
Neuromuscular blockers	paralyze skeletal muscles	pancuronium (Pavulon); rocuronium (Zemuron)

Drug Class	Purpose	Example(s) generic name (brand name)
Nonsteroidal anti-inflammatory drugs (NSAIDs)	reduce pain and inflammation	ibuprofen (Motrin, Advil); naproxen (Aleve, Naprosyn)
Opioid pain relievers	block pain signals in brain	morphine (Astramorph, Duramorph); oxycodone (Percocet, OxyContin)
Proton pump inhibitors	reduce stomach acid	esomeprazole (Nexium); lansoprazole (Prevacid); omeprazole (Prilosec)

- **Adverse drug reaction** is a broad term used to describe unwanted, uncomfortable, or dangerous effects resulting from taking a specific medication.
  - Most adverse drug reactions are dose related, but they can also be allergic or idiosyncratic (unexpected responses that are neither dose related nor allergic responses).
  - Adverse drug reactions are one of the leading causes of morbidity and mortality in health care.
  - They can be classified by severity as:
    - mild (e.g., drowsiness)
    - moderate (e.g., hypertension)
    - severe (e.g., abnormal heart rhythm)
    - lethal (e.g., liver failure)
  - Adverse drug reactions are classified into six types, which are described in Table 1.6.

Table 1.6. Adverse Drug Reactions

Type	Description	Example
A augmented	predictable reactions arising from the pharmacological effects of the drug; dependent on dose	diarrhea due to antibiotics; hypoglycemia due to insulin
B bizarre	unpredictable reactions; independent of dose	hypersensitivity (anaphylaxis) due to penicillin
C chronic	reactions caused by the cumulative dose (the dose taken over a long period of time)	osteoporosis with oral steroids
D delayed	reactions that occur after the drug is no longer being taken	teratogenic effects with anticonvulsants
E end of use	reactions caused by withdrawal from a drug	withdrawal syndrome with benzodiazepines
F failure	unexpected failure of the drug to work; often caused by dose or drug interactions	resistance to antimicrobials

- The following routes are used to administer medications:
  - buccal: placed between the cheek and gum via spray, gel, or tablet
  - inhalation: inhaled into the respiratory system via mist, spray, or mask
  - intradermal (ID): injected into the dermal skin layer at a 15-degree angle via a 25- to 27-gauge needle
  - intramuscular (IM): injected into the muscle at a 90-degree angle via an 18- to 23-gauge needle
  - intravenous (IV): injected into a vein via an 18- to 22-gauge needle
  - ophthalmic: placed in the eye via ointment or drops
  - oral: taken by mouth and swallowed via capsule, tablet, liquid, gel, or solution
  - otic: placed in the ear via drops
  - parenteral: any injected medication (SC, IM, ID, or IV)
  - rectal: placed in the rectum via applicator (cream or suppository)
  - subcutaneous (SC): injected into the subcutaneous tissue at a 45- to 90-degree angle via a 22- to 25-gauge needle
  - sublingual: placed under the tongue via gel or tablets
  - topical: placed on the skin via patch, ointment, cream, liquid, or spray
  - transdermal: placed on the skin via patch
  - urethral: placed in the urethra and bladder via catheter
  - vaginal: placed in the vagina via applicator (cream or suppository)
  - Z-track: a specific IM injection method used to prevent the medication from irritating the subcutaneous tissue.
- To prevent errors, the "six rights of medication administration" should be followed every time a patient is given any medication.
  - Right patient
  - Right drug
  - Right route
  - Right dose
  - Right time
  - Right documentation
- Medications can be packaged in a variety of ways depending on the medication form, intended use, shelf stability, and more.
  - **Tablets** and **capsules** are usually taken orally.
  - **Metered-dose inhalers (MDIs)** allow droplets of medication to be inhaled.
  - **Transcutaneous patches** deliver medication through the skin.

PRACTICE QUESTION

26. What physiological changes should an EMT expect to see in a patient who has taken clonazepam (Klonopin)?

ANSWER KEY

1. The meninges are connective tissue.
2. The neck is inferior, or below, the head.
3. Blood from the lungs is returned to the left side of the heart. When the left side cannot pump this blood back out to the body, fluid builds up in the lungs. Blood from the body is returned to the right side of the heart, so right-sided failure causes fluid to build up in the abdomen and extremities.
4. The P wave shows atrial contraction. If a rhythm shows abnormalities in the P waves, then the patient's atria are not functioning properly.
5. An AED will advise a shock is necessary when it recognizes V-tach or V-fib.
6. Air that has been inhaled through the nostrils enters the trachea and then passes through the bronchi and bronchioles. The pathway for the inhaled air ends in the alveoli, where gas exchange takes place.
7. Kussmaul breathing is deep, labored hyperventilation associated with metabolic acidosis. Patients with this type of breathing are likely experiencing diabetic or kidney disorders, with diabetic ketoacidosis being the most common cause.
8. The lumbar vertebrae are located in the lower back. The patient may have injured their lumbar vertebrae.
9. The patient likely has rheumatoid arthritis which has led to progressive, bilateral degeneration of the joints in her hands.
10. The patient most likely has a cramp is his gastrocnemius (calf) muscle, which is posterior on the lower leg.
11. The patient will likely have muscle weakness and limited range of motion that will limit his mobility. He may also have muscle spasms. If the MD is advanced, the patient may have difficulty breathing.
12. Myelin insulates nerve cells and increases the speed that signals travel through the nervous system. When the myelin sheath disintegrates, signals between nerve cells slow down or are not transmitted at all.
13. Orthostatic syncope is the temporary loss of consciousness caused by a sudden drop in blood pressure upon standing. If the patient reports fainting immediately after standing from a sitting or lying position, the EMT should suspect orthostatic syncope.
14. The liver produces bile, which helps break down fat in the small intestine.
15. The vasculature of the lower esophagus drains into the portal vein, which becomes hypertensive in patients with advanced cirrhosis. This hypertension prevents the blood from the capillaries in the esophagus from draining. As a result, they become dilated and may burst.
16. Antibodies attach to antigens and destroy pathogens that cause infection. Because the mother and child have likely been exposed to the same pathogens, the mother's antibodies can help protect the infant from pathogens to which he has been exposed.
17. Patients with leukemia have dysfunctional white blood cells, so they are prone to frequent infections. Leukemia also disrupts the production of platelets, so patients with leukemia may bruise easily or bleed excessively.
18. The pancreas controls blood glucose levels by producing and releasing insulin and glucagon.
19. Type 1 diabetes is an autoimmune disease in which the body destroys cells in the pancreas that produce insulin. People with type 1 diabetes do not produce enough

insulin. Type 2 diabetes is the result of developed insulin resistance: the body produces insulin, but cells do not respond appropriately.

20. Semen passes through the urethra as it exits the penis.
21. The fallopian tubes are the passages through which eggs travel from the ovaries to the uterus.
22. Untreated STIs can spread to other organs, including the uterus, ovaries, and testes. The resulting infections can create a range of serious health problems including severe pain and infertility.
23. Urine passes through the ureters from the kidneys into the urinary bladder.
24. Bloody urine and flank and back pain are symptoms of renal calculi (kidney stones).
25. The epidermis is the outermost layer of the skin.
26. Clonazepam (Klonopin) is a benzodiazepine that relaxes muscles and reduces anxiety. A patient who has taken clonazepam may appear drowsy and have slowed breathing and heart rate.

TWO: PATIENT ASSESSMENT and TRANSFER

Assessing the Scene
SCENE HAZARDS

- Provider safety is the most important aspect of patient care.
- The priority is to protect:
  1. yourself
  2. your partner
  3. the patient
  4. bystanders
- To ensure scene safety, a quick assessment, or **scene size-up**, should be conducted to determine:
  - scene hazards
  - number of patients
  - need for additional resources
  - mechanism of injury or nature of illness
- Scene hazards may include environment hazards, hazardous substances, violence, and rescue hazards.
  - **Environmental hazards** can include inclement weather, traffic, poor lighting, or loud noises.
  - **Hazardous substances** can include hazardous chemicals or biological agents, radioactive agents, or explosives.
  - **Violence hazards** can include violent patients or bystanders, active crime scenes, or animals.
  - **Rescue hazards** can include traffic, water, fire, or collapsed buildings.
- If the scene is safe, make patient contact and begin the patient assessment.
- When hazards are present, the EMT should remove the hazard or remove the patient from the hazard if this can be done safely.

HELPFUL HINT
Park upwind, uphill, and upstream of hazardous materials incidents.

HELPFUL HINT
If the scene is not safe for bystanders, EMTs should request additional resources (e.g., police) to move bystanders to safety.

- If the scene hazards cannot be addressed, request additional resources.
  - Fires: Request the fire department.
  - Rescue operations: Request the fire department and a technical rescue team.
  - Hazardous chemicals and biological agents: Request the fire department and a hazardous materials (HazMat) response team.
  - Traffic hazards and violent or active crime scenes: Request the police.
- At hazardous scenes, EMTs may need to **stage**: wait off-scene in a safe location with the crew until responders on the scene request EMT presence.

PRACTICE QUESTION

1. The EMT has arrived on the scene of a car that struck a utility pole. What hazards should the EMT look for before entering the scene?

MASS CASUALTY INCIDENTS

- If there is more than one patient, immediately request additional ambulances or EMS personnel.
- A **mass casualty incident** is an event in which the number of patients overwhelms the capabilities of the initial EMS responders.
- In a mass casualty incident, the first EMS responders on scene should triage patients.
  - **Triage** is the sorting of patients by their injuries to determine in what order they will be treated and transported.
  - The goal of triage is to direct immediate resources to patients with life-threatening but treatable injuries (red).
  - Patients with less serious injuries (yellow and green) can receive delayed treatment and may be transported longer distances.
  - Patients with a very small chance of survival (black) are treated last.

Table 2.1. SALT Triage Classifications

Priority	Color	Description
Minor	green	minor injuries that require minimal treatment, including abrasions, sprains, and minor fractures
Delayed	yellow	serious injuries whose treatment can be delayed for a short period, including fractures and burns without airway compromise or major bleeding
Immediate	red	treatable life-threatening injuries, including respiratory compromise and uncontrolled bleeding
Expectant	gray	injuries incompatible with life
Dead	black	not breathing after life-saving measures have been attempted

- **Incident Command System (ICS)** is a system of control and command that emergency responders throughout the United States use.
  - The ICS provides recognizable command structure in emergencies and helps organizations work together effectively.
  - The **incident commander (IC)** is in charge of managing the emergency response across all agencies or organizations.
  - The IC will divide workers into sections, branches, and/or divisions, each of which has a designated supervisor.
  - When an EMT is dispatched to the scene of a mass casualty incident, they should know who their designated direct supervisor is on the scene.

PRACTICE QUESTION

2. An EMT arrives at the site of a motor vehicle crash (MVC). When assessing the scene, he notes that a school bus was involved in the accident, and multiple students appear to be injured. What should be the EMT's priority at this scene?

HAZARDOUS MATERIALS

- A **hazardous material** poses a threat to the safety of emergency responders, patients, bystanders, or the environment.
- A scene with hazardous materials present is referred to as a **HazMat incident**.
- HazMat protocols differ between regions and organizations. The EMT should be familiar with their local protocols.
- EMTs need specialized training to respond to most HazMat incidents.
- Commons sources of hazardous materials on a scene include:
  - fuel containers (e.g., car gas tank)
  - tanker trucks
  - leaks or fires at industrial facilities
  - sewage or natural gas infrastructure
- The EMT should assess the scene for signs of hazardous materials. These may include:
  - chemical storage containers
  - Department of Transportation (DOT) placards
  - multiple non-traumatic patients
  - shipping papers or **material safety data sheets (MSDS)** identifying chemicals on scene
- If the EMT suspects hazardous materials are present on a scene, they should immediately request the appropriate additional resources.
- Hazardous materials are categorized as Level 0 – 4 based on their level of toxicity, with Level 0 materials causing little damage and Level 4 materials causing death after minimal contact.

Figure 2.1. DOT Placards

PATIENT ASSESSMENT AND TRANSFER

- HazMat scenes are divided into three zones:
  - **hot zone**: area of contamination
  - **warm zone**: where decontamination occurs
  - **cold zone**: clear of contamination
- EMTs should wear the appropriate personal protective equipment (PPE) in each containment area.

PRACTICE QUESTION

3. An EMT is the first responder at the scene of an MVC. At the scene, the EMT sees a tanker truck leaking large amounts of fluid onto the road. What should the EMT do first?

PERSONAL PROTECTIVE EQUIPMENT (PPE)

DID YOU KNOW?
Universal precautions were introduced in the 1980s to protect health care workers from blood-borne pathogens. These were later replaced by *body isolation standards*, which in turn were replaced by *standard precautions* in 1996. The three terms are often used interchangeably.

- **Standard precautions** are a set of infection prevention measures crafted by the Centers for Disease Control and Prevention (CDC) to protect health care workers from infections in blood, feces, mucus, and other bodily substances.
- EMTs should use standard precautions any time they interact with a patient or scene.
- Standard precautions are based on the idea that health care workers should assume all patients are carrying a microorganism.
- Standard precautions relevant to the EMT include:
  - Use PPE, including gloves, masks, gowns, and protective eyewear.
  - Wear gloves during any contact with patients.
  - Change gloves after contact with patients and before touching equipment or other patients.
  - Practice good hand hygiene by washing with soap and water or using antimicrobial foam.
  - Wear appropriate PPE if at risk of body fluids splashing or spraying.
  - Clean and disinfect surfaces and equipment that come in contact with patients' bodily fluids.
  - Use an N-95 respirator mask when patients are suspected or known to be carrying an airborne infection (e.g., measles).
- PPE may also include gear to protect EMTs from scene hazards.
  - PPE may include firefighting turnout gear, reflective vests, helmets, or steel-toed boots.
  - The PPE needed will be determined by the hazards on an emergency scene. For example, wear firefighting turnout gear with goggles and helmet when extricating a patient from a car; wear reflective vests while working on roadways.
  - Specialized rescue PPE (e.g., self-contained breathing apparatus) should only be worn by rescuers who are trained to wear it.

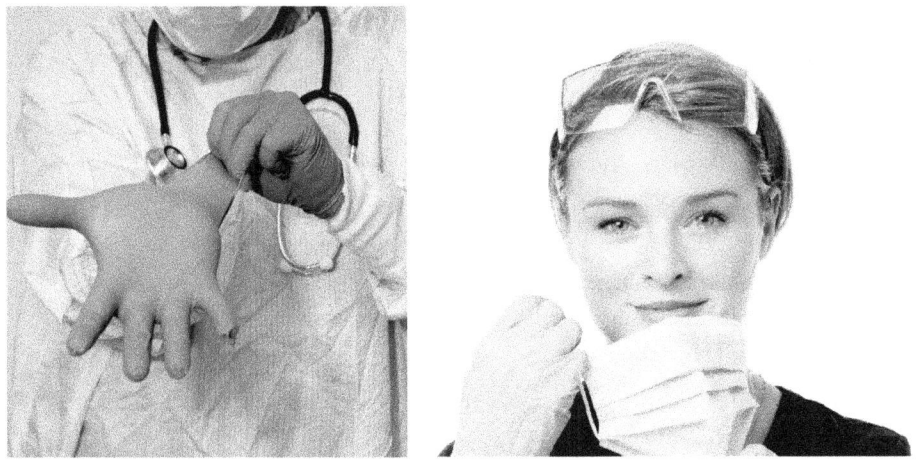

Figure 2.2. Personal Protective Equipment (PPE)

> PRACTICE QUESTION
>
> **4.** The EMT is caring for a patient who has been cut by a chainsaw. The patient has blood spurting from the leg wound. What PPE should the EMT wear during this patient encounter?

Assessing the Patient

- Providing a quality patient assessment will allow the EMT to form a **field impression**, the EMT's determination of the patient's likely condition.
- Patient assessment includes scene size-up, initial assessment, medical assessment or trauma assessment, and reassessment.
    - During the primary or **initial assessment**, the EMT looks for life-threatening conditions that need immediate attention.
    - A **medical assessment** is done on a patient with a medical ailment.
    - A **trauma assessment** is done on a patient with an injury.
    - **Reassessment** is done throughout the course of patient care to determine response to treatments or if any changes have occurred.

INITIAL ASSESSMENT

- The purpose of the initial assessment is to look for and address life-threatening issues.
- If life-threatening issues are found during the initial assessment, they should be promptly addressed, and the patient should be immediately transported to the ED.
- The initial assessment should always be completed in this order:
    1. general impression
    2. level of consciousness (LOC)

HELPFUL HINT

During the initial assessment, do not be distracted by injuries that are not immediately life threatening. Also, be aware that patients may be too distracted by their own injuries to accurately respond to questions about their condition.

DID YOU KNOW?
Most guidelines recommend checking the airway, breathing, and then circulation (**ABC**). However, some EMS systems are moving to address circulation first (**CAB**), particularly for cardiac arrest patients and patients with severe bleeding.

3. airway
4. breathing
5. circulation

- After determining that the scene is safe, the EMT can approach the patient. As the EMT approaches the patient, they can begin to form their **general impression**, or first impression, of the patient.
  - The general impression is an initial indicator of whether the patient is stable or unstable. A patient is considered **unstable** if their injury or illness is immediately life threatening.
  - During the general impression, the EMT should note the patient's age, sex, race, and general condition.
  - Look for obvious signs of distress, such as respiratory difficulty or indicators that the patient is in pain.

HELPFUL HINT
Use your senses to form a general impression.
- <u>Look</u> at the patient's appearance.
- <u>Listen</u> for sounds such as wheezing or gasping.
- Note foul <u>smells</u> that may indicate gangrene or other medical issues.

- After the general impression, determine the patient's **level of consciousness** (**LOC**), a measure of a person's responsiveness to stimuli.
  - LOC can be unaltered, altered, or unconscious.
    - **unaltered LOC**: alert and able to answer simple questions
    - **conscious with altered LOC**: alert but confused
    - **unconscious**: not responsive
  - LOC can also be described using the AVPU scale (Table 2.2).

Table 2.2. Assessing Level of Consciousness

Level of Consciousness	Designation	The patient will . . .
Alert	A	interact with EMTs without being prompted
Alert to Verbal Stimuli	V	respond only when they are spoken to
Alert to Painful Stimuli	P	respond only to painful stimuli
Unresponsive	U	not respond to any stimuli

HELPFUL HINT
Check for response to painful stimuli by applying pressure to the earlobe, supraorbital nerve, or trapezius muscle.

- The EMT may also determine the patient's Glasgow Coma Scale (from 3 to 15).

Table 2.3. Scoring on the Glasgow Coma Scale

Eye Opening (E)	Verbal Response (V)	Motor Response (M)
4 = spontaneous 3 = to sound 2 = to pressure 1 = none NT = not testable	5 = orientated 4 = confused 3 = to words 2 = to sounds 1 = none NT = not testable	6 = obeys command 5 = localizes 4 = normal flexion 3 = abnormal flexion 2 = extension 1 = none NT = not testable

- Next, check the **airway** and determine if it is open.
  - If the patient is alert, speak with the patient to determine if there is any obstruction to the airway.
  - If the patient cannot speak or is holding their hand on their throat in distress, they may have an airway obstruction.
  - If the patient is not alert, open the airway and check for good air exchange.
    - No spinal injury: use the head tilt–chin lift maneuver.
    - Possible spinal injury: use the jaw-thrust maneuver.
  - If the patient cannot maintain an open airway, use an airway adjunct to keep the airway open.
    - oropharyngeal airway if no gag reflex
    - nasopharyngeal airway if there is a gag reflex
- Once the airway has been opened, check for **breathing** to assure adequate ventilation.
  - Form a general impression of breathing (e.g., fast/slow, shallow/deep); do not obtain a specific rate in the initial assessment.
  - If breathing is not adequate, the EMT should provide the appropriate intervention. (See chapter 3, "Respiratory Emergencies," for a detailed discussion of artificial ventilation and oxygen delivery.)
  - Address injuries interfering with respirations (e.g., impaled object in the cheek or a flail rib).
- The final part of the initial assessment is **circulation**.
  - Look for major bleeding, and address it immediately if found.
  - Check for the presence of pulses. (Do not obtain a specific rate in the initial assessment.)
    - Unconscious patients: start with a carotid pulse in adults and children and a brachial pulse in infants.
    - Conscious patients: palpate a radial pulse. If no pulse is found, check the femoral or carotid pulse.
  - The EMT should compare central (carotid) and peripheral (radial) pulses. If the pressures differ, the patient could be suffering from shock.
  - Immediately begin CPR on unconscious patients with no pulse and prepare AED.
  - Check the patient's skin color, condition, and temperature.
    - skin color: pale, cyanotic, flushed, or jaundiced (yellow)
    - condition: diaphoretic, dry, or poor skin turgor
    - temperature: cold, warm, or hot

HELPFUL HINT
Do not palpate both carotid arteries at once, as it can reduce blood flow to the brain and cause syncope.

HELPFUL HINT
Pale skin that is cold and clammy is a potential sign of shock, which should be treated immediately.

PRACTICE QUESTION

5. An EMT is dispatched to a call for a 56-year-old male with chest pain. At the scene, the EMT finds the patient prone on the floor, and the patient does not respond to the EMT's questions. What should the EMT do next to further assess the man's LOC?

VITAL SIGNS

- EMTs must take a full set of vital signs to determine how to care for patients.
- A full set of vital signs includes:
  - alertness level
  - pulse
  - blood pressure
  - respirations
  - lung sounds
  - pulse oximetry (SpO_2)
  - pupillary response
  - blood glucose
- Vital signs do not have to be taken in order. The EMT should first choose vital signs relevant to the patient's chief complaint. For example, if a patient is complaining of difficulty breathing, evaluate the patient's respiratory rate, lung sounds, and pulse oximetry first.
- Determine **alertness level** by asking simple questions that everyone should know (e.g., What month is it? Where are you?).
  - The EMT should only ask questions they know the answers to.
  - The patient is described as "alert and oriented by" the number of questions answered correctly "of" the number of questions asked (e.g., A&O × 3 of 5).
- Check a patient's **pulse** (measured in beats per minute [bpm]) for rate, regularity, and strength.
  - Obtain a pulse rate with a pulse oximeter or by palpating the pulse.
  - Check carotid, femoral, brachial, radial, or pedal pulses (dorsalis pedis and posterior tibial).

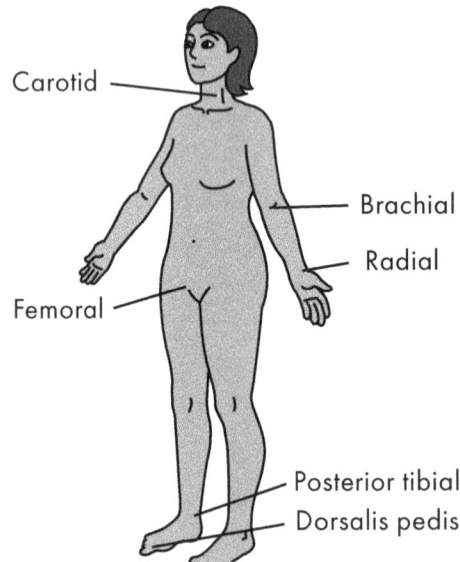

Figure 2.3. Location of Pulses

- Heart rate is described as normal, **tachycardia** (fast), or **bradycardia** (slow).

Table 2.4. Normal Heart Rate

Age	Beats per Minute (bpm)
Adults and adolescents	60 – 100
Children (2 – 10 years)	60 – 140
Infants and toddlers	100 – 190
Newborns (< 3 months)	85 – 205

- Pulse rhythm is described as **regular** (equal time between contractions) or **irregular** (missed beats or changes in time between beats).
- Pulse strength is described as normal, **bounding** (stronger than normal), or **thready** (weaker than normal).

- **Blood pressure (BP)** is the measurement of the force of blood as it flows against the walls of the arteries, measured in mm Hg.
  - **Systolic pressure** is the pressure that occurs while the heart is contracting; **diastolic pressure** occurs while the heart is relaxed.
  - Blood pressure can be taken at the brachial artery by auscultation, palpation, or automated blood pressure cuff.
    - An automated blood pressure cuff is placed on the patient's bicep and provides a readout of their blood pressure.
    - During auscultation, the EMT places the blood pressure cuff on the patient's bicep and the stethoscope on the brachial artery. The EMT should inflate the cuff and listen for **Korotkoff sounds**. The first sound will be the systolic pressure, and the absence of sound is the diastolic pressure.
    - To palpate blood pressure, the EMT places the blood pressure cuff on the upper arm and palpates a radial pulse. The cuff is inflated. The systolic pressure is determined when the EMT feels the radial pulse return as the cuff is deflating. Palpating blood pressure is the least accurate method.
  - A healthy adult blood pressure is a systolic value of 100 to 139 mm Hg and a diastolic value of 60 to 79 mm Hg.

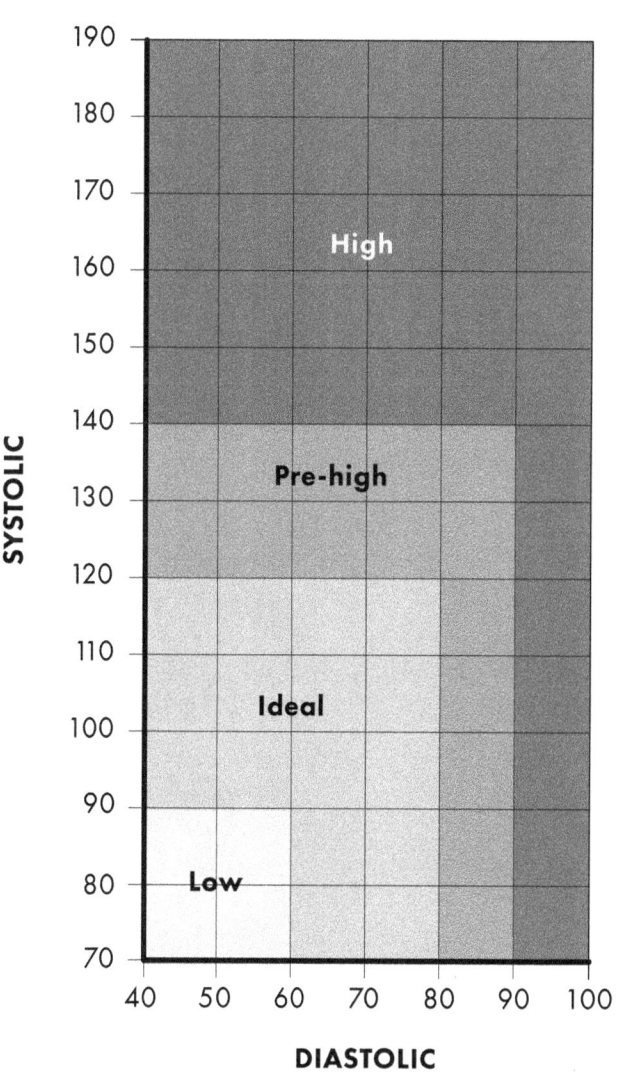

Figure 2.4. Classifying Blood Pressure

- For infants and children, the normal systolic blood pressure is 80 + 2 × patient's age in years; the diastolic pressure is about 2/3 the systolic.
- **Respirations** should be evaluated for rate, rhythm, depth, and quality.
  - Respiratory rate (measured in breaths per minute) can be described as normal, **tachypnea** (fast), or **bradypnea** (slow).
  - Respiratory rhythms can be normal, irregular, or **apneic** (no breathing).
  - Respiratory depth can be normal, **shallow**, or **deep**.
  - **Respiratory quality** can be normal or labored, with the patient working harder than normal to breathe. Evidence of labored breathing includes **tripod position**, using accessory muscles, bobbing the head, or flaring the nostrils.

Figure 2.5. Tripod Position

Table 2.5. Normal Respiratory Rate

Age	Breaths per Minute
Adult	12 to 20
Child 11 – 14 years	12 to 20
Child 6 – 10 years	15 to 30
Child 6 months – 5 years	20 to 30
Infant 0 – 6 months	25 to 40
Newborn	30 to 50

- **Lung sounds** should be taken by listening to the upper and lower lungs on the right and left side of the patient's back. Lung sounds may also be taken from the patient's front or side if the back is inaccessible.

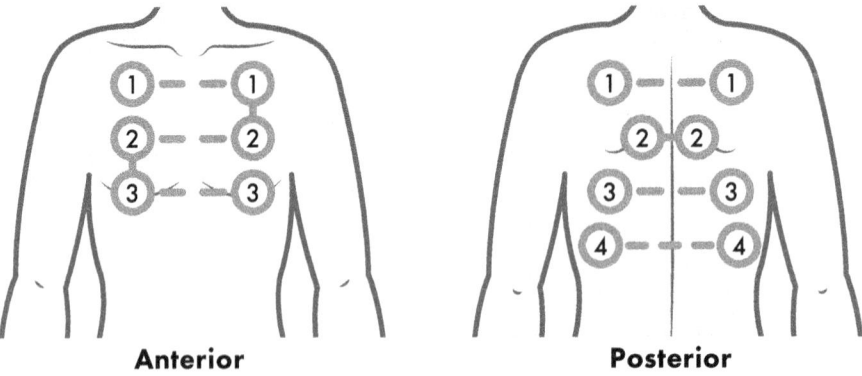

Figure 2.6. Respiratory Auscultation

Table 2.6. Lung Sounds

Sound	Description	Etiology
Normal	air heard moving through the lungs with no obstructions	normal function of the lungs
Wheezes	continuous musical-like sound; can occur on inspiration or expiration	air being forced through narrowed passages in the airway (e.g., asthma, COPD)

Sound	Description	Etiology
Rhonchi	low-pitched, coarse rattling lung sounds	secretions in the airway (e.g., pneumonia, cystic fibrosis)
Stridor	high-pitched wheezing sound	air moving through narrowed or obstructed passages in the upper airway (e.g., aspiration, laryngospasm)
Rales (crackles)	crackling, rattling sound that can be coarse or fine	fluid in the small airways of the lung (e.g., pulmonary edema, pneumonia)
Pleural friction rub	grating, creaking sound	inflamed pleural tissue (e.g., pleuritis, pulmonary embolism)
Diminished or absent breath sounds	decreased intensity of breath sounds due to lack of air in lung tissues	air or fluid around the lungs (e.g., pleural effusion, pneumothorax) or blocked airway

- **Pulse oximetry** (SpO_2) measures the percentage of red blood cells that are carrying oxygen.

Table 2.7. Pulse Oximetry (SpO_2)

Reading	Assessment
96% – 100%	normal
91% – 95%	mild hypoxia
85% – 90%	moderate hypoxia
Less than 85%	severe hypoxia

  o Pulse oximetry can provide false readings in patients who have suffered carbon monoxide poisoning: the actual oxygenation saturation will be lower.
  o Pulse oximetry may not work well on patients with cold hands, anemia, or nail polish.

- **Pupils** should be assessed for size and reactivity.
  o Pupils may be **equal** (the same size) or **unequal** (different sizes).
  o Pupil size is described as **constricted**, **mid-point** (normal size), or **dilated**.
  o The pupils' response to light is described as **reactive** or **non-reactive**.
  o Unequal pupils may indicate a brain injury.
  o Unreactive constricted pupils or pinpoint pupils may indicate opioid overdose.
  o Unreactive dilated pupils may indicate alcohol or drug usage.

- **Blood glucose** can be used to identify hypoglycemia or hyperglycemia.
  o Take the blood glucose of any patient who is unconscious or has altered LOC.

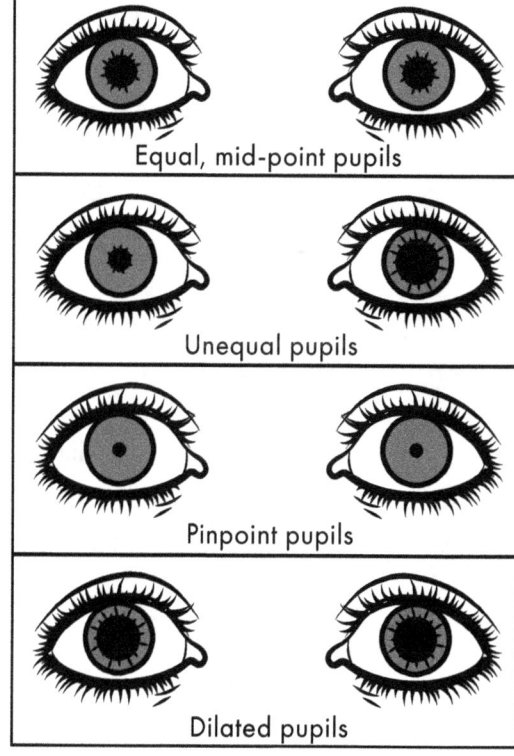

Figure 2.7. Pupil Assessment

- The EMT should use a **glucometer** to take a blood glucose: clean the patient's finger with an alcohol wipe, prick the patient's skin with a lancet, and apply a drop of blood to the test strip.
- The normal blood glucose range is 60 – 110 mg/dL.
- After the finger stick, dispose of the lancet in a sharps container.

HELPFUL HINT

False low-glucose readings can occur if the EMT does not allow the alcohol to dry before performing the finger stick.

PRACTICE QUESTION

6. An EMT is dispatched on a call for an adult female complaining of headache and difficulty breathing. The EMT finds the patient alert with unaltered LOC. The EMT gathers the following vital signs: heart rate 110 bpm, respiratory rate 22 breaths per minute, BP 190/100 mm Hg, SpO_2 92%. Which finding indicates a need for immediate medical treatment?

SECONDARY ASSESSMENT: MEDICAL PATIENTS

- **Nature of illness (NOI)** is the cause of the patient's current illness or **chief complaint** (the patient's main concern).
- If the medical patient is conscious, ask questions to determine a field impression and treatment strategy.
- Ask conscious patients about the history of the present illness. This can be done using the **OPQRST** mnemonic.
    - Onset: When did the symptoms start?
    - Provocation: What causes the pain? What were you doing when the pain started?
    - Quality: Please describe the pain.
    - Radiation: Where is the pain? Does it go anywhere?
    - Severity: On a scale of 1 to 10, with 10 being the worst pain you ever had, what is your pain level?
    - Time: When did the pain start?
- Take a **SAMPLE** history.
    - Symptoms
    - Allergies
    - Medications
    - Pertinent history
    - Last oral intake
    - Events leading to the incident
- Tailor the physical examination to the chief complaint, vital signs, history of present illness, and SAMPLE history. Examine the affected body system thoroughly.
- If the patient is unconscious, perform a rapid physical exam.

Table 2.8. Rapid Physical Exam of an Unconscious Patient

Area	What to Look For
Neck	jugular vein distension, medical alert tags
Chest	equal chest rise and fall, lung sounds
Abdomen	rigidity, distension
Pelvis	incontinence, symmetry
Extremities	symmetry, pulse, motor function, sensation, medical alert tags

- Attempt to obtain OPQRST and SAMPLE histories from bystanders or family.
- Complete a **reassessment** every 5 minutes for unstable patients and every 15 minutes for stable patients.
  - Look for trends in the vital signs to determine if the interventions are improving the patient's condition.
  - Reassess if there is any change in the patient's condition and after giving medications.

PRACTICE QUESTION

7. The EMT has completed the initial assessment and checked the vital signs on a conscious medical patient. What should the EMT do to complete the secondary assessment?

SECONDARY ASSESSMENT: TRAUMA PATIENTS

- **Mechanism of injury (MOI)** is how an injury occurred; use the mechanism of injury to obtain clues about possible injuries.
- A trauma patient could have multiple injuries; the patient should be systematically assessed so that injuries are not missed.
  - If the patient is alert and stable, obtain a SAMPLE history and perform a detailed assessment on scene.
  - If the patient is unstable, perform a **rapid head-to-toe assessment** looking for immediate life threats, and then immediately transport the patient to the hospital. The detailed assessment can be done en route.
- The detailed assessment should include checking the head, neck, chest, abdomen, pelvis, extremities, and posterior for **DCAP-BTLS**:
  - Deformity
  - Contusions
  - Abrasions
  - Punctures and penetrations
  - Burns

- - Tenderness
  - Lacerations
  - Swelling

Table 2.9. Revised Trauma Score

	Criterion	Revised Trauma Score Points
Glasgow Coma Scale	13 – 15	4
	9 – 12	3
	6 – 8	2
	4 – 5	1
	3	0
Systolic Blood Pressure	> 89 mm Hg	4
	76 – 89 mm Hg	3
	50 – 75 mm Hg	2
	1 – 49 mm Hg	1
	0 mm Hg	0
Respiratory Rate	10 – 29/min	4
	> 29/min	3
	6 – 9/min	2
	1 – 5/min	1
	0/min	0

- The EMT's goal is to get the trauma patient to the hospital within the **golden hour**: the first hour after a patient suffers a traumatic injury.
  - The concept of the golden hour is controversial. Multiple studies have suggested that time to initiation of definitive treatment has minimal impact on patient outcomes.
  - Patients with cardiac arrest, intracranial hemorrhage, and abdominal hemorrhage are most affected by delays in treatment.
- Assess the patient's **trauma score** (Table 2.9).
  - The trauma score will determine what level of trauma center the patient should be transported to.
  - A low revised trauma score indicates the need for a higher-level trauma facility.

Table 2.10. Trauma Center Levels

Level	Description
I	Provides complete care for any level of injury.
II	Able to initiate definitive care for all injured patients. Some procedures may require transfer to a Level I trauma center.

Level	Description
III	Able to assess, resuscitate, and stabilize injured patients. Patients requiring intensive care will be transferred to Level I or II trauma center.
IV	Provides advanced trauma life support (ATLS) before transferring patients to a higher level of care; common in remote areas with long transport times to higher-level trauma centers.
V	Provides ATLS before transferring patients to a higher level of care (designation used only in some states).

PRACTICE QUESTION

8. An EMT is assessing a construction worker who has fallen off a roof. During the initial assessment, the EMT determines that the patient is unconscious but breathing with a weak pulse. What type of assessment should the EMT perform next?

Moving the Patient

MOVING PATIENTS

- The EMT should choose the best device to move, lift, and transfer the patient.
    - When possible, use a **power stretcher** to avoid back injuries.
    - If the patient is in a bed, push the stretcher next to the bed. Then transfer the patient to the stretcher using a sheet.
    - Use a **stair chair** for conscious patients who need to be moved downstairs. When backing down the stairs, have a spotter to help maintain balance.
    - Use a **commercial sheet with handles** for patients who need to be moved through tight quarters.
    - Use a **backboard** to move unconscious or traumatic patients.
    - Use a **litter basket stretcher** to carry patients across rough terrain. There should be 4 to 6 EMTs carrying the litter basket stretcher.
- Use proper lifting techniques when moving patients.
    - When lifting, the EMT should keep their legs shoulder-width apart and lift with the legs.
    - The EMT should avoid lifting to the side or twisting.
    - The EMT should avoid reaching more than 15 to 20 inches from their body when lifting.
- The EMT should know their limitations and call for additional help if needed.
- Communicate with the patient and other EMTs when lifting and moving patients or heavy items.
- In all patient transfers and moves, EMT and patient safety must be a priority.

PRACTICE QUESTION

9. The EMT is evaluating a patient who is morbidly obese. The EMTs do not believe they can lift the patient without further assistance. What should they do?

LOAD-AND-GO

- Any patient in a potentially life-threatening condition is considered a **load-and-go** patient.
    - The load-and-go patient should be immediately moved to the ambulance and transported to the hospital.
    - Patient care should be completed en route to the hospital.
- Load-and-go patients have an issue that has been discovered during the primary assessment, including:
    - shock
    - heart attack
    - stroke
    - cardiac arrest
    - respiratory arrest
    - anaphylaxis
    - significant trauma
- Upon recognition of a load-and-go patient, request an advanced life support (ALS) intercept.
    - An **ALS intercept** is a request for an ALS unit to be sent to meet the EMTs. The patient is transferred to the ALS unit for treatment.
    - The EMT should not wait on scene with a load-and-go patient if the ALS intercept has not arrived. Attempt to meet the ALS unit en route to the hospital. If the hospital is closer than the ALS unit, transport the patient to the hospital.

PRACTICE QUESTION

10. An EMT is on scene with a 24-year-old male in respiratory arrest. An ALS intercept is en route, but the dispatcher reports they have been slowed by traffic. The patient has been loaded in the ambulance and is ready for transport. What should the EMT do next?

PATIENT TRANSFERS

- Transferring patients can be emergent, urgent, and non-urgent.
- **Emergent** moves are performed when there is an immediate threat to the safety of patients or EMTs.
    - Emergent moves may be used when:

- the patient needs to be removed from a hazard before treatment for a life-threatening condition
- there is a life-threatening condition that requires the patient to be repositioned before treatment
- the patient must be moved to get to other patients with life-threatening conditions
  - No spinal stabilization is used during emergent moves.
  - Emergent moves should be made by lifting or dragging the patient on the long axis to avoid aggravating possible spinal injuries.
  - Emergent moves include blanket drags, firefighter's carry, cradle carry, and one- or two-rescuer assists.
- **Urgent moves** are performed when the scene is safe, but the patient needs to be moved to treat a life-threatening condition.
  - Urgent moves include spinal injury precautions.
    - Use a long spine board if time allows.
    - Use the rapid extraction technique if the patient needs to be moved quickly.
- **Non-urgent moves** are patient transfers in which there is no immediate threat to the life or safety of the patient or EMT.
  - Choose a method that minimizes pain and discomfort for the patient.
  - Always use spinal stabilization if a spinal injury is suspected.
  - Possible methods include extremity lift, direct carry, and direct ground lift.

HELPFUL HINT
Urgent moves are common in MVCs when patients must be rapidly removed from the vehicle to receive care.

PRACTICE QUESTION

11. A firefighter EMT finds a victim in an active house fire. What type of transfer would they use to move the patient out of the home?

AIR TRANSPORT

- **Air transport** should be used when patients require medical care that cannot be provided quickly enough by ground transport.
- Air transport may be called when:
  - a long transport would mean life-saving care is provided outside the golden hour
  - an unstable patient will require a lengthy extraction from a motor vehicle
  - the patient is in a remote location
- Local protocols will dictate when the EMT should call for a helicopter.
- Guidelines for air transports include:
  - Locate a 100 × 100 ft. flat area for the helicopter to land. The area should be free of debris and overhead obstructions.
  - Do not approach the helicopter without permission from the crew.

- Approach from the front of the aircraft.
- If the helicopter is on a hillside, approach from the lower side.
- If the helicopter is requested at night, illuminate the landing site and any nearby hazards (e.g., power lines).

PRACTICE QUESTION

12. The EMT is caring for an MVC victim who is being extricated from the car. The patient is showing signs of shock. The time to extrication will be 20 minutes, and the distance to the hospital is 1 hour. How should the EMT plan for the patient to be transported?

ANSWER KEY

1. Possible hazards in this scenario include downed power lines, fluids leaking from the car, and traffic. Depending on the type of vehicle, the EMT may also need to check the car for hazardous cargo.

2. The EMT's priority should be to request additional resources. He should contact dispatch to request additional ambulances to the scene. He should contact police for traffic control and the fire department for extrication of victims if needed. After requesting the additional resources, the EMT should begin triaging the patients.

3. The EMT should park a safe distance away from the incident and immediately call for additional resources to handle a potential HazMat scene. The EMT should attempt to visually locate the DOT placard or other signs that may identify the truck's contents. The EMT may then begin containing the area to prevent injury to bystanders.

4. The EMT should be wearing gloves, goggles, a face shield, and a gown for this patient encounter. The spurting blood could come in contact with any uncovered clothing or skin.

5. The EMT should provide a painful stimulus, such as pinching the earlobe, to determine if the patient is responsive to pain. If he does not respond, he should be considered unresponsive, and the EMT may move on to assessing the ABCs.

6. A systolic blood pressure over 180 mm Hg is a hypertensive emergency. The patient should be transported immediately to the ED.

7. The EMT should obtain information on the history of the present illness and a SAMPLE history. The EMT should then focus the physical exam on the body system affected.

8. The patient is unstable and should receive a rapid head-to-toe assessment. The detailed assessment can be completed en route to the hospital.

9. The EMTs should acknowledge their limitations and contact dispatch to request additional EMTs to help lift the patient safely. This could also include requesting a specialized ambulance to transport the morbidly obese patient.

10. The EMT should begin transport to the hospital. If possible, they should meet the ALS intercept on the way to the hospital.

11. A house fire is an unsafe scene, so the firefighter EMT should use an emergent move to remove the patient from the hazardous environment. Depending on the scene and the patient's condition, the EMT may choose to use the blanket drag, firefighter's carry, cradle carry, or one-rescuer assist.

12. The EMT should request air transport to the hospital to ensure the patient arrives within the golden hour.

THREE: RESPIRATORY EMERGENCIES

Airway, Respiration, and Ventilation
OPENING AND SUCTIONING THE AIRWAY

- The EMT's priority task is establishing a **patent airway** (open and clear); this should always take precedence over other medical care.

- A conscious patient who is able to speak can help the EMT determine if their airway is open.
    - Conscious patients with a patent airway may remain in a comfortable position during assessment.

- Unconscious patients with a potentially compromised airway should be placed in the supine position so the EMT can assess and open their airway.

- Establishing a patent airway takes priority over the immobilization of the patient's head, neck, and spine: provide as much spinal immobilization to the trauma victim as possible without delaying assessment of the patient's airway.

- There are two common methods of manually opening the patient's airway: the head tilt–chin lift maneuver and the jaw-thrust maneuver.

- The **head tilt–chin lift maneuver** is the preferred method for opening the airway and correcting blockage.
    - Perform by placing one hand on the patient's forehead and tilting it back while simultaneously using the fingertips of the other hand to lift beneath the patient's chin.
    - This maneuver is contraindicated in patients with suspected head, neck, or spine injury.

- The **jaw-thrust maneuver** is used for suspected trauma patients to minimize movement of the cervical spine.

HELPFUL HINT
Place padding underneath the shoulders of a supine pediatric patient to counter neck flexion and prevent injury while opening the airway.

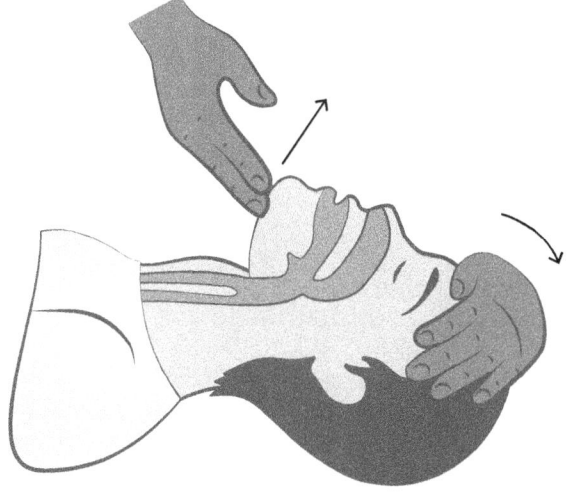

Figure 3.1. Head Tilt–Chin Lift Maneuver

- From a kneeling position at the top of the patient's head, place fingers behind the angles of the patient's jaw and lift the jaw without moving the patient's head, neck, or spine.

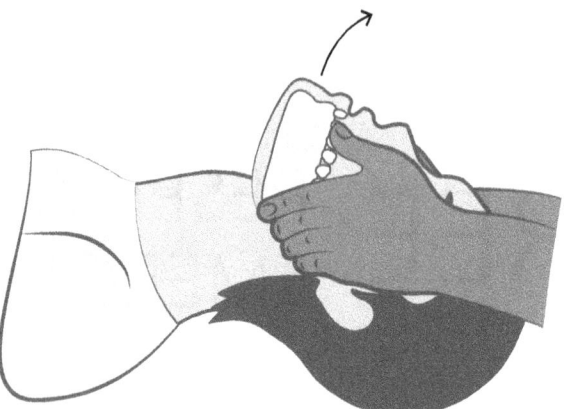

Figure 3.2. Jaw-Thrust Maneuver

- Excess secretions (including mucus, vomit, or blood) or foreign objects can block the patient's airway or be aspirated into the lungs.
- Secretions and foreign material should be **suctioned** after opening the airway but before inserting an airway adjunct.
- Suction devices consist of a catheter and/or tubing, a source of vacuum (such as a pump), and a collection canister.
  - Suction units can be portable or fixed (usually mounted inside the ambulance).
  - Suction devices should be able to generate at least 300 mm Hg of vacuum.
  - The disposable catheter, tubing, and collection canister are for single-patient use only.
- The two most common suction catheters are the rigid suction catheter and French tip.
  - **Rigid catheter**: Also called the Yankauer or tonsil-tip catheter, it has a large bore suitable for suctioning the oral airway.
  - **French catheter**: A flexible tip appropriate for suctioning lighter secretions such as those found in a nasal airway or stoma.
- The techniques for suctioning include:
  - Only place the tip of the catheter where it can be seen.
  - Position the tip of the catheter prior to applying suction.
  - Begin suctioning while withdrawing the catheter.
  - To reduce the risk of hypoxia, limit suction to 15 seconds for an adult, 10 seconds for a child, and 5 seconds for an infant.

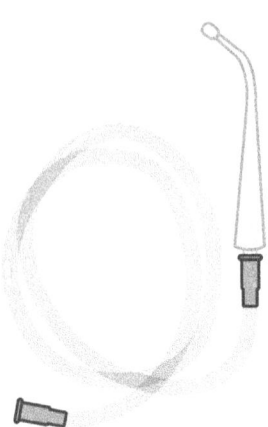

Rigid catheter

French catheter

Figure 3.3. Types of Catheters

DID YOU KNOW?
The word "French" refers to a scale that measures the outer diameter of the catheter. Abbreviated as "Fr," a larger number denotes a larger size catheter.

PRACTICE QUESTION

1. A patient is found unresponsive at the base of a ladder with blood dripping from his mouth. How should the EMT assess and open the airway?

AIRWAY ADJUNCTS

- **Airway adjuncts** assist in maintaining the patient's airway. They are used when:
  - The tongue is obstructing the airway.
  - More room is needed for suctioning.
- Airway adjuncts include oropharyngeal and nasopharyngeal airways.
- The **oropharyngeal airway (OPA)** is indicated in unconscious patients with no gag reflex.
  - Select the correctly sized OPA by measuring from the corner of the mouth to the earlobe.
  - For adult patients, begin by inserting the OPA upside-down with the tip toward the roof of the mouth, then rotate 180 degrees.
  - For pediatric patients, use a tongue depressor to move the tongue down while inserting the OPA with the tip at a 90-degree angle, and then rotate.

DID YOU KNOW?
The tongue is the most common airway obstruction, particularly in unconscious patients. When the muscles of the tongue relax, the tongue collapses and can block the airway.

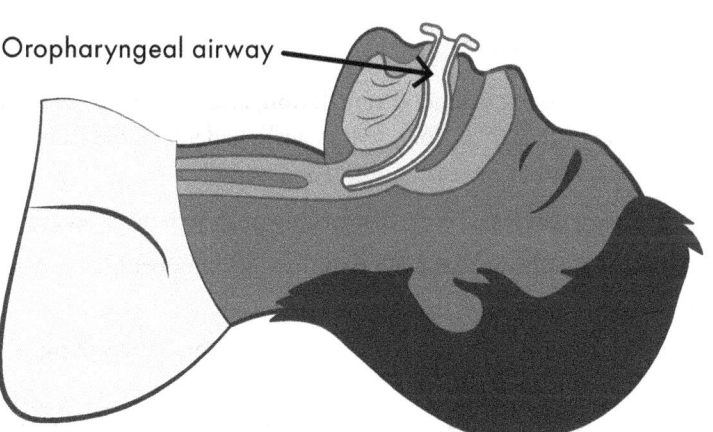

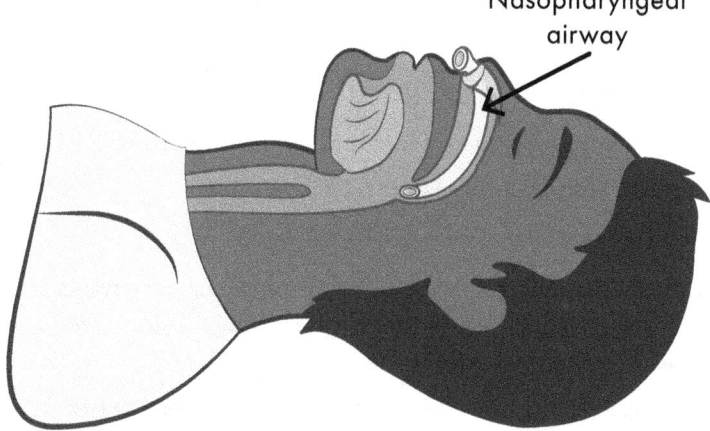

Figure 3.4. Airway Adjuncts

RESPIRATORY EMERGENCIES

- If the patient gags while the OPA is being inserted, remove the OPA, log roll the patient, and suction in case of vomiting.
- The **nasopharyngeal airway (NPA)** may be used when a patient's gag reflex prevents the insertion of an OPA.
    - Contraindications include severe facial trauma and significant resistance from both nostrils during insertion.
    - Select the correctly sized NPA by measuring from the nostril opening to the earlobe.
    - Apply a water-based lubricant to the NPA before insertion (do not use petroleum jelly).
    - Place the **bevel** (angled portion) of the tip of the NPA toward the **septum** (wall separating the two nostrils).
    - If resistance is met during insertion, attempt to use the other nostril.

PRACTICE QUESTION

2. An adult patient is found with a respiratory rate of 6 breaths per minute and is only responsive to painful stimuli in the form of a trapezius pinch. How should the patient's airway be managed?

ARTIFICIAL VENTILATION

- The EMT must provide **artificial ventilation**, also referred to as assisted or positive pressure ventilation, for patients with inadequate breathing resulting from severe respiratory distress, failure, or arrest.
    - **Respiratory distress**: labored breathing or shortness of breath
    - **Respiratory failure**: breathing that does not support life due to insufficient oxygen intake
    - **Respiratory arrest** or **apnea**: complete cessation of breathing
- Deliver 10 breaths per minute for adult patients and 12 – 20 breaths per minute for children and infants, with each breath delivered over a period of 1 second.
- Artificial ventilation techniques for the EMT, in order of preference, include:
    - mouth-to-mask
    - two-person bag-valve mask (BVM)
    - flow-restricted, oxygen-powered ventilation device (FROPVD)
    - automatic transport ventilator (ATV)
    - mouth-to-mouth
- **Mouth-to-mask**, preferably with high-flow supplemental oxygen, is the NREMT-preferred method due to the ease in which a single rescuer can achieve proper face seal and tidal volume.
    - Utilizing a pocket face mask, ensure an adequate seal to the patient's face while maintaining an open airway.
    - If available, connect oxygen to the mask inlet and flow at 15 liters per minute (lpm).

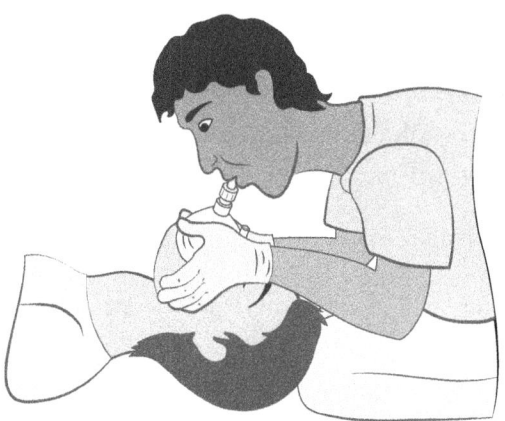

Figure 3.5. Mouth-to-Mask

- To conduct two-rescuer **bag-valve mask (BVM)** ventilation:
  - One rescuer at the top of the patient's head uses both hands to achieve a proper mask seal.
  - From either side of the patient, the second rescuer uses both hands to squeeze the bag.
  - Two-rescuer BVM ventilation is preferred over one-rescuer BVM.

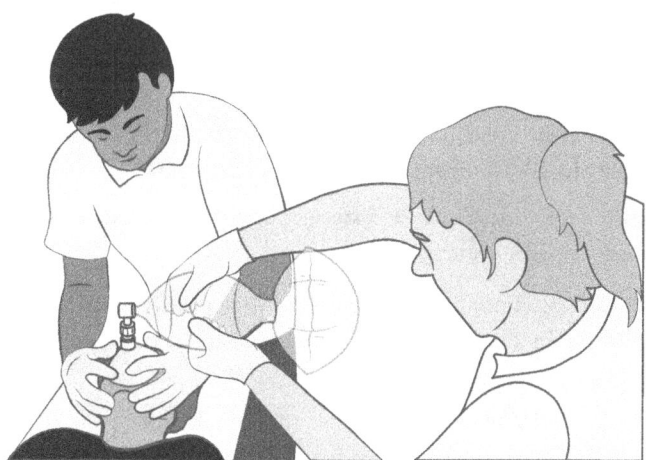

Figure 3.6. Two-Rescuer Bag-Valve Mask Ventilation

- One-rescuer BVM ventilation is problematic due to the difficulties of maintaining a patent airway and proper mask seal with one hand and achieving adequate tidal volume with the other.
  - The "EC" clamp technique is preferred for one-rescuer BVM ventilation: the EMT forms a "C" with the thumb and index finger surrounding the mask while the remaining three fingers form an "E" that clamps the patient's lower jaw.

RESPIRATORY EMERGENCIES

- A **flow-restricted, oxygen-powered ventilation device (FROPVD)** uses pressurized oxygen to deliver ventilations when the EMT depresses a trigger attached to the face mask.
  - Using a FROPVD increases the risk of gastric distention.
  - FROPVD generally cannot be used on children.
  - The use of FROPVDs is less common, and protocols are specific to each EMS system.
- An **automatic transport ventilator (ATV)** is similar to a FROPVD, except the EMT sets the ventilation rate and tidal volume rather than triggering each breath manually.
  - Special training is required to use an ATV.
- **Mouth-to-mouth** is not recommended unless no other methods are available.
- If artificial ventilation is effective:
  - The chest will gently rise and fall.
  - Lung sounds will be heard by auscultation.
  - Pulse oximetry will trend upwards.
- EMTs in some jurisdictions may be given advanced training in the use of **continuous positive airway pressure (CPAP)**.
  - CPAP is used for patients in respiratory distress.
  - Follow local protocol.
- A **stoma** is a permanent surgical opening in the patient's neck as the result of a laryngectomy, or larynx removal.
  - Patients with a **stoma** do not breathe through their mouth or nose.
  - Provide artificial ventilation for patients with a stoma by sealing the facepiece of a BVM or pocket mask over the stoma.
  - Close the mouth and nose of a stoma patient to prevent air escape while providing artificial ventilation.
- A **tracheostomy** is similar to a stoma, but it is typically temporary and found in patients who are on a ventilator or had recent trachea trauma.
  - Patients with a **tracheostomy tube** can be ventilated by removing the facepiece of a BVM or pocket mask and attaching the one-way valve directly to the end of the universal fitting of the trach tube.

PRACTICE QUESTION

3. An 8-year-old female patient with a clear airway is responsive and breathing at a rate of 38 breaths per minute. What intervention should the EMT perform next?

OXYGEN DELIVERY

- **Supplemental oxygen** administration is intended to maintain a pulse oximetry (SpO_2) level of 94% or greater.

- In recent years there has been a fundamental shift away from routinely giving oxygen to all patients.
- Indications for prehospital supplemental oxygen administration include:
  - SpO_2 < 94%
  - cardiac arrest
  - shock
  - altered LOC
  - any patient requiring artificial ventilation
- When indicated, supplemental oxygen delivery should be **titrated** (adjusted) to maintain SpO_2 levels of 94 – 96%, guided by a pulse oximeter.
- Oxygen delivery systems consist of a cylinder with an attached valve, a removable pressure regulator with a flow meter, and a delivery device typically consisting of flexible tubing connected to a facemask.
- The amount of oxygen in a cylinder is monitored by pressure, not volume.
  - Most cylinders, regardless of size, will hold approximately 2,000 **pounds per square inch (psi)** of oxygen when full.
  - Oxygen cylinders should be removed from service to be refilled once they reach 200 psi.
- To use an oxygen delivery system:
  - Slightly open or "crack" the valve on the cylinder to purge any debris.
  - Attach the regulator to the oxygen cylinder.
  - Open the cylinder valve, verify the pressure at the gauge, and check for leaks.
  - Attach the delivery device tubing, set the flow meter to the desired lpm, and titrate based on pulse oximetry.
- The **non-rebreathing mask** is the preferred method of prehospital oxygen administration.
  - Flow rate is 12 – 15 lpm.
  - Pre-fill the reservoir bag by placing a finger over the connection port prior to applying the mask to the patient.
  - For pediatric patients, choose a facepiece specific to infants or children.
- The **nasal cannula** is a low-flow option that may be used for patients who do not tolerate a non-rebreathing mask.
  - flow rate: 1 – 6 lpm
- The **Venturi mask** delivers specific amounts of oxygen and is not commonly used in the prehospital setting.
  - Flow rate varies.
  - The Venturi mask is most often used on COPD patients.
  - Follow local protocol.

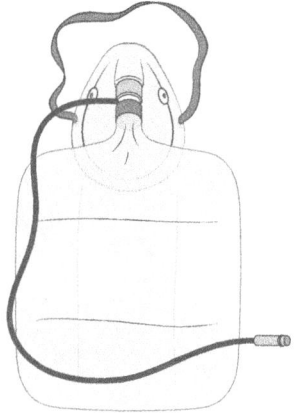

Figure 3.7. Non-rebreathing Mask

Figure 3.8. Nasal Cannula

- To provide supplemental oxygen to patients with a tracheostomy, place a non-rebreathing mask over the stoma opening.
- Oxygen administration hazards:
  - Oxygen is not a flammable gas, but it does accelerate combustion of other materials.
    - Never use or handle oxygen near ignition sources.
  - Oxygen cylinders are under significant pressure.
    - Always store oxygen cylinders on their side.

PRACTICE QUESTION

4. An awake and alert adult patient complains of nausea and a headache after accidentally leaving their car running in the garage for an extended period. The SpO_2 reading is 99% on ambient outside air, and the patient is not experiencing any difficulty breathing. Should the EMT administer supplemental oxygen? Why or why not?

Acute Pulmonary Edema

Pathophysiology

Acute pulmonary edema is the accumulation of fluid in the alveoli and lung tissue. This fluid inhibits gas exchange. Patients with pulmonary edema will struggle to breathe and will show symptoms related to hypoxia. Acute pulmonary edema is a life-threatening emergency that may lead to respiratory or cardiac arrest.

Pulmonary edema can be caused by a wide range of injuries and underlying disorders:

- Cardiogenic pulmonary edema occurs secondary to left-sided heart failure, also known as **congestive heart failure (CHF)**.
- Neurogenic pulmonary edema occurs secondary to a CNS injury.
- High-altitude pulmonary edema occurs after rapid ascent to altitudes greater than 8,200 feet.
- Inhalation of toxic gases or immersion injuries can also cause pulmonary edema.

What to Look For

KEY FINDINGS

- tachycardia
- dyspnea
- orthopnea
- crackles or wheezes
- cyanosis
- frothy pink sputum
- history of heart failure

OTHER FINDINGS

- chest pain
- pedal edema
- cough (dry or productive)
- fatigue and weakness
- dizziness

Medical Care

- Provide 100% oxygen.
- Use suction to keep airway clear.
- Keep the patient in a comfortable position.
- Use airway adjuncts as needed to maintain an airway.
- Transport the patient to the closest ED per protocols.
- Use CPAP if within local protocols.

PRACTICE QUESTION

5. Why does cardiogenic pulmonary edema cause hypoxia?

Airway Obstruction
Pathophysiology

Airway obstruction, or blockage of the upper airway, can be caused by a foreign body (e.g., teeth, food, marbles), the tongue, vomit, blood, or other secretions. Possible causes of airway obstruction include traumatic injuries to the face, edema in the airway, peritonsillar abscess, allergic reaction, and burns to the airway. Small children may also place foreign objects in their mouths. Patients or bystanders may be able to report the source of the obstruction to the EMT.

A complete airway obstruction is a life-threatening emergency that should be addressed immediately.

DID YOU KNOW?
Airway obstruction and respiratory distress account for approximately 13% of all EMS calls.

What to Look For

KEY FINDINGS

- visually observed obstruction in airway
- grasping at throat or mouth
- dyspnea
- stridor
- agitation or panic

OTHER FINDINGS

- excessive drooling in infants
- trouble swallowing
- loss of consciousness or altered LOC
- respiratory arrest

Medical Care

- If the patient can breathe and is stable:
    - Provide supplemental oxygen.
    - Suction as needed.
    - Transport the patient to the ED per protocols.
- For complete obstruction:
    - Follow BLS guidelines.
    - Suction as needed.
    - Use airway adjunct.
    - Provide rapid transport to the ED.
- Follow allergic reaction treatment guidelines if allergic reaction is suspected.

PRACTICE QUESTION

6. What are some common causes of upper airway obstruction?

Asthma

Pathophysiology

Asthma, an obstructive disease of the lungs, is characterized by long-term inflammation and constriction of the bronchial airways. Patients with asthma often experience exacerbations triggered by lung irritants, exercise, stress, or allergies. Asthma cannot be cured but can be managed through pharmacological measures and lifestyle changes.

Status asthmaticus is a severe condition in which the patient experiences intractable asthma exacerbations with limited pauses or no pause between the exacerbations. The symptoms are unresponsive to initial treatment, including prescribed medications, and can ultimately lead to acute respiratory failure. Status asthmaticus can develop over hours or days.

Patients with asthma may have a **prescribed inhaler** that contains a bronchodilator (usually albuterol). The most common prescribed inhaler for asthma is the **metered-dose inhaler (MDI)**.

To administer an MDI:

- Confirm the medication is prescribed to the patient.
- Verify how many doses the patient took prior to EMS arrival.

- Follow local protocols to obtain permission from medical control.
- Prepare the inhaler by shaking it vigorously.
- Coach the patient to exhale completely and then breathe in slowly and deeply while pressing down on the medication canister.
- If there is a spacer (valved holding chamber) with the MDI, the medication is first sprayed into the chamber.
  - If available, spacers should always be used because they typically increase the amount of medication that enters the patient's respiratory system.

What to Look For

KEY FINDINGS

- wheezing, particularly during exhalation
- frequent cough
- chest tightness
- dyspnea
- history of recent exposure to asthma triggers
- difficulty speaking full sentences

OTHER FINDINGS

- tachycardia
- hypertension
- abdominal pain due to overuse of abdominal accessory muscles

Medical Care

- Provide supplemental oxygen.
- Suction mucus from airway.
  - Do not take patient off oxygen for more than 15 seconds (adult) or 10 seconds (child).
- If the patient has their own inhaler, help administer the medication.
- Patients may require airway management with BVM.
- Use CPAP if within local protocols.
- Transport the patient to the ED per protocol.

PRACTICE QUESTION

7. An EMT is assessing a 4-year-old patient complaining of difficulty breathing after playing outside. The EMT hears wheezes during lung auscultation, and the child is struggling to speak. The child's mother states that both her children have asthma, and she always has an inhaler with her. She hands the EMT the patient's brother's MDI. What should the EMT do next with the medication?

RESPIRATORY EMERGENCIES

Chronic Obstructive Pulmonary Disease (COPD)

Pathophysiology

Chronic obstructive pulmonary disease (COPD) is characterized by a breakdown in alveolar tissue (emphysema) and long-term obstruction of the airways by inflammation and edema (chronic bronchitis). The most common cause of COPD is smoking, although the disease can be caused by other inhaled irritants (e.g., smoke, industrial chemicals, air pollution).

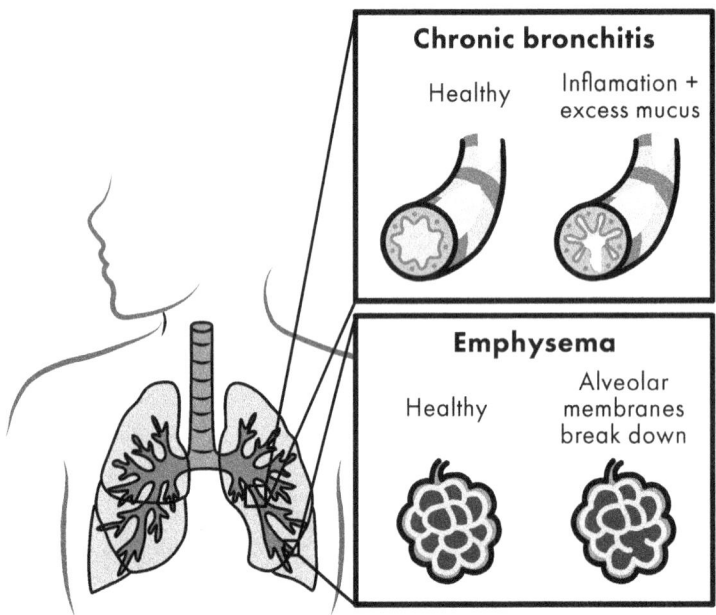

Figure 3.9. Chronic Obstructive Pulmonary Disease (COPD)

Patients with COPD may experience exacerbations characterized by increased sputum production, cough, and dyspnea. Exacerbations are most commonly caused by respiratory infections.

Many patients diagnosed with COPD will have a prescribed metered-dose inhaler. Some COPD patients will have multiple MDIs containing different medications. Follow the same protocols as outlined in the asthma section for assisting patients with MDI administration.

What to Look For

KEY FINDINGS

- chronic, productive cough
- dyspnea
- "dry" wheezing
- prolonged expiration
- history of COPD, recent respiratory infection, or smoking

OTHER FINDINGS

- crackles
- cyanosis
- altered mental status due to hypercapnia

Medical Care

- If the patient has an in-home inhaler, help administer medication.
- Provide supplemental oxygen.
  - Titrate supplemental oxygen to achieve 88 – 92% SpO_2 levels.
- Consider using CPAP if within local protocols.
- Keep the patient comfortable, and transport to the ED per protocols.

PRACTICE QUESTION

8. What are the common causes of COPD?

Pulmonary Aspiration
Pathophysiology

Pulmonary aspiration is the entry of foreign bodies, or material from the mouth or gastrointestinal tract, into the upper and/or lower respiratory tract. Aspiration is most common in young children and adults > 65, who have weaker muscles and less ability to expel objects from the airway. When patients report foreign body airway obstruction, EMTs should consider aspiration. Patients with an altered LOC are also at risk for aspirating fluids.

What to Look For

- dyspnea
- cough
- decreased lung sounds
- crackles if fluid was aspirated
- vomit, blood, or other fluid near the airway
- recent history of foreign body airway obstruction

Medical Care

- Suction or finger sweep the airway as appropriate.
- Provide oxygen as necessary, and keep the patient comfortable.
- Transport the patient to the ED per protocol.

PRACTICE QUESTION

9. Who is at highest risk for pulmonary aspiration?

Hyperventilation

Pathophysiology

Hyperventilation is an increased breathing rate (> 20 breaths per minute). During hyperventilation, more carbon dioxide (CO_2) is expelled than is produced, decreasing the amount of CO_2 found in the blood below normal (a condition known as **hypocapnia**). Hyperventilation may occur due to an underlying medical condition and functions as a way for the body to expel excess CO_2. It most commonly occurs for psychological reasons, a condition called **hyperventilation syndrome**. Patients experiencing hyperventilation syndrome typically describe the experience as a panic or anxiety attack.

Most episodes of hyperventilation syndrome resolve without injury or medical intervention. However, because the underlying cause of hyperventilation cannot be determined in the field, hyperventilation should be treated as an emergent condition.

What to Look For

- tachypnea
- dyspnea
- chest tightness
- dizziness or lightheadedness
- medical history of anxiety
- paresthesia in the hands, feet, or lips
- spasms in the hands or feet

Medical Care

- Provide reassurance to the patient.
- Evaluate the patient in a comfortable setting away from loud noise, emotional family members, and other stress-inducing elements.
- Provide verbal directions to the patient to help decrease their breathing rate.
- Provide supplemental oxygen if the breathing rate cannot be controlled.
- Transport the patient to the ED per protocols.

PRACTICE QUESTION

10. What is the most effective treatment for hyperventilation syndrome?

Pleural Effusion

Pathophysiology

A **pleural effusion** is the buildup of fluid around the lungs in the pleural space. (The pleurae are layers of tissue between the lungs and chest wall that normally have a small amount of fluid that acts as a lubricant during thoracic movement.) Excess fluid buildup can displace lung tissue and inhibit lung expansion. Pleural effusion occurs secondary to various other conditions, including heart failure, cancer, and infections.

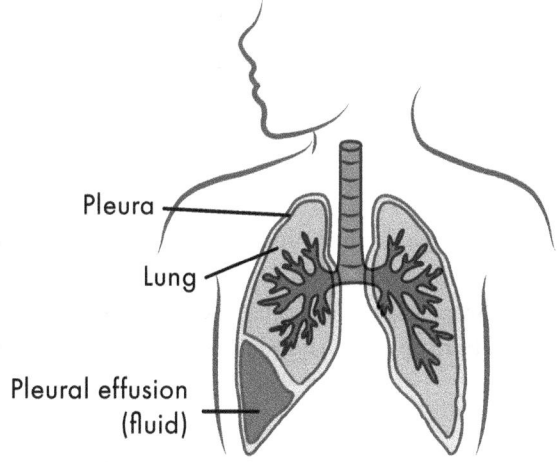

Figure 3.10. Pleural Effusion

What to Look For

- dyspnea
- dullness upon percussion of the lung area
- decreased breath sounds on affected side
- asymmetrical chest expansion
- pleuritic chest pain

Medical Care

- Provide oxygen if necessary and keep the patient comfortable.
- Transport the patient to the ED per protocols.

PRACTICE QUESTION

11. How does pleural effusion prevent lung expansion?

Pneumothorax

Pathophysiology

Pneumothorax is the collection of air between the chest wall and the lung (in the pleural space). It can occur due to a blunt or penetrative chest-wall injury, medical injury, underlying lung tissue disease, or hereditary factors. Pneumothorax is classified according to its underlying cause:

- **Primary spontaneous pneumothorax (PSP)** occurs spontaneously in the absence of lung disease and often presents with only minor symptoms.
- **Secondary spontaneous pneumothorax (SSP)** occurs in patients with an underlying lung disease and presents with more severe symptoms.
- **Traumatic pneumothorax** occurs when the chest wall is penetrated or when fractured ribs puncture a lung or the pleura.
- **Tension pneumothorax** is the late progression of a pneumothorax in which the increased pressure from the air in the pleural space causes the affected lung and eventually the heart and vena cava to be compressed. It causes significant respiratory distress in the patient and requires immediate intervention.

What to Look For

KEY FINDINGS

- sudden, unilateral pleuritic chest pain
- dyspnea
- tachycardia
- unequal chest rise and fall
- thoracic trauma or recent thoracic surgery

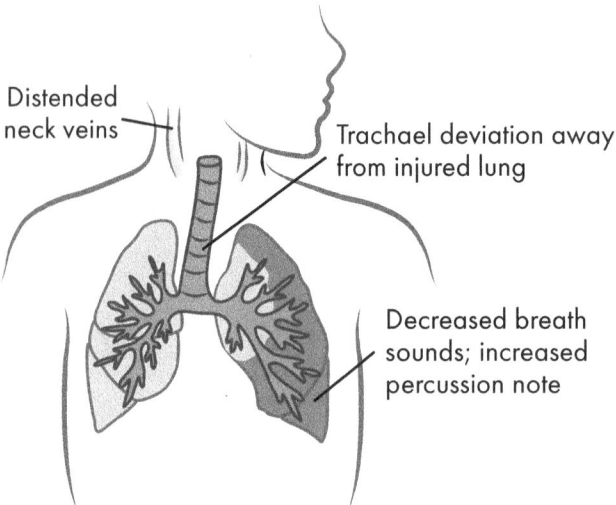

Figure 3.11. Signs and Symptoms of Tension Pneumothorax

KEY FINDINGS
- penetrating thoracic injury
- decreased breath sounds over the affected lung
- increased percussion note
- distended neck veins (late stage)
- tracheal deviation away from the side of the tension (late stage)

Medical Care

- Provide supplemental oxygen.
- Keep the patient in a comfortable position.
- Be prepared to manage the airway and provide respirations as needed.
- Apply an occlusive dressing to any open chest wounds.
- Transport the patient to the ED per protocols.

PRACTICE QUESTION

12. What is the primary difference between a simple pneumothorax and a tension pneumothorax?

Pulmonary Embolism

Pathophysiology

A **pulmonary embolism (PE)** occurs when an **embolus** (usually a blood clot or an air bubble) occludes an artery of the lungs. The occlusion prevents blood flow to affected areas of the lungs, preventing gas exchange.

The most common embolus is a blood clot caused by deep vein thrombosis (DVT). Other occlusions, such as tumor emboli, fat emboli, and amniotic fluid emboli, can also reach the lungs. People who are immobilized for long periods of time, pregnant, recently had surgery, or have a history of blood clots are at a higher risk of PE. PE is a life-threatening condition that requires immediate medical treatment. However, it can be difficult to diagnose in the field, and prehospital care is mostly supportive.

What to Look For

- pleuritic chest pain
- dyspnea
- tachypnea
- tachycardia
- hemoptysis
- hypotension

- hypoxia
- anxiety

Medical Care

- Provide supplemental oxygen.
- Place the patient in a comfortable position.
- Transport the patient promptly to the ED per protocols.

PRACTICE QUESTION

13. How does a DVT lead to a pulmonary embolism?

Respiratory Infections
Pathophysiology

The respiratory system is prone to **respiratory tract infections.** Upper respiratory tract infections affect air inputs in the nose and throat, and lower respiratory tract infections affect the lungs and their immediate pulmonary inputs.

- Viral infections of the respiratory system include influenza and the common cold; bacterial infections include tuberculosis and pertussis (whooping cough).
- **Pneumonia**, the inflammation of the lungs that affects alveoli, can be caused by bacteria, viruses, fungi, or parasites. It is often seen in people whose respiratory system has been weakened by other conditions.

Respiratory tract infections rarely require emergency medical care. However, they may exacerbate chronic conditions such as COPD, asthma, and heart failure. In addition, young children and older patients may require medical treatment for fever or dyspnea related to respiratory infections.

What to Look For

KEY FINDINGS

- fever
- dyspnea
- pleuritic chest pain
- difficulty swallowing
- dehydration

OTHER FINDINGS

- wheezing and crackles
- rhinorrhea

- congestion
- dry or wet cough

Medical Care

- Provide supplemental oxygen if necessary.
- Suction excess secretions if they are compromising the airway.
- Place the patient in a comfortable position.
- Transport the patient to the ED per protocols.

PRACTICE QUESTION

14. What is the difference between upper and lower respiratory tract infections?

ANSWER KEY

1. Open the airway using the jaw-thrust maneuver. The head tilt–chin lift maneuver is contraindicated due to suspected head, neck, or back injury. The blood in the patient's mouth should not be suctioned until after the airway has been opened.

2. Insert a nasopharyngeal airway. An OPA is contraindicated because the patient is responsive to painful stimuli and therefore not unconscious.

3. Although the patient is breathing, the rate is too fast and therefore inadequate. Perform assisted ventilations using the mouth-to-mask technique. (NREMT prefers mouth-to-mask over BVM, particularly when only one rescuer is present.) The insertion of an airway adjunct (OPA or NPA) is contraindicated in responsive patients. Suction is not needed because the airway is clear.

4. The EMT should administer oxygen with a non-rebreathing mask. The patient's signs and symptoms suggest the patient may have carbon monoxide poisoning. The pulse oximeter is likely mistaking carbon monoxide saturation for oxygen saturation, resulting in a false reading.

5. Cardiogenic pulmonary edema is an accumulation of fluid in the alveoli that results from congestive heart failure. The fluid interrupts gas exchange and prevents oxygen from passing into the blood, causing hypoxia.

6. Common objects that may obstruct the airway include the tongue, teeth, blood, saliva, vomit, food, and small toys. Edema can also cause airway obstruction.

7. Although the patient would likely benefit from an MDI treatment, the EMT cannot assist in the administration of medication that is not prescribed to the patient. This is true even if the patient is a child and the EMT has permission from the parents.

8. Most COPD cases are the result of long-term cigarette smoking. COPD may also be caused by lung irritants such as dust, chemicals, or smog.

9. Young children and the elderly are at higher risk for aspiration due to weaker muscles and a diminished ability to expel foreign body obstructions. Also, patients with an altered mental status are at risk for aspirating fluids such as blood or vomit.

10. Because most cases of hyperventilation syndrome involve anxiety, the preferred treatment is to reassure the patient and provide coaching to decrease the breathing rate.

11. The pleural space is made up of layers of tissue between the lungs and inner chest wall that move with the lungs as they expand and contract. During a pleural effusion, excess fluid in the pleural cavity compresses the lungs and prevents them from fully expanding.

12. The term *pneumothorax* applies to any case involving air in the pleural space. *Tension pneumothorax* is an advanced and dangerous stage in which the amount of air in the pleura causes the lung to completely collapse and the heart and vena cava to become compressed.

13. A DVT is a blood clot that forms in the deep veins, usually in the extremities. When a piece of the clot is dislodged, it travels through the veins to the heart, which then pushes it into the pulmonary arteries. As the pulmonary arteries branch and narrow, the clot will eventually stop and occlude the artery, a condition called a pulmonary embolism (PE).

14. An upper respiratory tract infection affects the structures of the nose and throat, while a lower respiratory tract infection primarily affects the lungs.

FOUR: CARDIOVASCULAR EMERGENCIES

The Role of EMTs in Cardiovascular Emergencies

- The American Heart Association (AHA) and the European Resuscitation Council have developed guidelines for two levels of care that can be provided during cardiac emergencies.
    - **Basic Life Support (BLS)** includes rescue breathing, CPR, and use of an AED. The purpose of BLS is to maintain the circulation of oxygenated blood until more advanced medical care can be provided.
    - **Advanced Cardiac Life Support (ACLS)** or **Advanced Life Support (ALS)** includes all the elements of BLS and also includes an invasive procedure such as IV administration of medications or endotracheal intubation. The purpose of ALS is to restart the heart's normal rhythm.
- EMTs are certified to provide BLS. During a cardiac emergency, the EMT may perform the following procedures:
    - rescue breathing
    - CPR
    - defibrillation with an AED
    - administration of nitroglycerin and aspirin (per local protocols)
- An **ALS intercept** is a unit staffed with ALS-certified personnel who are dispatched to meet BLS units when the patient requires advanced life support.

CARDIOPULMONARY RESUSCITATION (CPR)

- **Cardiopulmonary resuscitation (CPR)** consists of ventilations and chest compressions that keep oxygen-rich blood flowing to the brain and other vital organs during cardiac arrest.
- The process of providing CPR starts with the initial assessment.

DID YOU KNOW?
Chest pain and cardiac conditions account for approximately 13% of EMS calls.

HELPFUL HINT

Guidelines released by the AHA in 2017 state that CPR should be initiated when a patient in cardiac arrest has a ventricular assist device (VAD). The EMT should ensure that relevant supplies carried by the patient (e.g., backup batteries) are transported with the patient.

- ○ Assess scene safety: Start CPR only when the scene is safe for both the EMT and the patient.
- ○ Wear appropriate PPE (usually gloves, but other equipment may be required depending on the scene and patient).
- ○ Determine the patient's responsiveness.
  - · For adults and children, kneel next to the patient and shake their shoulders. For infants, tap their foot.
  - · Simultaneously ask the patient if they are OK.
  - · If the patient is unresponsive, request an ALS intercept and bring the AED to the scene.
- ○ Check for breathing and pulse at the same time for no more than 10 seconds.
  - · Look, listen, and feel for breathing and pulse.
  - · Lean over the patient placing your ear over the patient's mouth and nose while looking down the patient's chest, watching for breathing.
  - · At the same time, place your fingers on the patient's carotid artery on the same side of the neck where you are kneeling.
  - · If the patient is not breathing and has no pulse, start CPR.
- • The EMT should start **compressions** while their partner attaches the AED.

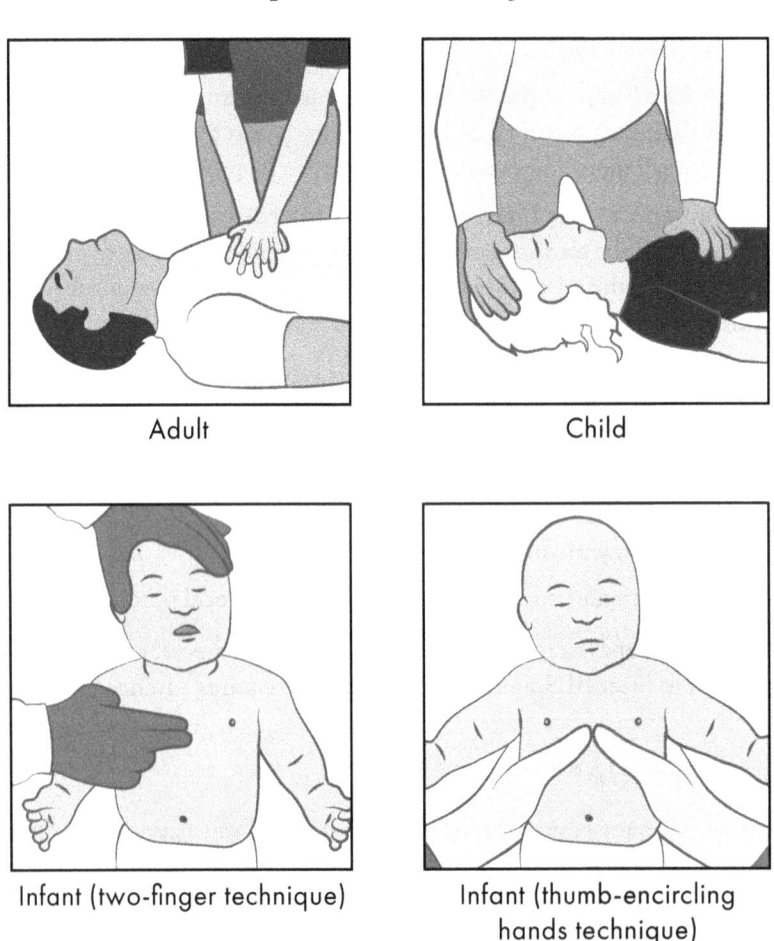

Figure 4.1. Hand Placement During CPR

80   EMT Study Guide

- o Move the patient to the supine position on a hard surface.
  - · Use caution in moving a patient who may have a spinal injury.
- o Place hands in the center of the chest on the lower half of the sternum.
  - · Use the two-handed method for adults.
  - · Use the one-handed method for children aged 1 to 8.
  - · For infants, use the two-finger technique (for one EMT) or thumb-encircling hands technique (for two EMTs).
- o Allow for full chest recoil between compressions.
- o Interrupt compressions for no more than 10 seconds.
- **Ventilations** are given via bag-valve mask (BVM) or through a barrier device. (See chapter 3, "Respiratory Emergencies," for detailed instructions on providing artificial ventilation.)
- One cycle of CPR is five sets of 30 compressions and 2 breaths.
  - o When two EMTs are performing CPR, they should switch roles every five cycles (roughly 2 minutes).
  - o The patient's breathing and pulse should be reassessed after every five cycles of CPR.

Table 4.1. Compression and Ventilation Guidelines for CPR

	Adult	Child	Infant
Compressions per minute	100 – 120		
Depth	2 – 2.4 inches	2 inches	1.5 inches
Compression-to-ventilation ratio	30:2	1 EMT: 30:2 2 EMTs: 15:2	1 EMT: 30:2 2 EMTs: 15:2

- An oropharyngeal airway (OPA) can be inserted in between cycles of CPR.
  - o Do not insert an OPA if CPR compressions will be delayed.
  - o If there is good compliance with BVM, the airway can be delayed.
- The EMT should continue CPR until the patient has **return of spontaneous circulation (ROSC)**, the patient is delivered to the hospital emergency department, or the patient is transferred to an ALS ambulance.

PRACTICE QUESTION

1. An EMT arrives on scene to find a 3-month-old infant who is pulseless and apneic. He and his partner call for an ALS intercept and begin providing CPR. What compression-to-ventilation ratio should they use?

AUTOMATED EXTERNAL DEFIBRILLATORS (AED)

- During **defibrillation**, also known as **unsynchronized cardioversion**, electrical current is used to reset the heart to a normal sinus rhythm.

- The electrical current is supplied randomly during the cardiac cycle, disrupting the heart's electrical rhythm and allowing normal sinus rhythm to restart.
- The automated external defibrillator (AED) will defibrillate ventricular fibrillation (V-fib) and ventricular tachycardia (V-tach). The AED will not defibrillate any other heart rhythms.
- Electrical defibrillators can be **monophasic** (unidirectional current) or **biphasic** (bidirectional current).
    - Monophasic devices deliver current at a more consistent magnitude and are more effective at lower energies.
- EDs can be semi-automatic or automatic.
    - When using a **semi-automatic defibrillator**, the EMT must depress the shock button to deliver a shock.
    - **Automatic defibrillators** will deliver the shock if indicated after a countdown.
    - Both defibrillators can be shut off to disarm a shock.
- The EMT should retrieve the AED as soon as the patient is found to be unconscious.
- When using a defibrillator, consider the safety of the EMT, their crew, and the patient.
    - Do not use an AED in an explosive or flammable atmosphere.
    - Make sure no one is touching the patient when the AED defibrillates the patient.
    - Do not use an AED in water; if patient is wet, dry patient's chest before use.
- As soon as the AED is available, attach it to the patient.
    - While one EMT is providing CPR, the another can attach the AED to the patient.
        - Remove clothes and jewelry from the patient's chest.
        - Dry the chest if the patient is wet.
        - If the patient has a hairy chest, shave the AED pad locations before application.
        - Turn on the AED.
        - Peel the pads off the plastic.
        - Place one pad on the upper-right chest.
        - Place the second pad on the lower-left chest (look at the picture on the pad or packaging).
        - For infants and small children, place one pad in the center of the chest and the other in the center of the back.
        - Plug the pads into the AED if they are not already attached.
        - While the AED is analyzing, briefly discontinue CPR.
        - If no defibrillation is indicated, continue CPR.
        - If defibrillation is indicated, provide CPR while the AED is charging.

HELPFUL HINT
Do not place the defibrillator pad over an implanted pacemaker or defibrillator. Place the pad at least 1 inch below the implanted device.

- Defibrillate the patient and immediately resume CPR.
- After two minutes of CPR, check for a pulse.
- The AED will automatically re-analyze the patient.
- Defibrillate if indicated; continue to provide CPR if a shock is not indicated.
- Repeat until ALS arrives or arrival at the hospital.

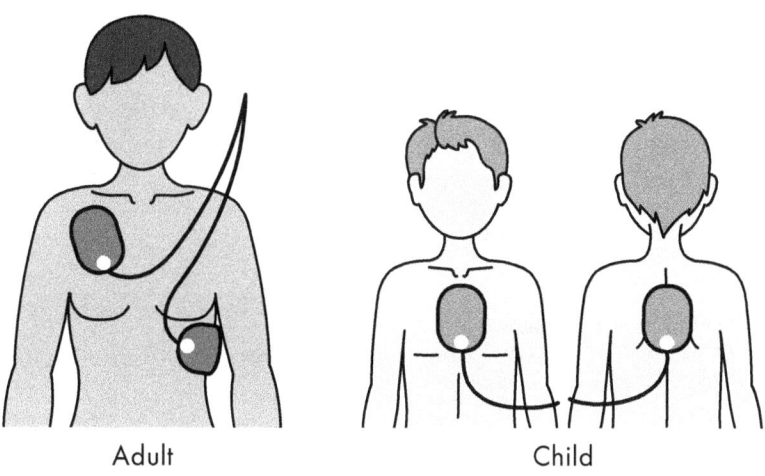

Figure 4.2. AED Pad Placement

- Document the time and response of AED application and defibrillations on the patient care report.

PRACTICE QUESTION

2. The EMT arrives and finds a 92-year-old male pulseless and apneic. CPR has been started and the AED was just brought to the patient's side. While one EMT is attaching the AED, what should the other EMT be doing?

ADMINISTERING MEDICATIONS IN CARDIAC EMERGENCIES

- Most EMS systems allow EMTs to administer nitroglycerin and aspirin to patients with chest pain.
    - **Nitroglycerin** dilates blood vessels and decreases the work of the left ventricle, allowing more blood to reach the heart muscle.
    - **Aspirin** is an antiplatelet that slows blood clotting and can help prevent further damage to the heart muscle caused by occluded blood vessels.
- Patients complaining of cardiac chest pain should be given nitroglycerin.
- Nitroglycerin is available in tablets or as a spray.
- Contraindications for giving nitroglycerin include:
    - BP < 100 mm Hg
    - head injury

HELPFUL HINT

Always check the expiration date on the medication before administering it.

- infant or pediatric patient
- patient use of vasodilators within the last 24 hours, particularly those prescribed for erectile dysfunction (e.g., sildenafil [Viagra] or vardenafil [Levitra])

- Procedures for administering nitroglycerin:
  - Determine the patient's baseline pain level (usually done on a scale of 1 to 10).
  - Administer the tablet or spray under the patient's tongue.
  - One tablet or spray can be given every 5 minutes for up to three doses.
  - Check blood pressure between each dose.
  - Reassess using the pain scale after 5 minutes to determine the effectiveness of the medication administration.

- Possible side effects of nitroglycerin include:
  - severe headache
  - drop in blood pressure
  - dizziness
  - flushing
  - tachycardia

- Patients with cardiac chest pain should also be given 324 mg of aspirin.

- Contraindications for aspirin include:
  - history of asthma
  - aspirin allergy
  - internal abdominal bleeding
  - bleeding disorders
  - pregnancy
  - recent surgery
  - recent administration of medication to slow clotting (e.g., aspirin or anticoagulant)

- Give the patient the aspirin by mouth. Patient should be told to chew and swallow the tablets.

- Side effects of aspirin may include:
  - nausea
  - vomiting
  - bronchospasm
  - bleeding

PRACTICE QUESTION

3. An EMT arrives on scene to find a 76-year-old male with chest pain. The EMT determines that the patient has a history of angina and asthma. The patient also indicates that he took Viagra four hours before calling for help. Which medications can the EMT not administer to this patient and why?

Acute Coronary Syndrome
Pathophysiology

Acute coronary syndrome (ACS) is an umbrella term for cardiac conditions in which blood flow to the heart is impaired. ACS is usually the result of atherosclerotic plaque or clots that partially or fully occlude the coronary arteries. ACS includes unstable angina, non-ST-elevation myocardial infarction (NSTEMI), and ST-elevation myocardial infarction (STEMI).

In **angina pectoris** (commonly called angina), the coronary arteries are temporarily unable to supply an appropriate amount of oxygenated blood to meet the oxygen needs of the heart. Angina can be classified into two categories: stable angina or unstable angina.

- **Stable angina** usually resolves in about 5 minutes, is resolved with medications or with rest, and can be triggered by exertional activities, large meals, and extremely hot or cold temperatures.

- **Unstable angina** can occur at any time and typically lasts longer (> 15 or 20 minutes). The pain is usually rated as more severe than stable angina and is not easily relieved by taking nitrates.

- A **myocardial infarction (MI)** is ischemia of the heart muscle that occurs when the coronary arteries are partially or completely occluded. MI is classified by the behavior of the ST wave.

- A **non-ST-elevation myocardial infarction (NSTEMI)** includes an ST depression, which reflects ischemia resulting from a partial blockage of the coronary artery.

- An **ST-elevation myocardial infarction (STEMI)** includes an elevated ST wave, indicating a complete occlusion of a coronary artery. STEMI is a life-threatening emergency that requires immediate intervention.

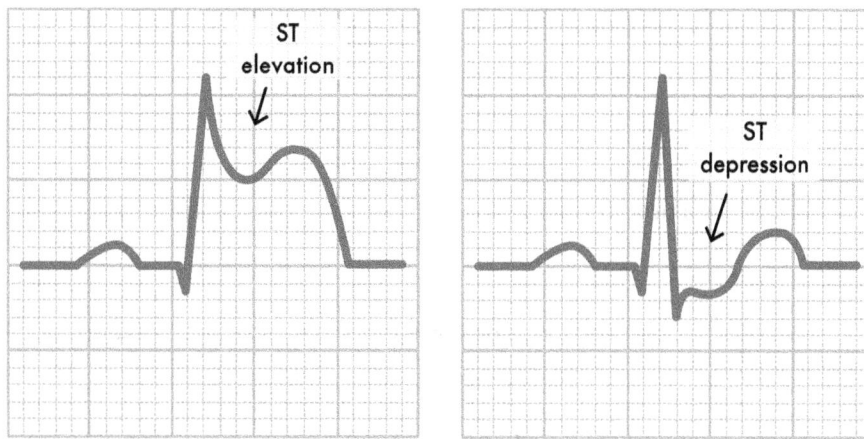

Figure 4.3. ST Depression and ST Elevation

What to Look For

KEY FINDINGS

- continuous chest discomfort or pain that may radiate to the back, arm, or jaw
- chest pressure or tightness
- syncope
- diaphoresis
- nausea or vomiting
- dyspnea
- pallor
- anxiety or feeling of impending doom

OTHER PRESENTATIONS OF MI

- Upper abdominal pain is more common in people > 65, people with diabetes, and women.
- Women are more likely to present with back pain or indigestion.
- Patients with a "silent" MI have no symptoms.

DID YOU KNOW?
Studies show that about two-thirds of patients who seek medical care for an MI will present with chest discomfort or pain. Groups who are less likely to report pain include women and people with diabetes.

Care and Transport

- All patients who report chest pain should be thoroughly assessed for symptoms of MI.
- Provide supplemental oxygen; titrate to 95 – 99%.
- Use adjuncts as needed to manage the airway.
- Administer aspirin and nitroglycerin per local protocols (see "Administering Medications" on page 83 for details).
- Provide rapid transport to ED.
- If the patient enters cardiac arrest during transport:
    - Stop the vehicle and begin performing CPR.
    - Administer one shock via AED as soon as possible.
    - Resume CPR.
    - Follow local protocols for calling ALS support and transporting patients.

PRACTICE QUESTION

4. What symptom, identified by the patient, is the most common and consistent with an MI?

Cardiac Arrest

Pathophysiology

Cardiac arrest (also called sudden cardiac arrest) refers to the complete cessation of all cardiac activity. Most cardiac arrests are caused by sustained V-fib following an MI. Cardiac arrest can also be caused by structural abnormalities in the heart (e.g., cardiomyopathies or valve dysfunction) or abnormalities in the heart's electrical systems. Most cardiac arrests in infants and children are caused by respiratory arrest.

HELPFUL HINT

Asystole and pulseless electrical activity (PEA) cannot be corrected with defibrillation. They can only be treated with administration of epinephrine, which must be done by ALS personnel.

What to Look For

- sudden loss of consciousness
- no pulse
- respiratory arrest or apnea

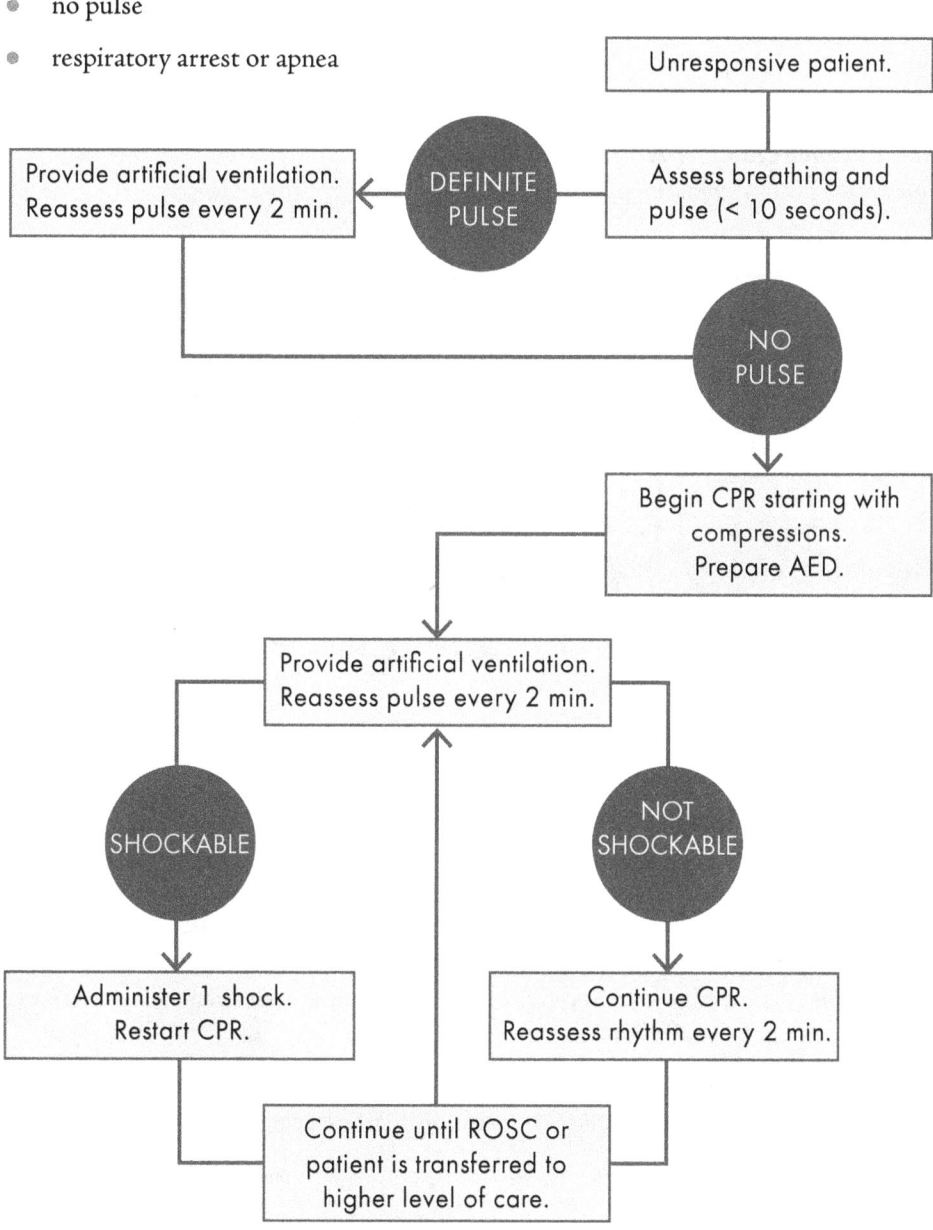

Figure 4.4. Basic Life Support (BLS) Algorithm

Care and Transport

- Follow BLS algorithm (see Figure 4.4).
- Patient will require immediate transfer to ALS care (ALS intercept or transport to hospital).

PRACTICE QUESTION

5. EMTs arrive on the scene to find a 68-year-old male who is unresponsive with agonal breathing and no pulse. The EMTs begin CPR and attach the AED to the patient. The AED indicates that no shock is needed. What should the EMTs do next?

Aortic Aneurysm

Pathophysiology

An **abdominal aortic aneurysm (AAA)**, often called a triple A, occurs when the lower aorta is enlarged. The AAA is the most common type of aneurysm. A **thoracic aneurysm** occurs when the portion of the aorta in the chest is enlarged.

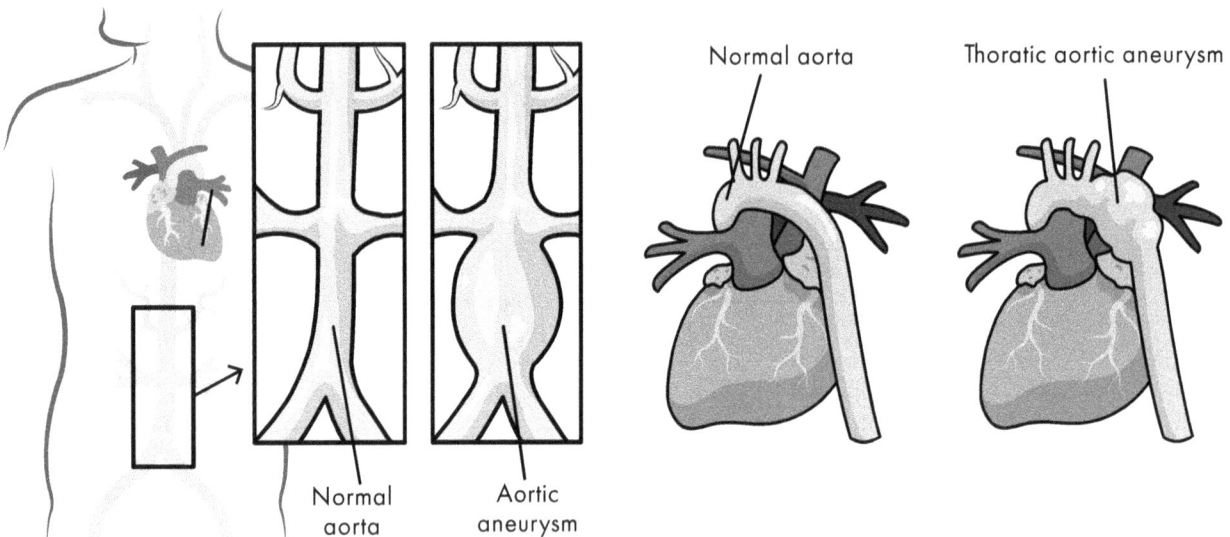

Figure 4.5. Abdominal Aortic and Thoracic Aneurysm

DID YOU KNOW?
Approximately 75% of aortic aneurysms occur in men.

Many patients with aortic aneurysms do not have any symptoms at all. The main concern for people with aortic aneurysms is **aortic rupture**, a complete tear in the wall of the aorta, or **dissection**, a tear in the innermost layer of the aorta that allows blood to enter the aortic media. Patients with an aortic rupture or dissection will rapidly enter hemorrhagic shock, and most will die within minutes.

Rupture or dissection in a thoracic aneurysm may present with similar symptoms to an MI and should be considered for patients with severe chest pain.

What to Look For

KEY FINDINGS

- sudden abdominal pain that radiates to the back (abdominal aneurysm)
- sudden chest pain (thoracic aneurysm)
- pain often described as "tearing"
- signs and symptoms of hemorrhagic shock

OTHER FINDINGS

- a pulsating feeling by the umbilicus (abdominal aneurysm)
- a blood pressure difference of greater than 20 mm Hg between the left and right arms
- anxiety or a feeling of impending doom

Care and Transport

- Provide oxygen.
- Gently move the patient.
- Transport the patient to the ED immediately.
- Prevent further damage to the artery.
    - Minimize patient movement.
    - If a rupture or dissected artery is suspected, do not palpate the abdomen or provide aggressive treatment.

> **HELPFUL HINT**
> Life-threatening conditions that can cause chest pain include:
> - MI
> - aortic dissection
> - pulmonary embolism
> - pneumothorax
>
> Non-life-threatening sources of chest pain include:
> - heartburn
> - costochondritis
> - muscle strains
> - rib fractures

> **PRACTICE QUESTION**
>
> 6. EMTs respond to a call for a 77-year-old male with chest pain. They arrive to find the patient curled on the floor. He describes the pain as tearing and says it started suddenly about 15 minutes ago. He rates the pain at 10 out of 10. Assessment shows a BP of 175/112 mm Hg in the right arm and 197/125 mm Hg in the left. How should the EMTs manage this patient?

Hypertensive Crisis

Pathophysiology

Hypertensive crises include hypertensive urgency and hypertensive emergencies. **Hypertensive urgency** is a BP greater than 180/120 mm Hg without evidence of organ dysfunction. A **hypertensive emergency** is a BP greater than 180/120 mm Hg accompanied by evidence of progressive organ dysfunction.

> **DID YOU KNOW?**
> Hypertensive crises increase the risk of stroke because of the potential damage to blood vessels in the brain.

What to Look For

KEY FINDINGS

- systolic blood pressure greater than 180 mm Hg
- diastolic blood pressure greater than 120 mm Hg

OTHER FINDINGS

- may be asymptomatic
- severe headache
- blurred vision
- bounding pulse
- ear ringing
- nausea and vomiting
- altered mental status

Care and Transport

- Continually monitor blood pressure.
- Keep patient calm and comfortable.
- Stable, asymptomatic patients may choose not to receive further care.
- Symptomatic patients require rapid transport to the ED.
- Request an ALS intercept for unstable patients who need immediate intervention to lower BP.

PRACTICE QUESTION

7. EMTs respond to a call for a 55-year-old male with a severe headache and an altered mental status. During assessment, they find the patient is dyspneic and has a BP of 202/130 mm Hg. How should the EMTs manage this patient?

Shock

Shock occurs when there is inadequate tissue perfusion. The resulting lack of oxygen circulating to major organs can lead to organ failure and death. Shock is classified by the underlying cause of the inadequate perfusion. The most common type of shock is hypovolemic.

Table 4.2. Types of Shock

Type	Description	Common Causes	Key Findings
Cardiogenic shock	occurs when the heart can no longer pump effectively, reducing blood flow and available oxygen throughout the body	<ul><li>MI</li><li>dysrhythmias</li><li>inflammation or infection in the heart</li></ul>	<ul><li>tachycardia</li><li>hypotension</li><li>cool, pale, moist skin</li></ul>
Hypovolemic shock (hypovolemia)	occurs when rapid fluid loss decreases circulating blood volume and cardiac output, resulting in inadequate tissue perfusion	<ul><li>trauma</li><li>excessive fluid loss through vomiting, diarrhea, or urination</li></ul>	
Hemorrhagic shock	a type of hypovolemic shock in which blood is lost rapidly	trauma	
Septic shock	occurs when a massive infection damages blood vessels	infection, most often in the urinary tract or respiratory tract	<ul><li>tachycardia</li><li>hypotension</li><li>warm, flushed skin</li></ul>
Neurogenic shock	caused by an injury or trauma to the spinal cord, typically above the level of T6, which disrupts the functioning of the automatic nervous system, producing massive vasodilation	trauma to neck	<ul><li>bradycardia</li><li>hypotension</li><li>warm, dry skin</li></ul>
Anaphylactic shock	caused by a severe histamine reaction causing dilated blood vessels, flushed skin, and respiratory compromise	allergen	<ul><li>tachycardia</li><li>flushed skin</li><li>hypotension</li><li>urticaria</li></ul>

Care and Transport

- Administer oxygen.
- Manage the airway as needed.
- Keep the patient warm.
- Transport to the ED immediately.
- Request an ALS intercept for unstable patients.

PRACTICE QUESTION

8. A 27-year-old woman was found lying on the couch complaining of the flu. The patient has had diarrhea and vomiting for the last 24 hours. During assessment, the EMTs find that she is hypotensive with cool, pale skin. What type of shock does the patient most likely have?

ANSWER KEY

1. The compression-to-ventilation ratio for 2-person infant CPR is 15 compressions to 2 ventilations.

2. While one EMT is attaching the AED, the other EMT should be continuing CPR. CPR should not be interrupted for more than 10 seconds.

3. The EMT cannot administer aspirin or nitroglycerin. The patient has a history of asthma, which prevents him from receiving aspirin. He has taken a vasodilator within the last 24 hours, which prevents him from receiving nitroglycerin.

4. An uncomfortable feeling of pressure, squeezing, fullness, or pain in the center of the chest is the predominant symptom of an MI.

5. The EMTs should continue CPR until the patient can be transferred to ALS providers. Depending on local protocols, an ALS intercept might be called to the scene or the patient may be transported to the ED.

6. The patient has signs and symptoms of an aortic aneurysm or dissection, including sudden, tearing chest pain and a blood pressure difference between the right and left arm. The patient needs oxygen and must be immediately transported to the hospital. During transport, the EMTs should be prepared for possible hemorrhagic shock and cardiac arrest in the patient.

7. The EMTs should keep the patient calm and provide oxygen if indicated. The patient is symptomatic and unstable, so he should be transported immediately to the hospital. Depending on local protocols, the EMTs may choose to request an ALS intercept.

8. The patient likely has hypovolemic shock due to fluid loss from vomiting and diarrhea.

FIVE: MEDICAL EMERGENCIES

Abdominal Pain

Abdominal pain is a common reason for calls to EMS systems. Most calls will be cases of **acute abdomen**, the medical term for sudden, severe abdominal pain. Acute abdomen is frequently accompanied by nausea and vomiting. EMTs should wear the appropriate PPE when handling vomit.

Patients with acute abdomen may also have **referred pain** in other locations, such as the shoulders or hands. Referred pain is caused by the proximity of nerves carrying pain signals to and from the spinal cord.

The specific cause of abdominal pain will be almost impossible to diagnose in the field. However, the EMT should be aware of possible causes of abdominal pain, particularly those that qualify as life-threatening emergencies.

DID YOU KNOW?
Abdominal guarding is the tensing of abdominal muscles in response to pressure. It is common in patients with severe abdominal pain.

Table 5.1. Causes of Acute Abdomen

Condition	Pathophysiology	Symptoms
Abdominal aortic aneurysm (AAA)	widening of the aorta in the abdomen	See chapter 4 for more information on symptoms and care of ruptured or dissected AAA.
Appendicitis	inflammation of the appendix	right lower quadrant pain; rebound tenderness; fever
Gallstones	blockage in the duct of the gallbladder leading to inflammation (cholecystitis)	right upper quadrant pain that is exacerbated by fatty meals; fever
Kidney stones	blockage in the urethra leading to inflammation of the kidney	unilateral flank pain (can be severe); hematuria
Pancreatitis	inflammation of the pancreas	upper abdominal and back pain; distension of abdomen
Peptic ulcer	erosion of the stomach by stomach acid	upper abdomen and back pain; heartburn
Ruptured ectopic pregnancy	rupture of the fallopian tube due to ectopic pregnancy	See chapter 9 for more information on symptoms and care of ruptured ectopic pregnancy.
Ruptured ovarian cyst	rupture of cyst in the ovary	sudden, severe, unilateral pelvic pain

Care and Transport

- Manage airway.
  - Patients with vomiting may require repositioning or suctioning.
- Provide oxygen as needed.
- Transport to ED per protocols.

PRACTICE QUESTION

1. What are some conditions occurring outside the gastrointestinal system that may cause acute abdomen?

Anaphylactic Shock

Pathophysiology

Anaphylactic shock (or anaphylaxis) is a life-threatening allergic reaction that causes symptomatic vasodilation and bronchoconstriction. The most common causes of anaphylactic shock are food allergens, medications, and insect venom.

The definitive treatment for anaphylaxis is an IM injection of epinephrine. Patients with known allergies may carry an epinephrine auto-injector (EpiPen). The EMT should know how to administer an EpiPen injection.

Mild cases of anaphylaxis may present with itching and urticaria (hives) with no accompanying respiratory compromise. These patients do not usually require emergency care and transport.

What to Look For

KEY FINDINGS

- respiratory distress (can be severe)
- wheezing
- throat tightness
- edema in face, lips, or tongue
- skin pallor or flushing
- hypotension
- history of recent exposure to allergen

OTHER FINDINGS

- weak thread pulse
- syncope or presyncope
- vomiting or diarrhea
- altered mental status
- sense of doom

Care and Transport

- Anaphylaxis requires immediate transport to ED.
- Provide high-flow oxygen and manage airway as needed.
- Follow local protocols when administering patient's epinephrine (EpiPen).
- ALS intercept may be called to administer epinephrine if needed.

> PRACTICE QUESTION
>
> **2.** What medication is used to treat anaphylactic shock and how does it work?

Gastrointestinal Bleeding

An **upper GI bleed** is bleeding that occurs between the esophagus and duodenum. A **lower GI bleed** is any bleeding that occurs below the duodenum. Lower GI bleeds occur less frequently than upper GI bleeds.

Upper GI bleeds can lead to **hematemesis**, the vomiting of blood. The blood may be bright red or brown and clotted (commonly referred to as coffee ground emesis). Lower GI bleeds can result in **hematochezia**, bright red blood in the stool. When blood is partially digested in the lower GI tract, it produces **melena**—dark, thick stools that contain the partially digested blood.

DID YOU KNOW?
More than 70% of GI bleeds occur in the upper GI tract.

Table 5.2. Causes of Gastrointestinal Bleeding

Location	Condition	Pathophysiology
Upper GI bleeding	esophageal varices	Veins in the esophagus dilate and rupture from the pressure caused by obstruction to venous flow, usually due to liver disease. Substantial bleeding can occur.
	esophagitis	Inflammation in the esophagus from infection or stomach acid that ruptures blood vessels. Often caused by **gastroesophageal reflux disease (GERD)**, a chronic condition in which stomach acid leaks into the esophagus.
	Boerhaave syndrome	Bleeding caused by rupture or perforation of the esophagus caused by forceful vomiting. Substantial bleeding can occur.
	Mallory-Weiss tear	Bleeding caused by small tears that occur at the gastroesophageal junction from forceful vomiting. The bleeding usually resolves on its own but may be substantial.
Lower GI bleeding	diverticulitis	Inflammation of the diverticula (small outpouchings in the GI tract) cause inflammation that can lead to necrosis and perforation.
	hemorrhoids	Inflammation of the blood vessels in the rectum that may present as bright red blood in stools. The bleeding is not usually substantial.

HELPFUL HINT
Pregnant people with morning sickness or hyperemesis gravidarum (severe and persistent vomiting) are at risk for Boerhaave syndrome and Mallory-Weiss tears.

Care and Transport

- Manage airway.
  - Patients who are vomiting or have hematemesis may require repositioning or suctioning.
- Provide oxygen as needed.
- Patients with signs and symptoms of a GI bleed should be transported immediately to the ED.

PRACTICE QUESTION

3. EMTs arrive at a call to find a 54-year-old woman vomiting bright red blood. While taking her history, the EMTs learn that she has recently been diagnosed with cirrhosis secondary to a chronic hepatitis C infection. What is the most likely location of the patient's bleed?

Headache

Pathophysiology

Headaches are pain caused by pressure or inflammation in the blood vessels and muscles of the head and neck. Most headaches do not require emergency care. However, headache can be a symptom of a serious underlying medical condition, including hemorrhagic stroke and hypertensive crisis. For this reason, patients complaining of headache should be transported to the hospital for further assessment.

Patients should be considered to have a possible life-threatening condition and transported immediately to the ED when headache is:

- severe with a sudden onset
- accompanied by other symptoms such as seizure, fever, or altered mental status
- accompanied by a stiff neck (indicates possible meningitis)

Table 5.3. Types of Headaches

Pathophysiology	Presentation
A **migraine** is a neurovascular condition caused by neurological changes that result in vasoconstriction or vasodilation of the intracranial vessels.	intense or debilitating headache; **prodrome** (changes in mood or bodily sensation) or **aura** (sensory disturbance) may precede migraine; nausea and vomiting; sensitivity to light and sound; paresthesia
Tension headaches are headaches caused by muscle tightness in the head and neck.	generalized mild pain without any of the symptoms associated with migraines, such as nausea or sensitivity to light
In **temporal arteritis**, the arteries in the temporal area become inflamed or damaged.	severe, throbbing headache in the temporal or forehead region combined with scalp pain that is exacerbated with touch; visual disturbances

Pathophysiology	Presentation
Post-traumatic headaches (PTHs) are headaches that begin within 7 days of a traumatic injury or upon the patient's regaining consciousness after a traumatic injury. They typically resolve within 3 months but can become chronic headaches.	signs and symptoms of migraine with recent history of head trauma
Cluster headaches are usually episodic, lasting from 1 to 3 months, with more than 1 episode of headaches a day. They can go into remission for months to years.	intense, recurring unilateral pain that often occurs at the same time every day; agitation; nasal congestion and excessive tear production
Sinus headaches are caused by fluid that builds up in the sinus cavities during an infection.	pain (described as pressure) in areas around sinus cavities; signs and symptoms of cold or allergies

PRACTICE QUESTION

4. What signs and symptoms accompany migraines but are not found with other types of headaches?

Hyperglycemia

Pathophysiology

Hyperglycemia occurs when serum glucose concentrations are elevated in response to a decrease in available insulin or to insulin resistance. The condition is most often associated with diabetes mellitus but can also be caused by medications (such as corticosteroids and amphetamines), infection, sepsis, and endocrine disorders.

Diabetic ketoacidosis (DKA) is a hyperglycemic state characterized by an insulin deficiency that stimulates the breakdown of adipose tissues. This process results in the production of ketones and leads to metabolic acidosis. DKA develops quickly (< 24 hours) and is most common in people with type 1 diabetes.

Hyperosmolar hyperglycemic state (HHS) is a severe hyperglycemic state characterized by extreme dehydration and the absence of acidosis. HHS develops gradually over days to weeks. HHS is more common in persons with type 2 diabetes and has a much higher mortality rate than DKA.

What to Look For

KEY FINDINGS FOR HYPERGLYCEMIA

- blood glucose > 200 mg/dL
- polyphagia
- polydipsia

DID YOU KNOW?

When assessing a patient with suspected hyperglycemia, look for signs of dehydration and take a detailed history of their fluid intake and output.

- polyuria
- dehydration
- weakness and fatigue
- altered mental status

KEY FINDINGS FOR DKA

- blood glucose 350 – 800 mg/dL
- Kussmaul respirations
- fruity odor on breath
- abdominal pain
- nausea and vomiting

KEY FINDING FOR HHS

- blood glucose > 800 mg/dL
- severe dehydration
- delirium
- seizure
- coma

Care and Transport

- Patients with hyperglycemia require insulin and IV fluids and should be transported immediately to the ED.
- Severely dehydrated patients may require an ALS intercept to begin fluid replacement and to monitor for dysrhythmias caused by electrolyte imbalances.

PRACTICE QUESTION

5. What signs and symptoms should the EMT look for to differentiate between diabetic ketoacidosis (DKA) and hyperosmolar hyperglycemic state (HHS)?

Hypoglycemia

Pathophysiology

Hypoglycemia occurs when blood sugar (glucose) concentrations fall below normal. Patients will typically show symptoms when serum glucose is < 70 mg/dL, but the onset of symptoms will depend on the patient's tolerance.

What to Look For

KEY FINDINGS

- blood glucose < 70 mg/dL

- tachycardia
- cold, clammy skin
- altered mental status
- presyncope or dizziness

OTHER FINDINGS

- shakes/tremors
- blurred vision
- fatigue or sleepiness
- lack of coordination or impaired gait
- seizures

Care and Transport

- Administer oral glucose per protocols.
- Transport to ED.

> PRACTICE QUESTION
>
> **6.** An EMT receives a call for an unconscious 34-year-old female. An EMT arrives on scene to find the patient unresponsive with regular, shallow breathing. The patient has a blood sugar of 38 mg/dL. How should the EMT manage this patient?

Sudden Infant Death Syndrome (SIDS)

Sudden infant death syndrome (SIDS) refers to the death of an infant where no cause is found. These infants are usually found in the morning and may have been deceased for several hours at the time of the call. These are among the most challenging calls that an EMT will face.

What to Look For

- The infant will be blue, unresponsive, and not breathing.
- The infant may show signs of rigor mortis or dependent lividity.

Care and Transport

- Because of the sensitive nature of these types of calls, each EMS system has its own protocols that mandate varying levels of treatment.
  - The most aggressive guidelines will allow for providers to "call" a death in the field with no resuscitation efforts if there are signs that resuscitation will be futile.

- Other guidelines are much more conservative and encourage resuscitation of all full-arrest pediatric patients with immediate transport to the ED, even if there are signs of death.
- If there are no obvious signs of death, resuscitation efforts should be initiated.

- Attend to grieving parents.
  - Allow parents to stay with the child during resuscitation efforts.
  - If no resuscitation efforts are made, explain why.
  - Do not offer speculation as to the infant's cause of death.
  - Provide support for parents by explaining what will happen next and calling other family members.

PRACTICE QUESTION

7. EMTs have responded to a call for an unresponsive 2-month-old infant. On arrival they find that the infant is blue and not breathing with obvious rigor mortis; they decide not to provide resuscitation. The parents ask the EMTs what happened to their baby. How should the EMTs respond?

Seizure
Pathophysiology

A **seizure** is caused by abnormal electrical discharges in the cortical gray matter of the brain; the discharges interrupt normal brain function.

- **Tonic-clonic seizures** start with a tonic, or contracted, state in which the patient stiffens and loses consciousness; this phase usually lasts less than 1 minute. The tonic phase is followed by the clonic phase, in which the patient's muscles rapidly contract and relax. The clonic phase can last up to several minutes.
- **Status epilepticus** occurs when a seizure lasts longer than 5 minutes or when seizures occur repeatedly without a period of recovered consciousness between them.
- **Atonic seizures** are characterized by a sudden loss of muscle tone, which causes the patient to suddenly fall. These seizures have been called "fall attacks" as the patient has no warning prior to falling.
- An **absence seizure** is characterized by a brief lapse in attention where the patient stares off into space and has no cognitive function. The period of "absentness" is brief, and the patient usually regains cognitive awareness within a few seconds.

Seizures may be caused by **epilepsy**, a chronic condition characterized by recurrent seizures. Seizures may also be caused by trauma or other medical conditions, including:

- fever
- hyper/hypoglycemia

- dysrhythmias
- intracranial hemorrhages
- electrolyte imbalances
- poisoning

What to Look For

- loss of consciousness
- alternating muscle contraction and relaxation
- urinary and fecal incontinence
- tongue biting and frothing at the mouth

Care and Transport

- Maintain a safe environment for the patient.
    - Clear possible hazards.
    - Loosen the patient's clothing around the neck.
    - Do not place anything inside the patient's mouth.
- Prevent aspiration.
    - Roll patient on their side (if no spinal injury is suspected).
    - Suction airway as necessary.
- Provide oxygen and artificial ventilation as needed.
- Transport to ED.
- ALS intercept may be needed for status epilepticus.

> PRACTICE QUESTION
>
> **8.** An EMT is documenting a call for a 34-year-old woman who required transport to a hospital for multiple seizures. What information about the seizure should the EMT document?

Stroke

Pathophysiology

A **stroke** occurs when blood flow to the brain is interrupted.

- An **ischemic stroke** occurs when blood flow within an artery in the brain is blocked, leading to ischemia and damage to brain tissue. The lack of blood flow can be caused by a thrombosis or an embolus.

- A **transient ischemic attack (TIA)**, is a sudden, transient neurological deficit resulting from brain ischemia. It does not cause permanent damage or infarction. Symptoms will vary depending on the area of the brain affected. Most

TIAs last less than 5 minutes and are resolved within 1 hour. A majority are caused by emboli in the carotid or vertebral arteries.

- A **hemorrhagic stroke** occurs when a vessel ruptures in the brain or when an aneurysm bursts. The blood that accumulates in the brain leads to increased intracranial pressure (ICP) and edema, which damages brain tissue and causes neurological impairment. The symptoms of hemorrhagic stroke usually develop over a few minutes or hours.

What to Look For

KEY FINDING FOR ISCHEMIC STROKE

- facial drooping, usually on one side
- numbness, paralysis, or weakness on one side of the body
- slurred speech or inability to speak
- confusion

KEY FINDINGS FOR TIA

- signs or symptoms of ischemic stroke that resolve on their own

KEY FINDINGS FOR HEMORRHAGIC STROKE

- severe, sudden headache (often described by the patient as the worst pain they've ever experienced)
- decreased LOC
- nausea and vomiting
- sudden onset of weakness
- difficulty speaking or walking

> **DID YOU KNOW?**
> **Bell's palsy** is facial drooping caused by inflammation of the facial nerve (cranial nerve VII). It is not life threatening and usually resolves without medical treatment. Bell's palsy is similar to the facial droop seen in stroke patients. However, patients with Bell's palsy will not show any other signs of stroke (e.g., weakness or altered LOC).

Care and Transport

- Manage patient's airway.
- Provide oxygen as needed.
- Transport immediately to a hospital with a stroke center.
  - Ischemic strokes may be treated with thrombolytic drugs that must be administered within 4.5 hours.
  - "Time is brain": the sooner the patient receives hospital treatment, the more likely they are to retain brain function.

PRACTICE QUESTION

9. An EMT receives a call for a 68-year-old man complaining of headache, dizziness, and left arm weakness. When the EMT arrives on scene, the patient reports that the symptoms started about 20 minutes ago and are gone now. The patient has clear speech and answers questions appropriately. He states that he feels fine and does not need to go to the hospital. How should the EMT respond?

ANSWER KEY

1. Acute abdomen—sudden, severe abdominal pain—may be caused by cardiovascular conditions, including a ruptured or dissected aortic aneurysm or an MI (particularly in women). It can also be caused by obstetrical or gynecological conditions, including a ruptured ectopic pregnancy or ruptured ovarian cyst.

2. Epinephrine at 0.3 mg IM (adults) is used to treat anaphylactic shock. Epinephrine is a sympathomimetic and works by dilating the airway, constricting peripheral blood vessels, and reducing swelling in the upper airways.

3. The patient most likely has esophageal varices—bleeding in the lower esophagus that is most often caused by liver cirrhosis.

4. Migraines are usually accompanied by extreme sensitivity to light and sound. They are usually preceded by a prodrome characterized by irritation or euphoria. They may also be preceded by an aura, which includes the sensation of strange lights, smells, or sounds or other sensory disturbances.

5. DKA develops rapidly and presents with hyperglycemia, Kussmaul respirations, abdominal pain, and vomiting. HHS presents with hyperglycemia and neurological changes, including delirium or coma. It may develop over many days or weeks.

6. The patient is hypoglycemic. Because she is unconscious, she cannot be administered oral glucose. She should be transported immediately to the ED where she can be given IV glucose.

7. The EMTs should explain that the infant has died, but the cause of death is still unknown. They should express sympathy and offer the parents the chance to hold the infant.

8. The EMT should include the length of the seizure, the activity witnessed during the seizure, the number of seizures, and the length of time between seizures. This information will be crucial for the physicians who will be following up with the patient.

9. The EMT should explain that the patient is showing symptoms of a transient ischemic attack (TIA), meaning he suffered a small stroke. He may have an underlying condition that is placing him at high risk for further strokes, so he should go to the hospital for further assessment.

SIX: ENVIRONMENTAL EMERGENCIES

Bites

Pathophysiology

Bites and stings can come from many different sources, including domestic animals, snakes, spiders, scorpions, ants, and marine animals.

- Wild or domestic animal bites can cause punctures, lacerations, and fractured bones. Wounds caused by animal bites are also at high risk for infection.
- While some snakes are venomous, most snakes are not; most bites should be treated like other animal bites.
- Insect bites and stings (e.g., bees, wasps, fire ants) do not typically require emergency care but may cause anaphylaxis.
- Jellyfish are venomous marine animals whose stings can cause intense pain, burning, and rashes.

DID YOU KNOW?
There are four common poisonous snakes in the United States: the rattlesnake, water moccasin, copperhead, and coral snake. The saying "Red on yellow kills a fellow, red on black the venom it lacks" can be used to identify coral snakes.

Care and Transport

- Assess scene safety.
    - Move patient away from source of the bite (e.g., wasp nest).
    - Have animal control remove animals that pose a risk to the patient or EMS crew.
- Uncover and clean injured area.
- Treat soft tissue injuries and fractures as needed.
- Treat allergic reactions and anaphylactic shock as needed.
- Specific interventions may be required for some bites.
    - Request shot records for domestic animals that cause injury.
    - Contact medical control to advise hospital of necessary antivenom if a poisonous snakebite is suspected.

- If a poisonous bite is suspected, splint the extremity to slow the toxin from being absorbed into the body.
- Rinse jellyfish stings with saltwater (not fresh water).
- Patients with fractures, bleeding, anaphylaxis, or bites with high risk of infection should be transported to the appropriate level of care.

PRACTICE QUESTION

1. An EMT is assessing a 24-year-old female who was bitten by a stray dog that ran away when EMS arrived. She has minor puncture wounds with controllable bleeding and little pain. The patient says that she does not need medical care or transport. How should the EMT respond?

Cold Exposure
FROSTBITE AND IMMERSION FOOT

Pathophysiology

Frostbite is injury to the dermis and underlying tissue caused by freezing temperatures. Frostbite most commonly affects fingers and toes. **Immersion foot** is the result of prolonged exposure to cold (but not freezing) temperatures, often in wet conditions. It typically affects the feet but can affect the hands as well.

Both frostbite and immersion foot are characterized by vascular system impairment that leads to cellular damage and inflammation. While frostbite is more likely to cause permanent damage to tissue, both injuries may cause ischemia in the affected extremity.

What to Look For

- Signs and symptoms will be localized in extremities.
- early-stage frostbite:
    - cold and white waxy skin
    - numbness, tingling, or throbbing sensation
- mild-stage frostbite:
    - skin hard or frozen to the touch
    - skin red and blistered when warmed and thawed
- severe-stage frostbite:
    - damage to underlying muscle, tendons, and bone
    - blue, blotchy, or white skin
    - blood-filled blisters as skin warms
    - necrotic areas that are black in appearance
- immersion foot:
    - numbness
    - cold and clammy skin

- pallor
- edema

Care and Transport

- Move patient to warm area.
- Remove any wet clothing.
- Handle affected areas carefully to avoid further damaging tissue.
- Splint and cover if the frozen body part is an extremity.
- Gently warm affected area using warm passive heating or warm water.
    - Do not use intense heat—the extremity will be numb, so the patient will not be able to sense burns or other injuries.
    - Do not rub the affected area.
- Administer oxygen via a non-rebreathing mask.
- Transport to ED.

> **PRACTICE QUESTION**
>
> 2. An EMT finds a 23-year-old male lying in the snow near his snowmobile. After walking for help and stepping in a creek, the man returned to his snowmobile to wait for help to arrive. On examination, the EMT finds his right foot to be pale, swollen, and clammy. How should the EMT care for this patient?

HYPOTHERMIA

Pathophysiology

Hypothermia occurs when core body temperature drops below 95°F (35°C), causing a reduction in metabolic rate and in respiratory, cardiac, and neurological functions. When body temperature drops below 86°F (30°C), thermoregulation ceases. If hypothermia persists, coma and respiratory arrest will result.

Fluid shifts during hypothermia can lead to hypovolemia, which is masked by vasoconstriction. When the patient is rewarmed and the blood vessels dilate, the patient will go into shock or cardiac arrest if the fluid volume is not replaced.

What to Look For

- intense shivering that lasts until core body temperature drops below 87.8°F (31°C)
- CNS symptoms:
    - lethargy
    - clumsiness
    - confusion and agitation
    - possible hallucinations
    - unconscious in late stage

- abdomen cool to the touch
- unreactive pupils
- rapid breathing and pulse in early stages
- decreased cardiac and respiratory function in late stages

Care and Transport

- If patient is alert and oriented, the priority intervention is to slowly warm the patient.
    - Remove the patient from the cold environment, and remove wet clothing.
    - **Passive rewarming** is moving the patient to a warmer environment and allowing the patient to warm themselves. This is achieved by removing wet clothing and applying blankets.
    - **Active rewarming** is applying heat packs to the neck, armpits, and groin. Check local protocols to determine if the EMT can utilize active rewarming.
    - Administer warmed, humidified oxygen.
- If patient has an altered LOC or is unconscious, the priority intervention is to manage the airway and breathing.
    - Open the airway if necessary.
    - Access pulse for 30 – 45 seconds. (The pulse can slow drastically for extremely hypothermic patients.)
    - If no pulse, follow BLS protocols.
    - If there is a pulse, provide high-flow oxygen via bag-valve mask or a non-rebreathing mask.
    - Passively rewarm the patient.
- Transport the patient to the hospital.

PRACTICE QUESTION

3. A 68-year-old female was shoveling the snow in her driveway and sat down to take a break. Her neighbor found her sitting in the chair outside shivering and lethargic. He took her into the house and called 911. When the EMT arrives, the woman is alert and oriented but still shivering. How should the EMT care for this patient?

Heat Exposure
Pathophysiology

Heat cramps occur when exercise or physical exertion leads to a profuse loss of fluids and sodium through sweating. When fluids are replaced but sodium is not, the resulting hyponatremia causes muscle cramps.

Heat exhaustion occurs when the body is exposed to high temperatures, leading to dehydration. It is not a result of deficits in thermoregulation or the central nervous system.

Heat stroke results when the compensatory measures for ridding the body of excess heat fail, leading to an increased core temperature. The resulting inflammatory process can cause multiple organ failure that, if not treated, leads to death.

There are two forms of heat stroke: classic and exertional. **Classic heat stroke** occurs as the result of prolonged exposure to high temperatures with no air conditioning or access to fluids. **Exertional heat stroke** occurs when exercising in extreme heat.

What to Look For

- Heat cramps cause a sudden onset of severe spasmodic muscle cramps:
    - seen in the extremity muscles
    - can last from a few minutes to hours
- heat exhaustion
    - temperature elevated but < 104°F (40°C)
    - sweating
    - dizziness or weakness
    - rapid shallow breathing
    - weak pulse
    - cold, clammy skin
- heat stroke
    - temperature > 104°F (40°C)
    - no longer sweating
    - hot, dry skin
    - confusion, delirium, or seizures

Care and Transport

- The priority intervention for heat exposure is to cool the patient.
    - Evaluate body temperature.
    - Remove the patient from the hot environment.
    - Cool the patient with cold packs in the neck, armpits, and groin; misting or fanning the skin; or cool-water immersion.
    - Cool as much of the body as possible.
    - Cool the patient first, and then transport the patient.
- Provide oral fluids if they can be tolerated.
- Provide oxygen via a non-rebreathing mask.
- Transport the patient to the hospital.
    - Patients with heat cramps that subside with cooling may not require transport.

HELPFUL HINT
Never give dehydrated or overheated patients fluids with carbonation, alcohol, or caffeine.

PRACTICE QUESTION

4. An EMT arrives at an outdoor construction site to find a 38-year-old male with hot, dry skin; rapid pulse; and a body temperature of 105°F (40.6°C). The patient is conscious and complaining of weakness. What should the EMT do first for this patient?

High-Altitude Emergencies
Pathophysiology

High-altitude illnesses are caused by rapid ascent to high altitudes. At higher altitudes, atmospheric pressure is lower, and less oxygen is available in the air. If the body is not able to compensate, less oxygen will reach tissues, resulting in hypoxia. EMTs working at high altitudes may see several types of high-altitude illnesses.

- **Acute mountain sickness** occurs 6 to 24 hours after patients quickly ascend to high altitudes (> 6,600 feet).

- **High-altitude cerebral edema (HACE)** is a rise in intercranial pressure due to increased fluid in the brain; it is often considered a progression from acute mountain sickness. HACE may be fatal if not treated promptly.

- **High-altitude pulmonary edema (HAPE)** is fluid in the lungs that occurs 2 to 4 days after ascent (> 8,000 feet).

DID YOU KNOW?
Descent is the definitive treatment for most high-altitude illnesses; symptoms will usually resolve 1 to 2 days after altitude is decreased.

What to Look For

- acute mountain sickness:
  - headache
  - dizziness
  - dyspnea
  - nausea or vomiting
- HACE:
  - often follows signs and symptoms of acute mountain sickness
  - altered mental status
  - uncoordinated motor function
  - coma
- HAPE presents with similar signs and symptoms as other types of pulmonary edema:
  - dry cough
  - dyspnea
  - crackles in lungs
  - cyanosis
  - production of frothy sputum

Care and Treatment

- Patients with signs and symptoms of high-altitude illnesses should immediately stop ascent.
  - Patients with signs and symptoms of mild acute mountain sickness may be able to stay at current altitude with support treatment.
  - Immediate descent is indicated for patients with signs and symptoms of HACE or HAPE.
- Administer oxygen via a non-rebreathing mask.
  - Be prepared to aggressively manage the airway of patients with signs and symptoms of HAPE.

PRACTICE QUESTION

5. An EMT is dispatched to a high-altitude hiking trail for a dyspneic and disoriented 25-year-old male. The patient's friend tells the EMT that the patient arrived in the area two days ago and has been complaining of severe headaches. What should the EMT expect to do for this patient?

Electrical Injuries
Pathophysiology

Generated electrical energy causes external and internal injury from the electrical current running through the body. Injuries will vary depending on the intensity of the current, voltage, resistance, the length of time exposed, entry and exit locations, and the tissue and organs affected by the electrical current.

Generated electrical injury can result in skin burns, damage to internal organs or tissue, respiratory arrest, or cardiac arrhythmias/arrest. Generated current will often cause subcutaneous or deeper tissue injury much greater than the areas indicated by the line of demarcation.

When a person is struck by **lightning**, the electrical energy can result in cardiac arrest, neurological deficits (both acute and long term), and changes in the level of consciousness. It differs from generated electrical energy in that it does not usually cause burns, rhabdomyolysis, or internal organ or tissue damage.

What to Look For

- electrical injury
  - burns with a clean line of demarcation at entry and exit points
  - involuntary muscle contractions
  - difficulty breathing or respiratory arrest
  - seizure or loss of consciousness
  - paralysis
- lightning injury

- confusion, amnesia, or loss of consciousness
- keraunoparalysis (weakness in limbs following a lightning strike)
- hearing loss due to tympanic membrane perforation
- cardiac or respiratory arrest

Care and Transport

- Ensure the safety of the crew and bystanders before caring for the patient.
  - Shut off power or remove the patient from the power source if it is safe to do so.
  - If there are downed power lines, be aware of objects in the environment that may conduct electricity (e.g., aluminum siding).
- Remove any burning or smoldering clothes.
- Check ABCs and follow BLS protocols.
- Treat burns and secondary wounds as needed.
- Transport immediately.

PRACTICE QUESTION

6. An EMT arrives at a scene to find an electrician who has been electrocuted by wires in a circuit breaker box. The patient is still in contact with the wires. What should the EMT do first?

Submersion Injuries

Pathophysiology

A **submersion injury** (drowning) is a respiratory injury or impairment that occurs as a result of being submerged in liquid. These injuries were previously known as "wet drowning" when water was aspirated or "dry drowning" when the patient had a laryngospasm but did not ingest or aspirate water. The term "near drowning" is another term that is no longer commonly used.

Diving into shallow water can cause spinal injuries. If the patient strikes their head on the bottom, the spinal injury may cause paralysis, which makes the patient unable to save themselves in the water.

DID YOU KNOW?
Only a small amount of fluid is required to cause a submersion injury. Young children, the elderly, and intoxicated persons have the highest risk of drowning and may drown in only a few inches of water.

Care and Transport

- The priority care for submersion injuries is to open the airway and follow BLS protocols.
- Assume a possible spinal injury if the patient is unconscious with no witnesses or if there is an obvious mechanism of injury (e.g., diving accident).
  - Move the patient's arms above their head and grasp their biceps to stabilize the neck while rotating them face up.

- Open the airway and provide rescue breaths while the patient is further stabilized and removed from the water.
- Once the patient has been immobilized and removed from the water, follow BLS protocols for CPR and AED use.

- If there is no reason to suspect a spinal injury, do not delay rescue breaths or CPR to immobilize the patient.
- Transport the patient to the hospital.

PRACTICE QUESTION

7. An EMT crew arrives at an apartment to find a pulseless, apneic 2-year-old. His parents tell the crew that they found their son with his face submerged in a bucket of mop water. What should the EMT do first for this patient?

ANSWER KEY

1. The EMT should tell the patient that he will not treat her without her consent. However, he should discuss with the patient the risk of infection from dog bites, including rabies. Since the dog has not been found, the patient will likely need prophylactic care for rabies and other possible infections.

2. The EMT should move the patient to a warm area as soon as possible. The EMT should then remove the patient's wet clothing and gently warm the foot using passive warming or warm water. The foot should be splinted if the patient is transported to the hospital.

3. The neighbor has already moved the patient to a warm environment. The EMT should continue passive warming by removing any wet clothing from the patient and wrapping her in blankets. The patient should then be gently moved to the ambulance and transported to the hospital.

4. The EMT's first action should be to cool the patient. He should be moved to a cool area, and the EMT may use ice packs, fans, and/or cool water to cool the patient. Once cooling measures have been taken, the EMT can give oxygen and fluids to the patient and prepare for transport.

5. The patient is showing early signs of high-altitude cerebral edema and will need to descend to a lower altitude immediately to prevent further injury.

6. The EMT should shut off power to the wires or have someone shut off power before administering patient care.

7. The EMTs should follow BLS protocols and begin CPR.

SEVEN: PSYCHIATRIC EMERGENCIES

Pathophysiology

- A **behavioral crisis** is a change in behavior during which the patient does not act in an acceptable or normal manner (as defined by family, friends, and/or cultural norms).
    - The EMS is usually contacted when a person with a behavioral crisis becomes a threat to themselves or others.
    - Examples of a behavioral crisis include a patient sitting at a bus stop eating raw chicken while talking to themselves, or a patient yelling at a tree.
- A **psychiatric emergency** is an acute incident in which the patient is in psychological distress.
    - The patient may be a danger to themselves or others.
    - An example would be a patient that has suffered a recent loss and is having suicidal ideations.
- Behavioral crises or psychiatric emergencies can be the result of:
    - psychiatric conditions (e.g., bipolar disorder)
    - underlying medical conditions (e.g., stroke)
    - psychosocial issues (e.g., depression after divorce)
- **Organic brain syndrome** refers to behavioral or psychological issues caused by an identifiable injury or disease process (e.g., Alzheimer's disease, TBI, drug exposure).
- **Functional disorders** are psychological or behavioral issues without an obvious physiological abnormality (e.g., depression).

HELPFUL HINT
Common medical conditions that cause altered behavior may include: hypo- or hyperglycemia, hypo- or hyperthermia, hypoxia, stroke, head injury, and exposure to toxins.

PRACTICE QUESTION

1. An EMS unit is flagged by a truck driver who says that the woman in the car behind him has been following him for several hours. He confronted her, and the woman stated she is supposed to follow him home. The EMT does a primary assessment and finds a 75-year-old woman who is unable to answer alertness orientation questions. What conditions should the EMT consider during further assessments?

Psychiatric Conditions

- **Anxiety** refers to feelings of fear, apprehension, and worry. Anxiety can be characterized as mild, moderate, or severe (**panic**).
  - Anxiety will impact other functions such as the respiratory, cardiac, and gastrointestinal systems. Patients may experience palpitations, chest pain, dizziness, or shortness of breath.
  - When a patient presents with anxiety, the EMT should always look for organic causes, as other life-threatening illnesses may present with similar symptoms.
- **Bipolar disorder** (formerly known as manic-depressive illness) is characterized by extreme shifts between mania and depression.
  - **Mania** is a state of high energy, increased activity, and feelings of elation and immortality. Mania is often a manifestation of bipolar disorder but can also result from an underlying medical condition (e.g., tumor, hyperthyroidism) or drugs/medications (e.g., cocaine, corticosteroids).
  - **Depression** is a mood disorder characterized by feelings of sadness and hopelessness.
- **Delirium** is a temporary cognitive change from baseline.
  - The patient exhibits confusion and disorientation with a decreased ability to focus or hold attention.
  - Common causes of delirium include medications, hypoxia, stroke, and metabolic disorders (e.g., hypoglycemia, hyponatremia).
- **Dementia** is a broad term for progressive, cognitively debilitating symptoms that interfere with independent functioning.
  - Patients may show decline in one or more cognitive domains, including language, memory, executive function, motor skills, or social cognition.
  - The most common causes of dementia are Alzheimer's disease (most common form of dementia in geriatrics) and vascular dementia (from stroke).
- **Post-traumatic stress disorder (PTSD)** occurs as a result of exposure to traumatic events. Patients with PTSD will have heightened anxiety, anger, and fear, particularly when exposed to triggers associated with the traumatic event. They may experience nightmares or flashbacks related to the event and show heightened sympathetic nervous system activity (e.g., tachycardia, hypertension).
- **Psychosis** is a mental state characterized by delusions, hallucinations, paranoia, suicidal or homicidal ideation, and disturbances in thinking and perceptions. Schizophrenia and severe episodes of either mania or depression can also result in psychosis.
- **Schizophrenia** is a chronic psychotic condition that is characterized by bouts of psychosis, hallucinations, and disorganized speech.
  - Positive symptoms of schizophrenia are those not normally seen in healthy persons. These include delusions, hallucinations, and disorganized speech.

DID YOU KNOW?
Postpartum depression can occur after childbirth. In addition to other symptoms of depression, patients may report trouble breastfeeding, inability to bond with the child, or intense anxiety about their child's safety.

- ○ Negative symptoms are disruptions of normal behaviors. These include social withdrawal, paranoia, and flattened affect.
- A **situational crisis** is an acute change or event in a patient's life that may lead to feelings of anxiety, fear, depression, or other mental or emotional illness concerns.
  - ○ Examples of a situational crisis include divorce, sexual assault, and loss of a family member.
  - ○ The EMT should understand that the crisis is as problematic as the patient perceives it to be: assessment should focus on the patient's response to the event, not the event itself.
- **Suicidal ideation** is characterized by feelings or thoughts of attempting or considering suicide.
  - ○ Patients exhibiting suicidal ideation may have vague thoughts without a distinct plan, or they may have a specific plan and the means to carry it out.
  - ○ When assessing patients having a behavioral or psychiatric emergency, the EMT should always screen for suicidal ideation.

PRACTICE QUESTION

2. What behaviors should an EMT expect to see in a patient with bipolar disorder who is having a manic episode?

Approaching a Behavioral Crisis

- When approaching a patient with altered behavior, the EMT should always be aware of scene safety.
  - ○ Do not enter violent scenes without law enforcement.
  - ○ Maintain situational awareness: look for patients, bystanders, exits, weapons, and other elements of the scene that may affect EMT safety.
  - ○ EMTs should identify themselves and avoid sudden movement that may alarm the patient.
  - ○ Watch for patient movements and never place the patient between the EMT and the exit.
  - ○ Do not leave the patient unattended.
- When assessing patients with altered behavior, the EMT should follow these steps.
  - ○ Complete an initial assessment (ABCs) to check for life-threatening issues.
  - ○ Complete a full set of vital signs and look for medical issues that may have caused the emergency (e.g., low blood glucose, low blood oxygen).
  - ○ Evaluate the patient's psychological state by asking the patient if they have:
    - tried to hurt themselves
    - a plan to commit suicide or attempted suicide
    - a history of psychiatric disorders

- recent increased stress levels or emotional trauma
- used or abused alcohol or drugs

- When communicating with patients with altered behavior, the EMT should take control of the scene and attempt to keep the patient calm.
  - Speak in a slow, clear voice.
  - Be compassionate and do not judge the patient.
  - Stay out of the patient's personal space except for necessary medical assessments.
  - Use active listening skills.
  - Be aware of the patient's response to bystanders (e.g., if the patient is agitated by family members, have them leave the scene).
  - Do not challenge or affirm patients with delusions or hallucinations. Instead, redirect the conversation toward what is real.
- Patients with psychiatric emergencies should be transported to the appropriate facility.
  - Cooperative patients may be transported using standard protocols.
  - Uncooperative patients may require restraints for transportation. (See "Using Restraints" below.)
  - Law enforcement or an ALS unit may be needed to restrain violent patients. Law enforcement officers may also ride in the back of the ambulance.
  - Document any statements the patient made about harming themselves or others and report these statements to the receiving facility.

> **DID YOU KNOW?**
> If a patient is a threat to themselves or others, EMS may transport the patient even if they do not consent to care. Medical control should approve the transport, and law enforcement should be called to provide support.

PRACTICE QUESTION

3. EMTs respond to a call about a man shouting and behaving erratically in a park. When the EMTs arrive, they find the man lying still on a bench. Law enforcement is on the scene and tells the EMTs that the man appears to be in a stupor and won't answer questions. What should the EMTs do first?

Using Restraints

- Patient **restraints** may be used when patients are a threat to EMS personnel or to themselves.
- Restraints should only be used when other de-escalation techniques have failed (i.e., as a last resort).
- Restraints may be physical (e.g., wristlets, chest harness) or chemical (i.e., sedation, usually benzodiazepines).
  - EMTs may apply physical restraints when necessary (usually with approval from medical control).
  - **Chemical restraints** must be administered by an ALS unit.

- Law enforcement should always be requested when a violent patient needs to be restrained.
- The safety of the patient should always be the primary concern when applying restraints.
    - To prevent **positional asphyxiation**, never restrain a patient in a position that may compromise their breathing (e.g., face-down).
    - Use reasonable force (only the force necessary) to apply restraints.
    - Use soft restraints.
    - Never sit on the patient to apply the restraints.
    - Never leave a restrained patient unattended.
- Steps to restrain a violent patient:
    - Communicate and plan with other crew members before attempting to restrain the patient.
    - The patient should be restrained supine with one arm restrained above their head and one at their side. Both legs should also be secured.
    - Attach restraints to non-moving parts of the stretcher.
    - If the patient is spitting, a surgical mask may be used (ensure the patient's airway can still be monitored).
    - A cervical collar can be used when patients attempt to bite EMS personnel.
    - Check distal pulses after application of the restraints; repeat pulse checks every 10 minutes.
    - If the restraints have a lock, keep a key with the EMT in the back of the ambulance.
- Once restraints have been applied, do not remove them unless required for medical care.
- Notify the receiving facility that restraints are being used and why.
- Request additional help at the hospital to transfer the patient to the hospital stretcher.

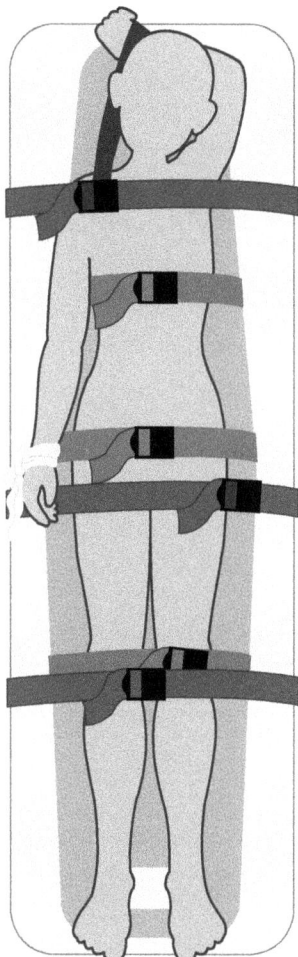

Figure 7.1. Restraint Positioning

PRACTICE QUESTION

4. EMTs respond to a call to find a patient yelling at and punching a tree. He repeatedly states he is going to hang himself from this tree. He is uncooperative and ignores all questions and direction from the EMT. What options does the EMT have to restrain and transport this patient?

ANSWER KEY

1. The patient's age and altered mental status suggest dementia (e.g., Alzheimer's disease). The EMT should also assess for an underlying medical condition, such as stroke or hypoxia, that would cause altered behavior. Finally, the EMT should also consider that the woman may be having an acute exacerbation of an underlying psychological issue (e.g., bipolar disorder).

2. People with bipolar disorder who are experiencing a manic episode will be highly energetic, often accompanied by euphoria or extreme irritability. They may be loud or aggressive and will likely have trouble focusing their attention.

3. The EMTs' priority should be to cautiously approach the patient and perform an initial assessment to look for life-threatening issues with the patient's airway, breathing, or circulation. If no life-threatening issues are found, the EMTs can proceed to assess for medical or psychiatric explanations for the patient's behavior.

4. If the man continues to refuse transport, the EMT should follow local protocols for restraint use. This may include physically restraining the patient with the help of law enforcement and transporting him in an ambulance or a police vehicle. Alternatively, the EMT may contact an ALS unit for chemical restraint.

EIGHT: TRAUMA

Amputation

Pathophysiology

An **amputation** occurs when a body part is separated from the body by surgical or traumatic means. Traumatic amputations typically occur in the extremities and may include fingers, toes, hands, feet, arms, or legs. Amputations are categorized as complete or incomplete (partial).

- **Complete amputations** occur when the body part is entirely separated from the body.
- **Incomplete** or **partial amputations** occur when the body part is non-functional but still technically connected by a tendon, ligament, or other tissue.

Severe hemorrhaging may be absent in some amputations due to the tendency for severed blood vessels to spasm and retract. Partial amputations or those with significant tissue damage (such as crush injuries) will likely result in more blood loss than cleanly severed body parts.

> **HELPFUL HINT**
> Trauma is often the result of situations that may be dangerous to the EMT, including violence, motor vehicle crashes (MVCs), or industrial accidents. Assess the scene both for safety and for information that may help treat the patient.

Care and Transport

- The primary concern during a traumatic amputation is bleeding control.
  - Apply direct pressure with a sterile dressing.
  - If bleeding continues, apply a tourniquet proximal to the amputation site.
- If the completely amputated body part is located, wrap it in sterile gauze moistened with saline and put it in a clean, sealed plastic bag. Then place the bag on ice (but do not freeze it).
- If amputation sites are contaminated with dirt or debris, irrigate with saline.
- Do not place ice directly against amputation injuries as this may cause tissue damage.
- Transport patient and amputated body part immediately.

PRACTICE QUESTION

1. What is the priority care for a patient with an amputation?

Blast Injuries

Pathophysiology

Blast injuries, or trauma caused by explosions, are grouped into four categories.

1. **Primary blast injuries** are caused by the over-pressurization shock wave that results from a high-explosive detonation (e.g., dynamite). Primary blast injuries result in **barotrauma** (injuries caused by increased air pressure) to hollow gas-filled structures such as the lungs, GI tract, and ear drums.

2. **Secondary blast injuries** occur from flying debris impacting the body and causing blunt or penetrative trauma.

3. **Tertiary blast injuries** result from the human body being thrown against a hard surface by the blast of an explosion.

4. **Quaternary blast injuries** are any symptoms not categorized as primary, secondary, or tertiary. Often, quaternary blast injuries are existing conditions (e.g., heart disease) that are exacerbated by the explosion. Quaternary blast injuries may also include burns or crush trauma.

HELPFUL HINT
Patients with primary blast injuries may not be able to hear your questions due to ruptured ear drums.

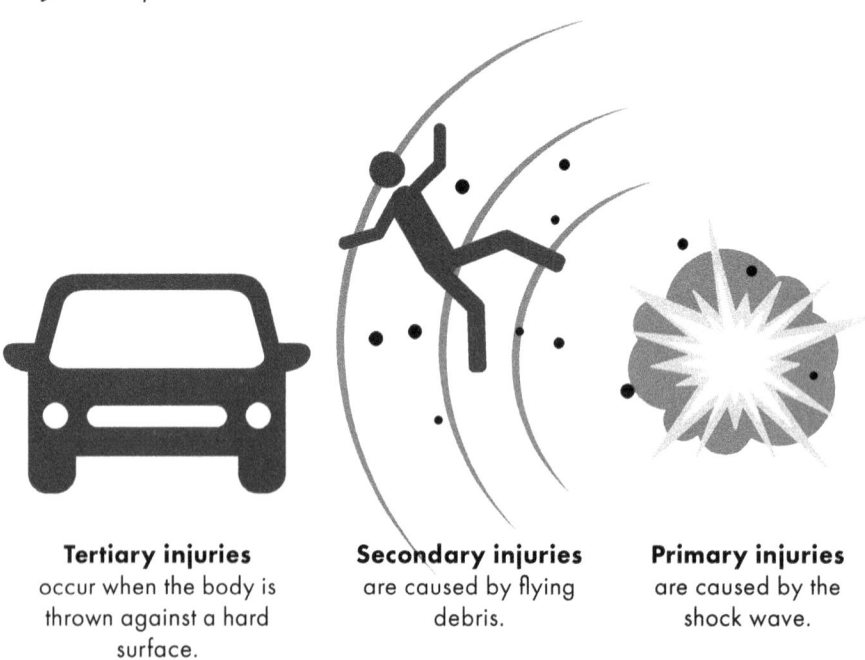

Tertiary injuries occur when the body is thrown against a hard surface.

Secondary injuries are caused by flying debris.

Primary injuries are caused by the shock wave.

Figure 8.1. Classification of Blast Injuries

Care and Transport

- Scene safety is paramount due to the risk of additional explosions.
    - Coordinate with fire, hazardous materials, and law enforcement for safety.

- o   If possible, move patients to a treatment area that has already been cleared by law enforcement.
- Patient care is symptomatic and often involves controlling bleeding from secondary blast injuries.
- Palpate and auscultate when primary blast injuries are suspected, as internal organs can be ruptured with no exterior signs.
    - o   Patients with suspected internal injury should be a priority transport to the ED.

PRACTICE QUESTION

2. What are the four types of blast injuries?

Bleeding
EXTERNAL BLEEDING
Pathophysiology

External bleeding, often caused by trauma such as lacerating or penetrating wounds, is categorized into three groups based on the source of the bleeding.

- **Arterial bleeding** is bright red blood that forcibly spurts each time the heart beats.
    - o   Arterial bleeding is difficult to control due to the pressure it is under.
    - o   As blood pressure drops, so will the force of the blood spurts.
- **Venous bleeding** is a steady flow of dark red blood.
    - o   The deoxygenated blood is darker in color than arterial blood.
    - o   The size of the vein and the wound will dictate how profuse the bleeding is.
- **Capillary bleeding** is slow and "oozing."
    - o   Capillary bleeding is usually from minor abrasions.
    - o   Capillary bleeding is easy to control, and the blood may clot on its own without intervention.

Care and Transport

- To reduce the likelihood of exposure, wear a mask, eye protection, a gown, and sleeves in addition to gloves.
- Determine severity by estimating the volume and rate of blood loss compared to the size, age, and medical history of the patient.
- The first and most effective step in controlling external bleeding is to apply direct pressure.
    - o   Apply temporary pressure with a gloved hand.
    - o   To create a pressure dressing, place sterile gauze pads over the wound and wrap tightly with a bandage.

- Check for a distal pulse before and after applying the pressure dressing to ensure circulation has not stopped.
- Do not remove dressing once applied. If bleeding continues, apply additional dressing.
- If pressure dressings do not effectively control bleeding, apply a tourniquet proximal to the wound.
- Other interventions may be used to prevent bleeding per local protocols.
  - **Hemostatic agents** are chemicals that promote coagulation. They can be applied as granules or dressings and are helpful in cases where a pressure dressing or tourniquet cannot be applied due to the location of the injury.
  - A **pelvic binder** can be used to decrease bleeding in patients with pelvic fractures.
  - **Air splints** can be used to immobilize fractures in the extremities and to slow bleeding.
  - **Traction splints** can reduce bleeding from femur fractures.
  - The effectiveness of **pneumatic anti-shock garments (PASG)**, also known as **medical/military anti-shock trousers (MAST)**, has been criticized in recent years, and their use has become increasingly less common.
- Administer high-flow oxygen to all patients with severe bleeding.
- Transport patients with arterial or uncontrolled bleeding to the ED immediately.

HELPFUL HINT
Estimated blood loss for a patient with an open fracture to the femur or pelvis is 1500 to 2000 mL. These patients are at high risk for hemorrhagic shock.

PRACTICE QUESTION

3. An EMT is dispatched to an MVC involving one car with a single occupant. On arrival, the EMT finds the patient in the driver's seat. He is agitated and repeatedly tells the EMT that his leg is broken and he needs to get out of the car. The EMT does a rapid head-to-toe assessment and finds an open femur fracture with significant blood loss. What is the priority EMT action for this patient?

INTERNAL BLEEDING

Pathophysiology

Internal bleeding describes any bleeding inside of the body. Most internal bleeding is caused by blunt trauma such as falls or MVCs; broken bones may also cause internal bleeding. There may not be any obvious external signs of internal bleeding, and the severity of internal bleeding is difficult to determine since large amounts of blood may be pooling inside internal cavities.

HELPFUL HINT
The risk of internal bleeding is elevated with some medications, particularly anticoagulants (blood thinners).

What to Look For

- contusions
- edema
- pain associated with internal organs

- rigid or tender abdomen
- blood in the vomit or stool
- signs of shock

Care and Transport

- Obtain an accurate history of possible traumatic mechanisms of injury in the days leading up to the symptoms.
- Treatment for internal bleeding is mostly supportive.
- Treat for shock.
- Splint and stabilize broken bones.
- Transport rapidly to an appropriate emergency center.

> PRACTICE QUESTION
> 4. Why is internal bleeding difficult to assess?

Burns
Pathophysiology

Burns are tissue injuries caused by heat, chemicals, electricity, or radiation. In addition to the primary tissue damage, severe burns can lead to life-threatening secondary complications such as hypothermia and infection. Significant **circumferential burns**, which wrap entirely around a body part, can cause constriction of blood vessels and nerves due to edema.

External burn injuries are classified by depth.

- **Superficial** (first degree): Damage is limited to the epidermis and does not result in blisters (e.g., sunburn).
- **Partial-Thickness** (second degree): Damage includes the dermis and epidermis accompanied by severe pain.
- **Full-Thickness** (third degree): All layers of the skin are damaged and there is likely underlying tissue damage. The patient may not feel pain in areas of significant nerve damage.

The severity of external burns is also dependent on the amount of damage, known as **body surface area (BSA)**. The **rule of nines** (Figure 8.2) is used to estimate BSA and is different for pediatrics than adults. The **rule of palm** (also known as the **rule of one**) may also be used to estimate BSA, particularly with smaller burns. The size of the *patient's* palm (not the EMT's) is approximately 1 percent of their body surface area.

The overall severity of burn injuries is classified based on depth and BSA plus any complicating factors.

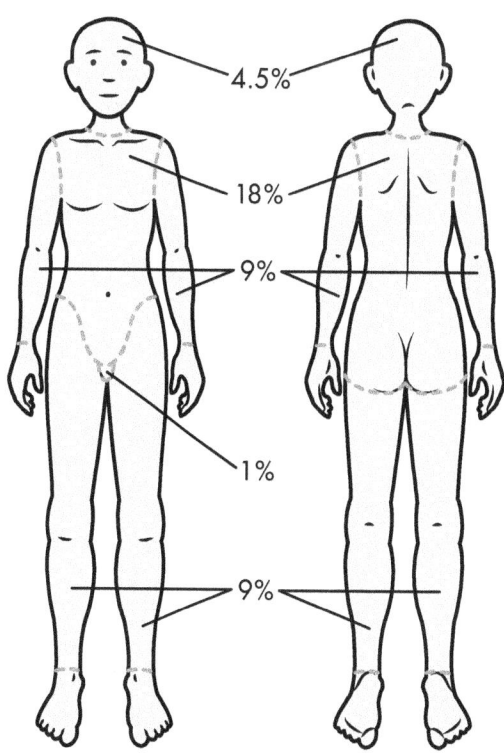

Figure 8.2. Rule of Nines for Calculating Total Body Surface Area (TBSA) of Burns

- **Minor**
  - full-thickness burns less than 2 percent
  - partial-thickness burns less than 15 percent
  - superficial burns 50 percent or less
- **Moderate**
  - full-thickness burns 2 to 10 percent
  - partial-thickness burns 15 to 30 percent
  - superficial burns greater than 50 percent
- **Severe/Critical**
  - full-thickness burns more than 10 percent
  - partial-thickness burns more than 30 percent
  - any burns to the respiratory tract
  - any full-thickness burns to the face, hands, feet, or genitals
  - any burns associated with traumatic or musculoskeletal injury
  - any circumferential burns
  - for patients under age 5 or over age 55, any burn that would otherwise be considered moderate

Care and Transport

- Look for signs of airway compromise such as burns to the face, soot in the nose or mouth, singed nasal hair, or coughing due to smoke inhalation.
- Aggressively manage the airway of any patient with possible airway burns.
- Priority care for burn injuries is to stop the burning.
  - Thermal: Remove the patient from the heat source.
  - Chemical: Brush off any dry powders or flush any liquids with water (irrigate for at least 20 minutes).
  - Electrical: Turn off electrical appliance if safe to do so or have electrical utility company isolate power.
- Dressings may be applied based on type and severity of burn.
  - Superficial and minor partial-thickness thermal burns may be treated initially with moist dressings, but apply dry sterile dressings once the skin has cooled.
  - Due to the risk of hypothermia, use only dry dressings for any burns more severe than minor partial-thickness.
  - Use sterile dressings whenever possible to lessen the risk of infection.
- Certain interventions should be avoided.
  - Do not apply ice or ointments to burn injuries.
  - For chemical burns, do not attempt to apply a "neutralizing" material.

HELPFUL HINT
For chemical burns, check the product label or safety data sheet (SDS) to ensure the chemical is not water-reactive before irrigating (if this can be done without significant delay).

- ○ Never attempt to remove anything that has melted to a patient's skin.
- Treat patients with high body surface area burns for shock and keep them warm.
- Transport the patient to the appropriate burn care center.
- With chemical burns, document the chemical name and its properties. Do not bring dangerous chemicals or their containers into the ambulance or hospital.

> PRACTICE QUESTION
>
> 5. An EMT arrives on a scene to find a 5-year-old patient with partial-thickness thermal burns on 2 percent of his body caused by placing his hands in boiling water. The patient has an elevated heart and respiratory rate and is in obvious pain. What is the priority EMT action for this patient?

Crush Injuries

Pathophysiology

Crush injuries occur when sufficient force is applied to the exterior of the body to compress and rupture internal organs, tissues, and bones. The major risk with crush injuries is internal bleeding and associated shock.

Crushing pressure that is sustained for a long period of time (> 60 minutes) can lead to **rhabdomyolysis**, the rapid breakdown of muscle tissue that releases large amounts of waste products into the circulatory system. When reperfusion occurs, these waste products flood the rest of the body, causing kidney failure (a condition sometimes called **crush syndrome**).

HELPFUL HINT
Rhabdomyolysis caused by crush injuries is the second most common cause of death following an earthquake (second only to direct trauma).

Care and Transport

- Extract patient as soon as it can be done safely.
- Manage fractures and bleeding as needed.
- Patients at risk for crush syndrome require paramedic-level care and transport.

> PRACTICE QUESTION
>
> 6. An EMT arrives on the scene of an MVC. The driver's right leg is trapped under the vehicle, but he is alert and has no complaints other than pain. The fire department will not be able to extract him until specialized equipment arrives. Why should the EMT request higher-level care for this patient?

Facial Injuries

Pathophysiology

Facial injuries are typically caused by traumatic impact with another object secondary to motor vehicle crashes, recreational or sports activity, violent incidents, or falls. Facial injuries may include penetrating trauma (e.g., stab wounds), soft tissue injuries (e.g., lacerations), broken or avulsed teeth, or fractures. Facial bones subject to fracture from blunt force trauma include:

- zygomatic bones (cheeks)
- nasal bones
- maxilla (upper jaw)
- mandible (lower jaw)
- frontal bone (forehead)

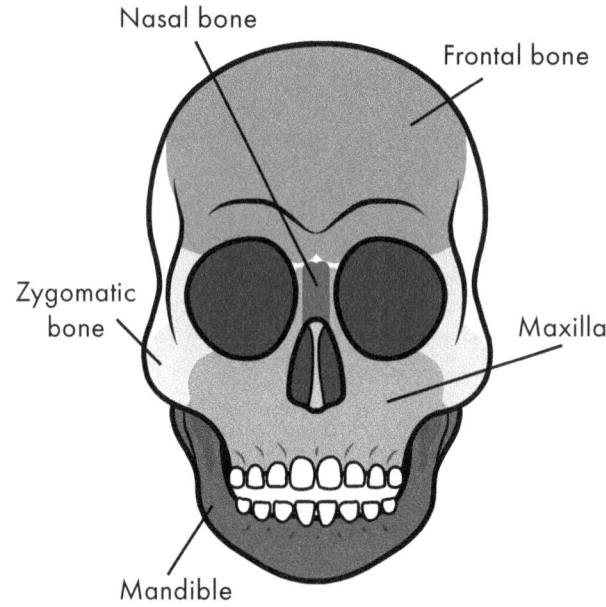

Figure 8.3. Bones of the Face

What to Look For

- The primary concern with facial injuries is airway compromise from fluid, broken bones, teeth, or swelling.
- Observe for signs of traumatic brain injury or associated head, neck, or back injury.
- Document any obvious deformities or asymmetries in the patient's facial structures.
- For dental injuries, observe the scene for any avulsed teeth.

Care and Transport

HELPFUL HINT
For **epistaxis** (nosebleeds), instruct the patient to lean forward and pinch nostrils. Do not let the patient lean back or tilt their head back as this may cause the blood to flow into the stomach.

- Follow appropriate protocol for suspected head, neck, or back injury.
- Be prepared to continuously suction the airway.
- Control any bleeding.
- Impaled objects not obstructing the airway should be secured in place.

- Avulsed teeth should be gently handled by the crown (not the root), rinsed (but not scrubbed) with sterile saline, and transported in sterile saline or in sterile gauze moistened with sterile saline.

PRACTICE QUESTION

7. Describe the process of assessing and caring for a nosebleed.

Eye Injuries

Pathophysiology

Eye injuries occur when there is direct contact with the eye and can be caused by trauma or chemical exposure. Very small foreign objects can easily disturb the **sclera** (outer surface of the eyeball), and foreign objects can cause abrasions to the **cornea** (transparent covering of the pupil and iris). The eyes are also subject to penetrative trauma.

What to Look For

- Assess eye movement by having the patient keep their head still while following the tip of a finger or pen with only their eyes.
- Ask the patient to read print of a size they can normally read without difficulty.
- Have the patient perform the eye movement and reading tasks with both eyes open, then repeat for each individual eye while keeping the other one closed.
- Check for blood or foreign objects in the eyes.
- Ask if the patient normally wears eyeglasses or contacts and if they were on at the time of injury.

Care and Transport

- For chemical exposure, irrigate the eyes immediately and continuously with copious amounts of water.
- Small amounts of debris in the eye, such as dust, can typically be removed by irrigation.
- Cover eyes injured by blunt trauma with a gauze bandage using minimal pressure.
- Do not remove objects impaled in the eye in the prehospital setting.
  - Stabilize impaled objects in place using rolled or folded gauze pads.
  - Add rigid stabilization, such as a paper cup, over the object and gauze.
- Patients with significant eye injury, such as impaled objects, may benefit from having both eyes covered in order to reduce the natural tendency for both eyes to move together.
- Transport patients with significant eye injuries to the ED.

PRACTICE QUESTION

8. How is eye movement assessed?

Falls
Pathophysiology

Fall injuries vary considerably, from an elderly patient rolling out of bed to a construction worker falling 20 feet off a roof. Fall injuries may be secondary to medical conditions such as sudden cardiac arrest, syncope, or seizures. Falls greater than 15 feet or three times the patient's height are considered severe. Geriatric patients are at much higher risk for significant injury from falls of any height.

What to Look For

- Attempt to determine the scope of injury by looking for:
    - the height of the fall
    - what type of surface the patient fell on
    - if the patient braced for the fall
    - if an object interrupted the fall
    - what part(s) of the body took direct impact
- Assess for signs and symptoms of common fall injuries including:
    - loss of consciousness
    - TBI
    - internal or external bleeding
    - broken bones

Care and Transport

- Follow appropriate protocol for suspected head, neck, or back injury.
- Splint any broken bones and treat any soft tissue injuries.
- Treat for shock as needed, particularly when internal bleeding is suspected.
- Transport to an appropriate emergency facility.

HELPFUL HINT
Remove jewelry or other constrictive items when swelling is likely to occur (e.g., fractures, burns, soft tissue injuries).

PRACTICE QUESTION

9. What are the indications of a severe fall injury?

Motor Vehicle Crash
Pathophysiology

All **motor vehicle collision** incidents involve three distinct impacts: 1) the vehicle initially impacting an object, 2) the occupant(s) impacting the vehicle, and 3) the organs of the occupant(s) impacting the inner surfaces of the human body. Depending on the speed involved, patients may have multi-system trauma, brain injury, broken bones, internal bleeding, amputations, burns, or abrasions ("road rash").

Motor vehicle crashes (MVCs) are classified by the motion of the vehicle. EMTs should be familiar with the types of crashes and the most common injuries caused by each.

- **Head-On (frontal)**: A vehicle in forward motion strikes a stationary object or another vehicle traveling in the opposite direction.
  - Unrestrained drivers may travel up-and-over or under the steering wheel, striking either the windshield or the underside of the dashboard.
  - The driver may also strike the steering wheel with their head, chest, or abdomen.
  - Occupants in other seating positions may strike the dashboard or the back of the seat in front of them.
  - Common injuries include trauma to the head, neck, chest, and abdomen, and fractures in the knees, femur, and pelvis.
- **Rear-End**: A vehicle at rest (or nearly at rest) is struck from behind by another vehicle.
  - Occupants of the rear-ended vehicle often experience head or neck injuries (e.g., hyperextension), particularly when the headrests are not properly positioned.

> **HELPFUL HINT**
> Seatbelts protect occupants from injuries caused by impact with the vehicle. However, they may cause other injuries, including hip dislocations, lumbar fractures, and damage to abdominal organs.

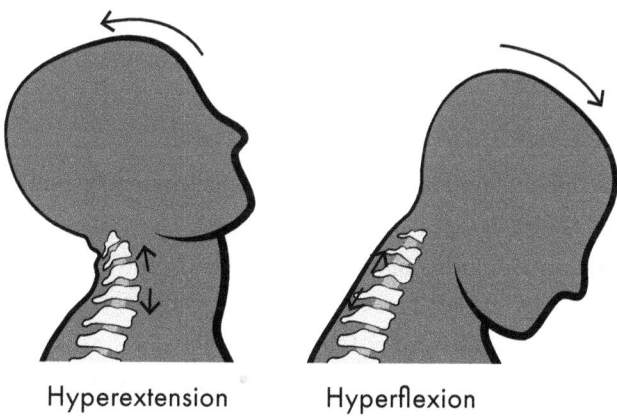

Figure 8.4. Hyperextension and Hyperflexion in the Neck

- **Lateral, T-Bone, Side-Impact,** or **Broadside**: A vehicle is struck by another traveling in a perpendicular direction.
  - Neck injuries are common as the head tends to remain still while the body is forced laterally.
  - Direct traumatic injury due to intrusion is more likely for the occupants on the side of the vehicle where the impact occurred.
- **Rollover**: A vehicle may roll onto its side or roof, or it may roll multiple times.
  - Injuries in rollover accidents are unpredictable.
  - Unrestrained occupants in rollover crashes have a high potential of ejection.

TRAUMA 133

- **Rotational:** A vehicle spins, while remaining upright, after striking an object or being struck.
    - Rotational injuries are similar to those found in side-impact crashes.

What to Look For

- Observe the crash scene and attempt to determine the mechanism of collision and number of patients.
    - In significant MVCs, unrestrained occupants who are ejected may be some distance from the impact site.
    - Pedestrians, bicycle riders, and motorcyclists may become trapped underneath vehicles.
    - Look for clues such as blood on a broken windshield, a bent steering wheel, or impact depressions on the dashboard.
- Attempt to determine where each occupant was sitting and whether they were properly restrained.
- Ask witnesses and occupants to estimate vehicle speed.
- Conduct a rapid trauma assessment as motor vehicle collisions often involve injury to multiple parts of the body.
- Look for signs and symptoms of underlying medical conditions exacerbated by trauma.

Care and Transport

- Follow appropriate steps for suspected spinal injury.
    - Maintain manual in-line stabilization for trapped occupants requiring advanced extrication.
    - The rescuer maintaining in-line stabilization during mechanical extrication should have appropriate personal protective equipment such as long sleeves and pants, eye protection, gloves, and a helmet.
    - Protect the patient against sparks, broken glass, and other debris present during mechanical extrication.
- Treat patients based on signs and symptoms.
- Transport patients to an appropriate hospital based on severity and extent of injuries.

PRACTICE QUESTION

10. What are the common mechanisms of injury in a head-on motor vehicle collision?

Neck Injuries

Pathophysiology

With the exception of spinal injuries, which are discussed separately, the main source of injury to the neck is an open wound due to trauma (e.g., cutting, gunshot wound). Neck injuries may be self-inflicted or caused by an outside force; they typically include lacerations or penetrations. Neck injuries may involve the jugular veins, carotid arteries, esophagus, larynx, or trachea.

Care and Transport

- The main priorities for neck injuries are to:
  - maintain the airway
  - control significant bleeding
  - prevent air embolism
- Apply pressure to the wound to control bleeding.
  - Take care not to apply so much pressure that all veins/arteries or the airway are obstructed.
- Place an occlusive dressing over any open neck wounds to prevent an air embolus from entering the blood vessels.
- Use bandages to secure any impaled objects in place, and do not attempt to remove the objects.
- Be prepared to suction excess secretions for patients with esophageal injury who may experience difficulty swallowing.
- Transport immediately to an appropriate medical facility.

> PRACTICE QUESTION
>
> 11. What is the EMT's priority when managing a patient with a penetrating neck wound?

Orthopedic Injuries

DISLOCATIONS

Pathophysiology

Dislocations involve bones being separated or "disrupted" from the joint they are a part of. Most dislocations are caused by sudden, abnormal force placed on the joint. Common causes of dislocations include falls, motor vehicle collisions, and athletics; common sites include shoulders, fingers, hips, and knees.

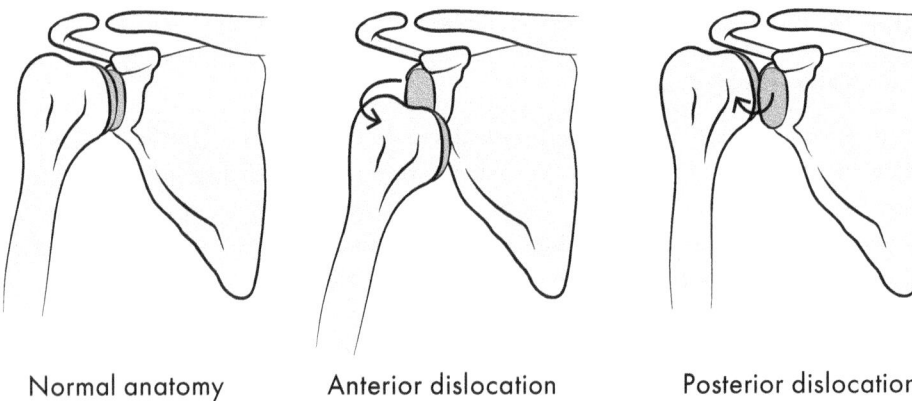

Normal anatomy | Anterior dislocation | Posterior dislocation

Figure 8.5. Shoulder Dislocation

Dislocations usually result in damage to ligaments and tendons and may damage muscles and blood vessels. Significant damage may still have occurred even if the joint was restored (sometimes done by the patient or bystanders before EMS arrival).

HELPFUL HINT
Patellar dislocation is most often caused by a sudden twisting motion with the foot planted. It often self-reduces. **Knee dislocation** involves dislocation of the tibia relative to the femur. It is caused by high-energy impact and is usually associated with major damage to tendons and vasculature.

What to Look For

- intense, localized pain at the joint
- deformity of joint
- loss of function or range of motion
- absent pulses distal to injury (with blood vessel damage or constriction)

Care and Transport

- The primary objective for dislocations is stabilization.
- Take spinal immobilization measures if indicated.
- Assess distal pulses, motor function, and sensation.
- If distal pulses are absent, manually realign the joint and reassess for circulation.
  - Realign by applying **manual traction** (gently pulling the limb away from the body).
  - Do not attempt to correct the dislocation by putting the bones back in place.
  - If distal pulses cannot be restored by realignment, patient transport should be a high priority.
- Select an appropriate size and type of splint to immobilize above and below the joint.
  - Reassess pulses, motor function, and sensation after the splint is in place.
- Transport to an appropriate medical facility.

PRACTICE QUESTION

12. What is the goal of realigning a dislocated shoulder joint?

FRACTURES

Pathophysiology

A **fracture** is a break in any bone. They are most commonly caused by trauma. Broken bones can cause serious internal damage, including significant blood loss and damage to nerves, tendons, or ligaments. Fractures are categorized as open or closed.

- **Open** (also known as compound): The broken bone has punctured the skin and is protruding outside of the body.
- **Closed**: The skin surrounding the break remains intact.

Compartment syndrome occurs when the pressure within a compartment (areas within the body separated by fascia tissue) becomes high enough to prevent perfusion. Most cases of compartment syndrome are caused by fractures that lead to blood collecting within the compartment. However, compartment syndrome can also be caused by hematomas, infections, or crush injuries. If left untreated, compartment syndrome can cause tissue necrosis.

> **HELPFUL HINT**
> Commonly fractured bones include the clavicle, radius/ulna, femur, and tibia/fibula. The most common area affected by compartment syndrome is the calf.

Assessment

- localized pain
- swelling
- deformation
- crepitus (grating of broken bones)
- The cardinal symptom of compartment syndrome is pain at the site that is disproportionate with the injury.

Care and Transport

- Take spinal immobilization measures if indicated.
- Control any external bleeding from open fractures.
- The care for fractures is stabilization, primarily achieved by splinting.
    - Stabilize broken bones at the joints above and below the injury.
    - Position the splinted limb as close to anatomically normal as possible.
    - Do not reposition the limb if there is resistance or evidence of further injury.
    - Reassess pulses, motor function, and sensation after the splint is in place.
- **Femur fractures** have the potential for large blood loss and are also very painful for the patient.
    - Use traction splints to stabilize femur fractures.
    - Continually reassess distal pulse, motor function, and sensation before and after splinting.
    - Transport immediately to an appropriate medical facility.
    - Contraindications for traction splints include open fracture, pelvic fracture, or any significant injury to distal bones or joints.

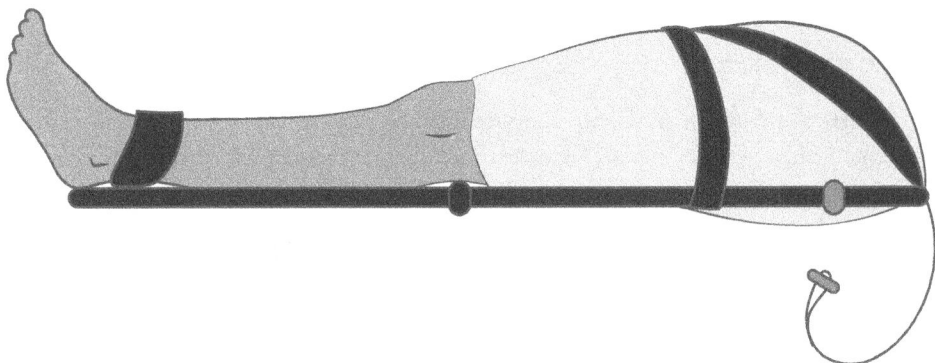

Figure 8.6. Traction Splint for Femur Fracture

PRACTICE QUESTION

13. A 6-year-old boy fell while running and caught himself with outstretched hands. He is now complaining of intense pain in his shoulder and is holding his arm across his chest. What possible injuries should the EMT suspect?

SKULL FRACTURES

Pathophysiology

Skull fractures are caused by trauma such as falls, violent incidents, motor vehicle collisions, and recreational activity. Skull fractures are subdivided into several categories:

- **Linear:** A single fracture line with no accompanying depression or movement of cranial bones.
- **Depressed:** The skull is indented, and the patient is at high risk for brain damage.
- **Basilar:** A fracture located at the base of the skull.
- **Compound:** A skull fracture that breaks the skin.

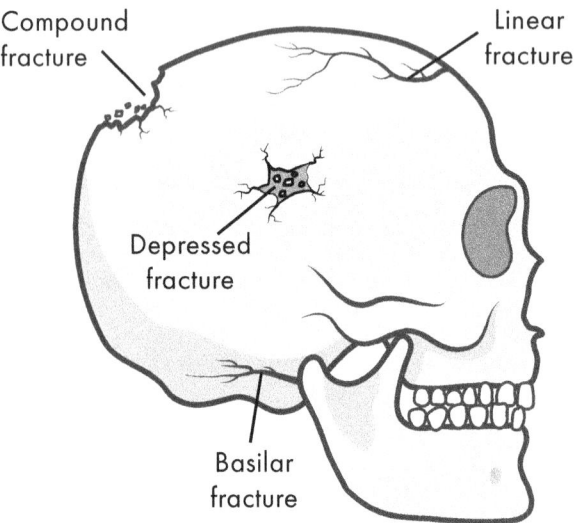

Figure 8.7. Types of Skull Fractures

- **Diastatic:** Limited to infants, the fracture widens the suture lines of the cranial bones before they fuse together.

What to Look For

- Skull fractures and brain injuries are assessed similarly since the two often accompany each other.
- The most obvious sign of skull fracture is deformity.
- It may be difficult or impossible to assess the difference between a skull fracture and a head laceration without fracture.

Care and Transport

- Initiate spinal immobilization measures.
- Control bleeding.
  - Do not apply pressure to depressed skull fractures.
- Keep the patient calm and treat for shock.
- Transport patients with known or suspected skull fracture to the ED immediately.

> PRACTICE QUESTION
>
> 14. What is a diastatic skull fracture?

STRAINS AND SPRAINS

Pathophysiology

A **strain** is the overstretching or tearing of muscles and/or tendons. The most common strains are the hamstring and lower back, with the latter often resulting from improper lifting technique. A **sprain** is the overstretching or tearing of ligaments. The most common sprains are the ankle, wrist, and knee.

Both injuries are usually caused by general overuse, a sudden force, or manual stretching. While strains and sprains are not life-threatening, improper care can lead to long-term joint or muscle complications and loss of quality of life.

What to Look For

- localized pain
- delayed swelling
- loss of range of motion
- Patients can usually attribute their injury to a specific activity.
- Strains may result in muscle twitching or spasm.
- Sprains are more likely to include discoloration or bruising.

- Complete tears may result in the patient feeling a "pop" at the time of injury and a deformity due to the tissues contracting or "rolling up."

Care and Transport

- Priority care for strains and sprains is splinting and immobilization.
- If the patient requests transport to a medical facility, provide supportive care and place in a position of comfort.

PRACTICE QUESTION

15. What is the difference between a sprain and a strain?

Penetration Injuries and Impaled Objects
Pathophysiology

Penetration injuries and impaled objects involve any foreign object completely puncturing the skin of the body. **Penetrating injuries** may be objects that have entered and remain in the body, leaving only an entrance wound. The object may also enter and pass through the body, leaving both entrance and exit wounds (**perforating wound** or **perforation**). **Impaled objects** are a subset of penetration injuries and describe objects that have punctured the skin and remain protruding from the body.

Penetration injuries are classified by velocity:

- **Low-Velocity**: Typically limited to objects propelled by hand or a bodyweight fall onto an object.
- **Medium-Velocity**: Handguns, shotguns, some rifles (including air rifles), and bows and arrows will produce medium-velocity wounds.
- **High-Velocity**: Limited to high-powered rifles, high-velocity projectiles will likely produce secondary internal damage known as **cavitation** or pressure-related damage resulting from the pressure wave that accompanies very fast-moving projectiles.

Regardless of velocity or location on the body, penetration injuries may be difficult to locate and are not always accompanied by pain or profuse external bleeding.

Care and Transport

HELPFUL HINT
The rapid trauma assessment should always include anterior and posterior portions of the body to verify the total number of entrance and exit wounds.

- Attempt to determine the size and characteristics of penetrating objects no longer in the body (e.g., caliber of firearm, length of knife).
- Expose the patient (remove clothing and equipment), taking care not to cut or tear through holes in clothing created by the penetrating object.
  - For violent incidents, the victim's clothing is considered evidence and should be left in the custody of law enforcement after being removed from the patient.

- Secure in place foreign objects that have impaled or otherwise penetrated the body, with the following exceptions:
  - objects that are obstructing the patient's airway
  - objects that are preventing the EMT from performing CPR when CPR is necessary
- Control bleeding with direct pressure and sterile dressings.
- Impaled objects that are too large or stationary to allow the patient to be moved will require specialized personnel and tools to cut the object. Follow medical direction and local protocol.
- Treat for shock as needed and transport to an appropriate facility as soon as possible.

PRACTICE QUESTION

16. What is the difference between perforating and non-perforating puncture wounds?

Sexual Assault

Pathophysiology

Sexual assault includes any sexual contact to which an individual does not explicitly consent. It can happen to people of any age, race, sex, gender identity, sexual orientation, marital status, or mental status. Sexual assault may result in injuries to the anus or genital regions and may be accompanied by trauma to other areas of the body (e.g., damage to airway caused by strangulation).

Care and Transport

- Notify the appropriate law enforcement agency in every case of known or suspected sexual assault.
- Most sexual assault survivors know their attackers. Ensure law enforcement has declared the scene safe for first responders if there is a risk the attacker may return.
- Provide a safe and private environment for the patient.
  - Remove any bystanders or non-essential persons from the area where the sexual assault patient is to be assessed.
  - Do not separate pediatric sexual assault patients from parents or guardians. If the pediatric patient accuses a parent of sexual assault, follow the direction of law enforcement and do not leave the child alone with the parent.
  - Sexual assault patients may be uncomfortable discussing what happened or allowing the EMT to examine them.
  - The EMT and the sexual assault patient should never be left alone together.

- If possible, the EMT and the sexual assault patient should be the same gender unless the patient specifically requests otherwise.
- Encourage victims of sexual assault to refrain from showering/bathing or discarding clothing, which should be treated as evidence.
- Control any external bleeding.
  - Sexual assault patients who are conscious and alert may wish to apply their own dressings, particularly to trauma of the genitalia.
  - Do not dispose of dressings or similar medical equipment used on sexual assault patients as it may be considered evidence.
- Provide supportive care.
- If possible, transport the patient to a medical facility with an on-duty **sexual assault nurse examiner (SANE)**, a registered nurse (or advanced practitioner) certified to treat victims of sexual assault.

PRACTICE QUESTION

17. A male EMT is the first responder on scene and approaches a woman who has been sexually assaulted. The woman refuses care and states that she just wants to take a shower and go to sleep. How should the EMT respond?

Soft Tissue Injuries
Pathophysiology

Closed soft tissue injuries are mainly caused by blunt force trauma that does not result in broken skin. A **contusion**, also referred to as a bruise, is temporary and indicates minor damage to the blood vessels in the dermis that will heal on its own. **Hematomas** are similar to contusions: they involve the collection of blood underneath the unbroken skin. However, hematomas involve larger amounts of blood and often need surgical intervention to heal. If left untreated, the internal pressure created from hematomas can be life threatening.

Open soft-tissue injuries are those in which the skin has been broken.

- An **abrasion**, often called a "scrape" or "scratch" by the layperson, involves only the outer layer of skin being damaged by friction. Bleeding may be minimal, but pain can be significant.
- A **laceration** is a tearing of the skin. They are commonly referred to as a "cut" but may also result from blunt trauma.
- **Avulsions** are flaps of skin that have been partially or completely severed.
  - **Degloving** describes an avulsion where the skin surrounding an appendage has been peeled or rolled back onto itself.
  - Degloving is often the result of constrictive jewelry being forcefully removed, such as after getting caught on an external object.

Assessment

- discoloration
- swelling
- pain at site
- Deep hematomas might not have visible discoloration.

Care and Transport

- Care for soft tissue injuries is supportive.
  - Splint the injury site, checking for distal pulses, motor function, and sensation before and after.
  - Treat for shock and transport to an appropriate medical facility.
- The priority care for open soft-tissue injuries is to control bleeding and help prevent infection.
  - Expose the open soft-tissue injury.
  - Control any major bleeding with direct pressure and sterile dressing.
  - Quickly yet gently clean minor bleeds by using sterile gauze to wipe away debris that could lead to infection.
  - Minimize movement or completely stabilize the injury site to reduce bleeding and further injury.
  - Gently put back in place partial avulsions after cleaning the wound site.
  - Total avulsions should be packaged separately in the same manner as a total amputation.

PRACTICE QUESTION

18. An EMT arrives on the scene of an industrial accident in which the skin on the patient's left finger was totally avulsed after his wedding ring became caught in equipment. What interventions should the EMT plan to provide?

Spine Injuries
Pathophysiology

Spinal injuries may occur by different means, such as MVCs, falls, sports or recreational activities, and blunt or penetrative trauma. Spinal injury can result in the fracture, dislocation, compression, bruising, or severing of the spinal anatomy. Spine injuries are classified by mechanism.

- **Compression** occurs when the head is pressed down onto the spine (e.g., diving injury, unrestrained occupants in MVCs).
- **Extension** occurs when the head is forced backward (e.g., rear-end MVC with an improperly set headrest).

- **Flexion** occurs when the head is forced forward (e.g., frontal collision when the torso is secured but the head is not).
- **Rotation** occurs when the head is moved in a sideways motion (e.g., hard collisions in contact sports).
- **Distraction** is the elongation or stretching of the spine; it typically only occurs in hangings.

What to Look For

- loss or reduction of motor or sensory function in the extremities
- paralysis
- pain, tenderness, or deformities along the spine
- signs and symptoms of complications caused by damage to spinal nerves
    - impaired breathing
    - priapism
    - loss of bowel or bladder control
    - neurogenic shock (hypotension with a normal or slightly low heart rate)

HELPFUL HINT
The treatment of life-threatening conditions, including the removal of the patient from an imminently dangerous scene, takes priority over spinal stabilization.

Care and Transport

- Follow protocols for spinal immobilization. (See chapter 12, "The Psychomotor Exam," for detailed instruction on spinal immobilization.)
- Patients with suspected spinal injury should be transported to an appropriate receiving facility, such as a trauma hospital.

PRACTICE QUESTION

19. What are the most reliable indications of spinal cord injury?

Traumatic Brain Injuries
Pathophysiology

Traumatic brain injury (TBI) is caused by direct or indirect contact with the brain. Direct contact with the brain typically happens as the result of a penetrating head wound or blunt force head trauma resulting in cranial fracture. Indirect brain contact involves an impact to the head wherein the force is transferred to the brain.

TBI may result in **intracranial hemorrhage** (bleeding within the skull). This bleeding is named for its location:

- **Epidural hematoma**: blood between the skull and the dura mater (usually associated with skull fracture)
- **Subdural hematoma**: blood between the brain and the dura mater
- **Subarachnoid hematoma**: bleeding within the subarachnoid space

- **Intracerebral hemorrhage**: blood pooling within the brain tissue

The brain is tightly encased within the skull, and there is minimal room for swelling or blood. Significant brain injury will cause increased **intercranial pressure** (**ICP**), the pressure within the skull. In severe cases of increased ICP, the brain may shift into the **foramen magnum** (the opening in the base of the skull where the spinal cord enters) in a process known as **cerebral herniation syndrome**.

A **concussion** is a mild brain function disruption in which the acute symptoms have a rapid onset but gradually improve.

What to Look For

- signs and symptoms of TBI:
    - altered LOC or mental status
    - headache
    - trismus (clenched teeth/jaw)
    - cerebrospinal fluid (CSF) leaking from the ears or nose
    - Battle's sign (bruising behind the ears) (associated with skull fracture)
    - discoloration under the eyes ("raccoon eyes")
- signs and symptoms of intercranial hematoma:
    - posturing (stiff legs, arms stiff or drawn up toward the chest, fists or fingers clenched)
    - unequal or unreactive pupils
    - seizure
    - hypertension
    - decreased respiratory effort
- **Cushing's triad** is a sign of increased ICP and/or herniation syndrome:
    - hypertension
    - bradycardia
    - altered respiratory pattern
- signs and symptoms of concussion:
    - briefly altered LOC
    - headache
    - nausea or vomiting
    - amnesia
    - general disorientation

Care and Transport

- Patients with suspected head injury are unreliable witnesses, so look for bystanders or rely on context clues.

HELPFUL HINT

Recent research has identified three "H bombs" to avoid in patients with TBI: hypoxia, hyperventilation, and hypotension. Addressing these three issues in prehospital care significantly increases survival rates.

- Provide manual stabilization of the head and neck.
- Reverse Trendelenburg position (head elevated) may be indicated by local protocol or medical direction.
- Aggressively manage airway and oxygen saturation.
  - Have suction ready in case patient vomits.
- Do not apply pressure to the skull if fracture is suspected.
- Do not apply pressure to areas with CSF leakage.
- Transport immediately to the ED.

PRACTICE QUESTION

20. What is Cushing's triad, and what interventions should the EMT expect to provide for patients with the symptoms associated with it?

ANSWER KEY

1. The EMT's primary concern with an amputation is controlling bleeding. While cleanly severed amputations may bleed less due to the blood vessels contracting, incomplete amputation or amputations involving arteries can lead to hemorrhage and shock.

2. Primary blast injuries are caused by the shock wave from a high-explosive detonation. Secondary blast injuries are from explosion fragments impacting the body. Tertiary blast injuries are from the body being thrown by the blast, and quaternary blast injuries are all of those not otherwise categorized.

3. Significant bleeding from an open femur fracture is a life-threatening injury that must be addressed before the patient can be moved or further assessed. If possible, the EMT should apply a pressure dressing to the patient before he is removed from the car. A tourniquet or hemostatic agent may also be used depending on the position of the patient and local protocols. The patient should then be removed from the car using a rapid extraction technique and immediately loaded for transport.

4. Assessing internal bleeding is challenging because the cause and the source of the bleed cannot be seen and may be unknown. The amount of blood hemorrhaging into internal cavities cannot be determined in a prehospital setting. Signs and symptoms may be minimal and are consistent with other conditions, such as shock or simple blunt force trauma.

5. The priority action for the EMT is to stop the burning process by cooling the area with a cool, wet dressing. Once the area is cool, the burn should be covered with a dry, sterile dressing, and the patient should be transported to the ED.

6. Because the driver's leg will be trapped under the car for an extended period of time, he is at high risk for crush syndrome. He will require fluids and analgesics while he remains trapped, and paramedics will need to monitor for and treat damage to the kidneys once he has been extracted.

7. For patients with epistaxis (nosebleed), have the patient lean forward and pinch the nostrils if this can be done without further pain or injury. The patient should never be instructed to lean back or tilt their head back as this could cause blood to drain into the stomach, leading to vomiting.

8. Eye movement is assessed by having the patient keep their head still while following an object, such as the tip of the EMT's finger, side-to-side as well as up and down using only their eyes. This assessment should be performed using both eyes followed by each eye individually while the other is covered.

9. Falls from greater than 15 feet or more than three times the patient's height are automatically considered severe. However, elderly patients may experience a severe fall from much lower height. Any fall resulting in spinal injury, loss of consciousness, significant internal or external bleeding, or brain injury should also be considered severe.

10. The driver of a vehicle in a head-on collision may travel up-and-over the steering wheel, striking the windshield and causing injury to the head or neck. The driver may also travel under the steering wheel, striking the underside of the dashboard and causing fractures of the knee, femur, or pelvis. The chest or abdomen may strike the steering wheel, causing rib fractures or trauma to the lungs or heart.

11. The EMT's priority should be maintaining the airway. The EMT will also need to control bleeding and prevent air emboli from entering the venous system.

12. The EMT should attempt to realign a dislocated shoulder if the pulse distal to the injury is absent. The goal of realigning the joint is to return circulation to the affected extremity. Realignment may also help alleviate pain.

13. The mechanism of injury and the patient's complaint could be consistent with either a fracture or a dislocation. The EMT should suspect either a shoulder dislocation or a fracture to the clavicle, humerus, or scapula.
14. A diastatic skull fracture is the widening or enlargement of the cranial sutures present in newborns and infants. Since the cranial bones fuse together in early childhood, diastatic skull fractures are only found in infants.
15. Sprains and strains are differentiated by the part of the anatomy they affect. Sprains are injuries to the ligaments, which connect bone to bone. Strains are injuries to either the muscles or tendons, the latter of which connect bone to muscle.
16. A perforating puncture injury is the result of an object that has left an entrance wound and an exit wound. A perforating wound may be caused by an object that entered and exited the body completely, such as a "through-and-through" gunshot wound. Impaled objects can also be perforating. A non-perforating puncture injury only has an entrance wound.
17. The EMT should assure the woman that he will not assess or treat her without her consent. He or his partner should then call for a female EMT to examine the woman and should ensure that the appropriate law enforcement personnel are en route. While he waits for further resources, he should suggest to the woman that she refrain from removing her clothes or showering, but he should not attempt to restrain her if she wants to leave.
18. The EMT should gently remove debris from the wound and control bleeding with direct pressure and a sterile dressing. The avulsed skin should be packaged in sterile moist dressing and transported with the patient.
19. In conscious patients, the most reliable signs of spinal cord injury are paralysis, loss or reduction in motor function, and/or loss or reduction in sensory function in the extremities.
20. Cushing's triad consists of hypotension, bradycardia, and irregular change in breathing. Cushing's triad is a sign of increased ICP and impending or actual cerebral herniation. Treatment may include positioning the patient in reverse Trendelenburg and hyperventilation with supplemental oxygen.

NINE: OBSTETRICAL EMERGENCIES

Anatomy and Physiology of Pregnancy

- After an egg is fertilized with sperm, it develops into an embryo, which implants itself on the wall of the uterus.
- After approximately eight weeks, the embryo is described as a **fetus**.
- The fetus is surrounded by a fluid-filled membrane called the **amniotic sac**.
- The **placenta** is a blood-rich temporary organ attached to the wall of the uterus that provides nutrients and gas exchange for the fetus and eliminates waste.
- The placenta is attached to the fetus by the **umbilical cord**.
- During **labor**, the cervix dilates and thins to allow the fetus to pass. Then, **contractions** of the muscular walls of the uterus push the fetus through the cervix and out the birth canal (**delivery**).
- Labor and delivery occurs in 3 stages.
    - Stage 1: cervix dilates and contractions begin (12 – 16 hours).
    - Stage 2: cervical dilation is complete, pushing begins, and the fetus is delivered (2 – 3 hours).
    - Stage 3: the placenta is delivered (10 – 12 minutes).
- **Full-term pregnancy** is 40 weeks and is divided into the first trimester (1 – 12 weeks), second trimester (13 – 26 weeks), and third trimester (27 – 40 weeks).
    - **Preterm labor** occurs between 20 and 37 weeks.
    - Post-term pregnancy occurs when the fetus has not been delivered by 42 weeks.

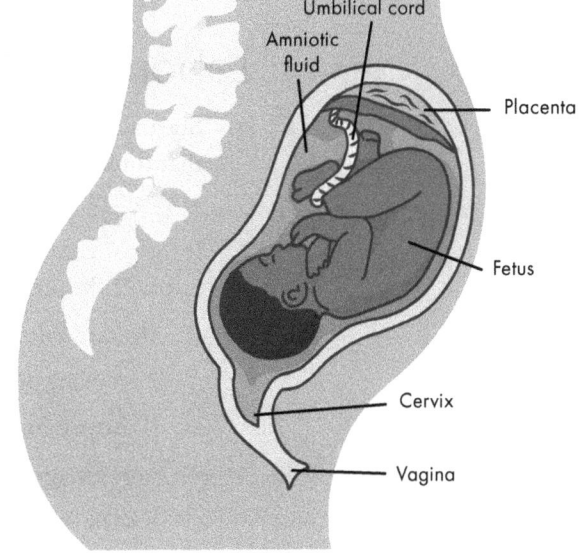

Figure 9.1. Fetus in Third Trimester

- The likelihood of survival is very low for fetuses delivered before 24 weeks but increases with gestational age.
- With access to appropriate neonatal care, around 90 percent of fetuses delivered at 27 weeks survive.

- Normal position for the fetus during delivery is head down. **Breech** position is when the fetus has its feet or buttocks downward.
- During pregnancy, the woman will experience physiological changes that may affect the delivery of medical care. These changes include:
  - increased blood volume (as much as 50 percent by the end of pregnancy)
  - increased heart rate (normal increase is around 15 beats per minute)
  - increased respiratory rate
  - increased oxygen demand and decreased lung capacity
  - increased clotting speed
  - displaced GI and respiratory organs

DID YOU KNOW?
During pregnancy, the top of the uterus (fundus) may be as high as the xiphoid process. This limits movement of the diaphragm and chest wall, which may cause difficulty breathing.

PRACTICE QUESTION

1. What changes from normal should the EMT expect to see when taking vital signs for a patient who is 38 weeks pregnant?

Labor and Delivery

- Start assessment of a pregnant patient by assessing ABCs. Conditions that threaten the life of the mother should be addressed before any further assessment is done.
- If the patient has no life-threatening conditions, take vital signs and assess the status of the pregnancy by asking the patient:
  - the due date
  - how many pregnancies the patient has had
  - if the patient has received prenatal care
  - how far apart the contractions are (time the contractions as well)
  - if their "water broke" (did the amniotic sac rupture)
  - if they feel the need to push or move their bowels
- Physically examine the vaginal opening for **crowning** (the emergence of any part of the baby from the vaginal opening).
- EMTs must assess pregnant patients to decide whether to load and go or stay to deliver the baby.
- Load and go if birth is not imminent.
- The EMT should stay and deliver the baby if birth is imminent. Signs that birth is imminent include:
  - crowning

- contractions 2 minutes apart or less
- feeling the urge to push or having a bowel movement
- if the mother has had multiple births and expresses that the baby is coming

● Load and go and call for an ALS intercept for complicated deliveries, which include:
- crowning that reveals a body part other than the head (including the umbilical cord)
- unstable patient vital signs
- the birth is not progressing
- preterm labor
- no prenatal care
- labor induced by trauma or drugs
- multiple births (twins or triplets)
- meconium staining

● Follow these steps to prepare the patient for birth.
- Move the patient to a private area.
- Use PPE (face masks, gloves, gown, face shield, and eye protection).
- Remove patient's clothes and undergarments that obstruct the view of the vaginal opening.
- Use sterile sheets when available to drape the patient.
- Elevate the mother's buttocks with the knees drawn up.

● During delivery:
- The EMT should allow the patient to push out the child while the EMT gently guides the head and shoulders out.
- Place the newborn on the patient to warm the baby before the cord is cut.
- When the cord is no longer pulsing, clamp 10 inches and 7 inches from the baby, and cut between the clamps.
- Deliver the placenta; do not pull on the cord.

● After delivery, assess the mother and address any bleeding or tearing.
- If the placenta delivers, massage the mother's abdomen to help contract the uterus (this will slow vaginal bleeding).
- Control bleeding by placing a 5 × 9 gauze on the vaginal opening, and instruct the mother to lower and put her legs together.
- There may be torn tissue on the perineum: advise the mother that this is normal and dress the wound with a sanitary pad.

HELPFUL HINT
ALS should always be called for a birth in the field.

DID YOU KNOW?
Meconium is the fetus's feces. If meconium is released into the amniotic fluid, the fetus may inhale it, causing asphyxiation.

PRACTICE QUESTION

2. An EMT arrives at a scene to find a 27-year-old woman having contractions. She has had four previous live births and states that she thinks the baby is about to come out. What should the EMT do?

Pregnancy and Delivery Complications

- **Umbilical cord prolapse** occurs when the cord presents alongside (occult) or ahead of (overt) the presenting fetus during delivery. Exposure of the cord makes it vulnerable to compression or rupture, which disrupts blood flow to the fetus.
- **Preeclampsia** is a syndrome caused by abnormalities in the placental vasculature that cause hypertension and proteinuria (protein in urine).
    - Signs and symptoms of preeclampsia include hypertension, edema, severe headache, and rapid weight gain.
    - Preeclampsia can lead to life-threatening complications, including eclampsia, pulmonary edema, and abruptio placentae (placental abruption).
    - In most cases, preeclampsia will resolve after delivery, but symptoms can develop up to 4 weeks postpartum.
- **Eclampsia** is the onset of tonic-clonic seizures in women with preeclampsia.
- In an **ectopic pregnancy**, the fertilized egg implants in a location other than the uterus.
    - In > 95% of cases, implantation occurs in the fallopian tubes (tubal pregnancy), but implantation can also occur in the ovaries, cervix, or abdominal cavity.
    - A tubal pregnancy may rupture the fallopian tube, causing a life-threatening hemorrhage.
    - Ectopic pregnancy should be considered for female patients with abdominal pain.

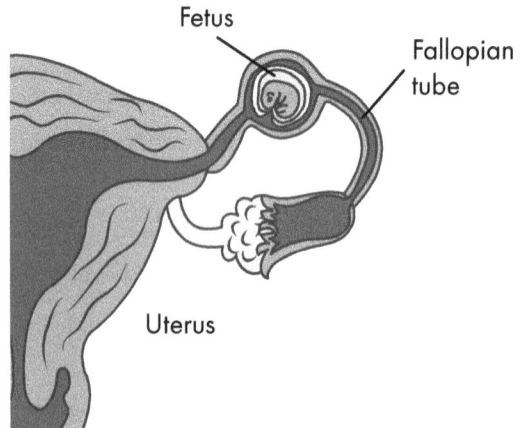

Figure 9.2. Ectopic Pregnancy (Tubal Pregnancy)

- **Hyperemesis gravidarum** is severe nausea and vomiting that occurs during pregnancy and leads to dehydration, hypovolemia, and electrolyte imbalances.
- **Abruptio placentae** (placental abruption) occurs when the placenta separates from the uterus before delivery.

- Abruption can lead to life-threatening hemorrhage.
- Blood loss due to abruption can be difficult to quantify as blood may accumulate behind the placenta (concealed abruption) rather than exiting through the vagina.

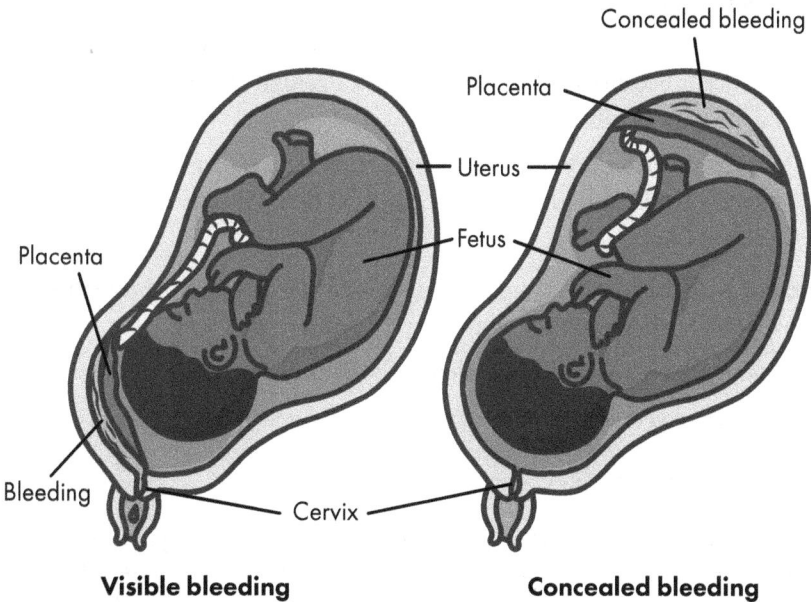

Figure 9.3. Abruptio Placentae

- **Placenta previa** occurs when the placenta partially or completely covers the cervix.
    - Placenta previa is usually asymptomatic and is found on routine prenatal ultrasounds.
    - The presence of previa makes the placenta susceptible to rupture or hemorrhage and necessitates a cesarean delivery.
- In **placenta accreta**, the placenta attaches abnormally deeply in the uterine lining and cannot detach following delivery. Placenta accreta can lead to hemorrhage and requires a hysterectomy.
- **Postpartum hemorrhage** is bleeding that occurs any time after delivery up to 12 weeks postpartum and exceeds 1000 ml or that causes symptoms of hypovolemia.
    - Primary hemorrhage occurs during the first 24 hours after delivery, usually as the result of trauma, retained tissue in the uterus, or failure of the uterus to contract.
    - Secondary hemorrhage occurs between 24 hours and 12 weeks postpartum, usually as the result of dilated arteries in the uterus, retained tissue, or infection.
- Postpartum patients are frequently discharged soon after delivery and may develop **postpartum infections** at home that require further treatment. Possible

sites of infection include the endometrium (endometritis), surgical incisions, breasts (mastitis), and urinary tract.

- **Spontaneous abortion** (miscarriage) is the loss of a pregnancy before the twentieth week of gestation. (Death of the fetus after the twentieth week is commonly referred to as a stillbirth.)
    - Spontaneous abortions are a common complication of early pregnancy. They can occur because of chromosomal or congenital abnormalities, material infection or disorders, or trauma.
    - **Septic abortion** occurs when the abortion is accompanied by uterine infection; it is a life-threatening condition that requires immediate medical intervention.
- Patients with pregnancy complications should always be transported to the appropriate facility and may require an ALS intercept.
    - Manage bleeding and hypovolemic shock as needed.
    - Provide oxygenation and airway management as needed.

PRACTICE QUESTION

3. A 24-year-old patient is 28 weeks pregnant and is complaining of severe headache. During assessment, the EMT finds that her blood pressure is 170/95 mm Hg, and she has pitting edema on her ankles. What condition should the EMT suspect?

Care of the Neonate

- Dry and stimulate the infant, and then wrap them in a blanket to keep them warm.
- Assess the neonate.
    - Evaluate the airway, and suction mouth and then nose as needed.
    - If the neonate's HR is less than 100 bpm, provide assisted ventilation via BVM with room air.

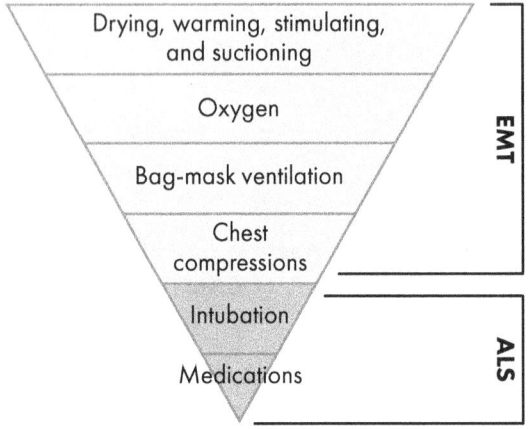

Figure 9.4. Inverted Pyramid of Neonatal Care

- ○ Use BVM with 100% oxygen if HR and respirations do not respond.
- ○ Start CPR if the neonate is not breathing or has an HR less than 60 bpm.
- Evaluate the neonate's **Apgar score** at 1 minute and 5 minutes; neonates should score between 8 and 10 by the 5-minute evaluation.

Table 9.1. Apgar Scores

Criteria	Score
Appearance	0: blue 1: extremities blue, trunk pink 2: pink all over
Pulse	0: 0 1: < 100 bmp 2: > 100 bmp
Grimace	0: no reaction 1: facial grimace 2: sneeze, cough, or cry
Activity	0: no movement 1: slight activity 2: moving around
Respirations	0: none, slow 1: irregular, weak cry 2: good breathing, strong cry

PRACTICE QUESTION

4. The EMT is evaluating a neonate at 1 minute after birth. The neonate is crying loudly, with a pulse of 160, and he is moving around well. His trunk is pink, but his extremities are blue. What is the Apgar score for this neonate?

OBSTETRICAL EMERGENCIES

ANSWER KEY

1. The EMT should expect the patient's heart rate and respiratory rate to be increased. Some patients may also show a slight increase in BP resulting from increased cardiac output.

2. If the patient states that she believes the baby's birth is imminent, the EMT should call ALS, stay on the scene, and prepare for delivery.

3. The patient has symptoms of preeclampsia.

4. The Apgar score is 9: 1 for the appearance, 2 for the pulse, 2 for the grimace, 2 for the activity, and 2 for the respiratory effort.

TEN: PHARMACOLOGY AND TOXICOLOGY

Pharmacology
MECHANISM OF ACTION

- **Pharmacology** is the science of drugs and their effects on the human body. **Pharmacodynamics** is the branch of pharmacology that involves how a drug affects the body.

- A drug's **mechanism of action** describes the biochemical pathways affected by the drug. The majority of drugs act on the system in two ways:
    - mimicking or suppressing normal physiological processes in the body
    - inhibiting the growth of certain microbial or parasitic organisms

- Drugs cannot change the fundamental physiological processes that occur in the body—they can only change the rate at which they occur. Drug action occurs when the drug binds to receptors on a protein molecule in the body to activate or block a physiological process.
    - An **agonist** binds to receptors and stimulates activity. For example, nitroglycerin is an agonist that results in the activation of enzymes that dilate blood vessels. Endogenous agonists (e.g., serotonin, epinephrine) are the molecules produced by the body that naturally bind to receptor sites.
    - An **antagonist** binds to a receptor to block activity. For example, ACE inhibitors block the angiotensin-converting enzyme (ACE), which normally causes blood vessels to constrict. The result is dilation in the blood vessels.
    - Some drugs are **partial agonists**, meaning they only partially activate receptors.

- The **brand name** of a drug is the name it is given by the pharmaceutical company that funded its research and development. This company holds the drug's patent for up to twenty years after its initial development, but when the patent expires, other pharmaceutical companies can produce the drug.

HELPFUL HINT

Anticholinergic drugs block activity at acetylcholine receptors in the parasympathetic nervous system. They relax smooth muscles and are used to treat conditions like asthma, overactive bladder, and tremors. Some antipsychotics and SSRIs are also anticholinergic drugs.

- A **generic drug** is the therapeutic equivalent of the brand-name drug.
  - It must have the same active ingredient, strength, and dosage form as the brand-name drug, but the inactive ingredients do not need to be the same.
  - The names of generic drugs are often shortened versions of a drug's **chemical name**, which describes its molecular structure.

QUICK REVIEW QUESTION

1. Naloxone is an opioid antagonist. How does it reverse the effects of opioid overdose?

Common Medications

Drugs are grouped into **classes** based on their chemical structures and the conditions they treat. The major drug classes, their general purpose, and examples of each are given in the table below.

Table 10.1. The Fifty Most Commonly Prescribed Medications in the United States

Generic Name (Brand Name)	Drug Class (Indication)	Adverse Effects and Contraindications
atorvastatin (Lipitor) simvastatin (FloLipid, Zocor) rosuvastatin (Crestor) pravastatin (Pravachol)	HMG-CoA reductase inhibitors (high cholesterol)	**ADR**: muscle/joint pain **Pregnancy**: Category X
levothyroxine (Synthroid)	synthetic hormone (hypothyroidism)	**BBW**: weight reduction **ADR**: dysrhythmias, dyspnea, headache, nervousness, irritability, weight loss
lisinopril (Prinivil, Zestril)	ACE inhibitor (hypertension)	**BBW**: fetal toxicity **ADR**: cough, hypotension, dizziness **Interactions**: other drugs that lower BP
metformin (Fortamet, Glucophage) glipizide (Glucotrol)	antidiabetic (type 2 diabetes)	**ADR**: hypoglycemia, diarrhea, nausea, headache
amlodipine (Amvaz, Norvasc)	calcium channel blocker (hypertension, dysrhythmias)	**ADR**: headache, edema, tiredness, dizziness **Interactions**: other drugs that lower BP

Generic Name (Brand Name)	Drug Class (Indication)	Adverse Effects and Contraindications
metoprolol (Toprol XL, Lopressor) carvedilol (Coreg) atenolol (Tenormin)	beta blocker (hypertension)	**ADR**: dizziness, fatigue, weight gain **Interactions**: other drugs that lower BP
albuterol (Ventolin HFA, Proventil HFA, Combivent Respimat, DuoNeb, ProAir HFA)	bronchodilator (asthma, COPD)	**ADR**: headache, tachycardia, dizziness, sore throat, nasal congestion **Interactions**: beta blockers, digoxin, MAOI, tricyclic antidepressants
omeprazole (Prilosec) pantoprazole (Protonix)	proton pump inhibitor (acid reflux)	**ADR**: headache, abdominal pain, nausea, diarrhea, vomiting **Interactions**: digoxin, clopidogrel, benzodiazepines, warfarin
losartan (Cozaar)	angiotensin II receptor blocker (hypertension)	**BBW**: fetal toxicity **ADR**: dizziness, headache, fatigue **Interactions**: potassium supplements, other drugs that lower BP
gabapentin (Gralise, Neurontin)	anticonvulsant (seizures, neuropathy)	**ADR**: drowsiness, dizziness, edema, angioedema (pregabalin), suicidal thoughts, emotional changes **Interactions**: alcohol, other CNS depressants
acetaminophen and hydrocodone (Norco, Vicodin, Lortab) tramadol (Ultram) oxycodone (OxyContin)	opioid (pain)	**ADR**: constipation, light-headedness, dizziness, nausea and vomiting **Interactions**: other CNS depressants
hydrochlorothiazide (Microzide) furosemide (Lasix)	diuretic (hypertension, edema)	**ADR**: hypotension, weakness, dizziness, blurred vision **Interactions**: alcohol, other antihypertensive drugs, NSAIDs

continued

Table 10.1. The Fifty Most Commonly Prescribed Medications in the United States (continued)

Generic Name (Brand Name)	Drug Class (Indication)	Adverse Effects and Contraindications
sertraline (Zoloft) escitalopram (Lexapro) fluoxetine (Prozac) trazodone (Desyrel) citalopram (Celexa)	selective serotonin reuptake inhibitor [SSRI] (mood disorders)	**BBW**: increased risk of suicidal thoughts/behaviors **ADR**: insomnia, headache, agitation, dizziness, drowsiness, dry mouth, nausea, vomiting
bupropion (Wellbutrin, Zyban)	dopamine/norepinephrine-reuptake inhibitor (mood disorders, smoking cessation)	
duloxetine (Cymbalta) venlafaxine (Effexor)	serotonin-norepinephrine reuptake inhibitor (mood disorders)	
montelukast (Singulair)	bronchodilator (asthma)	**BBW**: neuropsychiatric symptoms **ADR**: respiratory infection, fever, headache, sore throat, cough
fluticasone (Flonase, Flovent)	nasal/oral corticosteroid (asthma, allergies)	**ADR**: headache, nasal/throat irritation, nosebleed, cough, worsening of infections
amoxicillin (Augmentin)	antibiotic [penicillin]	**ADR**: diarrhea, nausea
acetaminophen (Tylenol)	analgesic, antipyretic (pain, fever)	**BBW**: hepatotoxicity **ADR**: nausea and vomiting
prednisone (Sterapred)	oral corticosteroid (inflammatory or auto-immune conditions)	**ADR**: fluid retention, hyper/hypoglycemia, hypertension, changes in behavior/mood, weight gain, worsening of infections
amphetamine and dextroamphetamine (Adderall) methylphenidate (Ritalin)	ADHD treatment	**ADR**: insomnia, headache, tachycardia, mood changes, decreased appetite, vomiting, dry mouth

Generic Name (Brand Name)	Drug Class (Indication)	Adverse Effects and Contraindications
insulin glargine (Lantus)	insulin (diabetes)	**ADR**: hypoglycemia, injection site reactions
ibuprofen (Advil, Motrin) meloxicam (Mobic)	NSAID (pain, fever)	**BBW**: cardiovascular thrombotic events, GI bleeding **ADR**: abdominal pain, diarrhea, upset stomach **Pregnancy**: Category D (> 30 weeks)
tamsulosin (Flomax)	alpha-1 blocker (BPH)	**ADR**: orthostatic hypotension, sexual disorder, dizziness, headache
alprazolam (Xanax) clonazepam (Klonopin)	benzodiazepine (anxiety)	**ADR**: drowsiness, sedation, fatigue, memory impairment **Interactions**: other CNS depressants
potassium	supplement	**ADR**: nausea, vomiting, flatulence, abdominal pain/discomfort, diarrhea
clopidogrel (Plavix) aspirin	anticoagulant	**ADR**: bleeding **Interactions**: omeprazole/esomeprazole (clopidogrel), NSAIDs
ranitidine (Zantac)	histamine H2 antagonist (acid reflux)	**ADR**: headache, constipation, diarrhea, nausea, vomiting **Interactions**: warfarin
cyclobenzaprine (Flexeril)	muscle relaxant	**ADR**: drowsiness, dizziness, dry mouth, nausea and vomiting **Interactions**: other CNS depressants
azithromycin (Zithromax)	antibiotic [macrolide]	**ADR**: diarrhea, nausea
allopurinol (Lopurin, Zyloprim, Aloprim)	antigout	**ADR**: rash, nausea, vomiting, drowsiness
BBW: black box warning **ADR**: adverse drug reactions		

HELPFUL HINT

Aspirin is an NSAID that also slows platelet aggregation, which prevents clotting. It is often prescribed to prevent thrombus formation (e.g., MI, stroke), but it can also be taken for pain, fever, or inflammation.

QUICK REVIEW QUESTION

2. What adverse drug reaction should EMTs be aware of when caring for a patient taking clopidogrel (Plavix)?

Adverse Drug Reactions

- **Intended effects** are the desired or expected responses to a drug.
- **Adverse drug reactions** are unwanted responses to a drug. Adverse drug reactions can range from mild (e.g., drowsiness) to lethal (e.g., liver failure).
- Adverse drug reactions are classified into six types, which are described in the table below.

HELPFUL HINT
The term side effects is sometimes used to refer to mild adverse drug reactions, like fatigue or weight gain.

Table 10.2. Adverse Drug Reactions

Type	Description	Example
A augmented	predictable reactions arising from the pharmacological effects of the drug; dependent on dose	diarrhea due to antibiotics; hypoglycemia due to insulin
B bizarre	unpredictable reactions; independent of dose	hypersensitivity (anaphylaxis) due to penicillin
C chronic	reactions caused by the cumulative dose (the dose taken over a long period of time)	osteoporosis with oral steroids
D delayed	reactions that occur after the drug is no longer being taken	teratogenic effects with anticonvulsants
E end of use	reactions caused by withdrawal from a drug	withdrawal syndrome with benzodiazepines
F failure	unexpected failure of the drug to work; often caused by dose or drug interactions	resistance to antimicrobials

QUICK REVIEW QUESTION

3. A patient who has recently started taking lisinopril to treat hypertension is reporting dizziness and weakness. How would this adverse drug reaction be categorized?

Drug Interactions

- Medications may interact with other medications or health conditions. These **drug interactions** can increase or decrease the action of the drug, which changes the therapeutic effects of the medication.

- There are three main types of drug interactions: drug-drug, drug-disease, and drug-nutrient.
- In a **drug-drug interaction**, a person takes multiple medications.
  - The drugs may be duplicates, resulting in toxicity or increased effect.
  - Combining drugs with opposite effects may reduce the effectiveness of one or both medications.
- **Drug-disease interaction** occurs when a medication taken for one disease causes or exacerbates a different disease. For example, calcium channel blockers (to treat hypertension) must be used cautiously in patients with chronic kidney disease because they can impair kidney function.
- **Drug-nutrient interactions** occur when drugs interact with other consumable substances, including foods, alcohol, and nutritional supplements. For example, alcohol and grapefruit juice both change the absorption and effectiveness of antibiotics.

> **HELPFUL HINT**
> Drug-drug interactions are common when patients take medications that contain multiple drugs. For example, a patient taking Norco and OTC Nyquil might not realize that both medications contain acetaminophen.

> **HELPFUL HINT**
> **Monoamine oxidase inhibitors (MAOIs)** are a class of antidepressants that are effective in treating mood disorders, but they are rarely used due to their potential for drug-drug interactions. Most drugs that affect serotonin, norepinephrine, or dopamine levels are contraindicated for patients taking MAOIs.

QUICK REVIEW QUESTION

4. What concern should an EMT have when a patient reports taking monoamine oxidase inhibitors (MAOIs) for depression?

Drug Administration

- **Indications** are the signs and symptoms that make it appropriate for a patient to receive a medication. For example, nitroglycerin is indicated for patients with chest pain or suspected MI.
- **Contraindications** are specific signs, symptoms, or situations that make it unsafe to administer a medication. Contraindications for nitroglycerin administration include hypotension and recent use of erectile dysfunction medications.
- **Dose** is the amount of medication given in a single administration. Manufacturers carefully gauge medication dosages to balance the desired therapeutic effect against possible adverse reactions.
- Drugs are available in many different forms.
  - **Pill** is a general term for a solid medication that is ingested.
  - Specific types of pills include **tablets** (compressed powders) and **capsules** (medication enclosed in a dissolvable container).
  - Liquid medications may be ingested (**enteral**) or injected (**parenteral**).
  - Drugs may also be given as a gas or solid powder to be inhaled.
- **Route** is how the medication enters the body. The following routes are used to administer medications:
  - **buccal** (BUC): in the cheek
  - **inhalational** (INH): through the mouth

- intramuscular (IM): into the muscle
- intranasal (NAS): through the nose
- intravenous (IV): into the vein
- oral (PO): by mouth
- rectal (PR): into the rectum
- subcutaneous (subcut): under the skin
- sublingual (SL): under the tongue
- transdermal (TOP): through the skin
- vaginal (PV): into the vagina

HELPFUL HINT

EMTs are only able to administer a limited list of specific drugs (per local protocols). Usually these include:
- nitroglycerin and aspirin for cardiac chest pain
- prescribed inhaled bronchodilators (e.g., albuterol) for asthma
- epinephrine (EpiPen) for anaphylaxis
- oral glucose for hypoglycemia

- EMTs should follow the six rights of medication administration to prevent medication errors.
  - Right Patient—Is this the appropriate patient for the medication? Is this the appropriate situation to use the medication?
  - Right Medication—Is this physically the correct medication?
  - Right Dose—Is the amount of medication appropriate for this patient?
  - Right Route—Is the way the medication is entering the body correct and appropriate?
  - Right Time—Is this the right time in the sequence of the care of this patient to give the medication?
  - Right Documentation—Have the indications for giving the medication been documented? Have the vital signs before and after administration been documented? Has the response to the medication been documented?

QUICK REVIEW QUESTION

5. A patient has a prescription for nitroglycerin 0.4 mg SL. How should the patient take this medication?

Drug Overdose

Assessment and Care for Patients with Suspected Poisoning

- During scene size-up, determine scene safety and look for clues that suggest what substance may have led to the emergency.
  - The patient may have left drugs, medication bottles, or drug paraphernalia (e.g., syringes) nearby.
  - Look for sources of inhaled pollutants, and unusual odors, such as those indoor fires, natural gas valves, or open chemical containers (e.g., chlorine).
  - Industrial settings should have material safety data sheets for on-site chemicals and may also have specific emergency care equipment (e.g., eye wash station, antidotes).

- For suspected hazardous substances, request a HazMat team.
  - Do not treat the patient until they have been decontaminated. The HazMat team will move and decontaminate the patient.
  - A HazMat team should always enter the scene first when toxic gas (e.g., carbon monoxide) is suspected.
- For ingested poisons or medications, contact medical control and poison control (if permitted by local protocol). They can be contacted enroute to expedite care at the scene.
- Perform a primary assessment and manage ABCs. Provide immediate transport to patients with life-threatening issues.
- Take a history focusing on the suspected poison.
  - What poison or drug was involved?
  - When did the exposure occur?
  - How much of the poison or drug was the patient exposed to?
  - What route did the poison take to enter the body (ingestion, inhalation, absorption, or injection)?
  - How long was the patient exposed to the poison or drug?
  - What treatments has the patient or family attempted?
  - What are the patients' signs and symptoms?
- Get a complete set of vitals, including a glucose reading.
- Transport the patient to the hospital.

HELPFUL HINT
Poison control is a resource; they do not have the authority to give online medical direction. Contact your medical control prior to beginning any treatments contrary to your local protocols.

QUICK REVIEW QUESTION

6. The EMT sees three patients lying outside of a industrial facility with a green mist coming from a tank close to the patients. The patients have green residue covering their clothes and skin. What should the EMT do first?

Toxidromes

- **Drug overdose** occurs when a patient has taken a toxic amount of a drug.
- The most common drugs involved in overdoses requiring medical care are opioids (both legal and illegal), psychostimulants (e.g., cocaine, methamphetamine), and benzodiazepines.
- **Toxidromes** are groups of signs and symptoms present in patients who have large amounts of toxins or poisons in the body. General signs and symptoms are given below, but these may vary based on the specific drug (or combination of drugs) ingested.

HELPFUL HINT
In 2019, 70% of drug overdose deaths involved an opioid.

Table 10.3. Signs and Symptoms of Toxidromes

Toxidrome	HR	BP	RR	Temp	Bowel Sounds	Pupils	Skin	Mental Status
Anticholinergic antihistamines, antipsychotics, tricyclic antidepressants (TCA), scopolamine, atropine, some medications used for COPD and asthma	↑	↑	—	↑	↓	↑	dry	agitated and delirious
Cholinergic anticholinesterase, insecticides and pesticides, nerve agents (e.g., sarin)	—	—	—	—	↑	↓	moist	—
Hallucinogenic LSD, psilocybin ("magic mushrooms"), mescaline, DMT, *salvia divinorum*, dextromethorphan (DXM), PCP	↑	↑	↑	—	↑	↑	—	disoriented
Sympathomimetic cocaine, amphetamines, methamphetamines, hallucinogenic amphetamines (MDMA, MDA), khat and related substances (methcathinone, "bath salts"), cold medications, diet supplements containing ephedrine	↑	↑	↑	↑	↑	↑	moist	agitated and delirious
Sedative-hypnotic benzodiazepines, barbiturates, antipsychotics, zolpidem (Ambien), clonidine, GHB	↓	↓	↓	↓	↓	—	dry	lethargic and confused

HELPFUL HINT

Presentation of anticholinergic overdose:
hot as a hare: hyperthermia
red as a beet: flushing
blind as a bat: blurred vision
dry as a bone: dry skin
mad as a hatter: agitation or delirium
full as a flask: urinary retention

HELPFUL HINT

Presentation of cholinergic overdose:
DUMBELS
Diarrhea
Urination
Miosis
Bronchorrhea, Bradycardia, Bronchoconstriction
Emesis
Lacrimation
Salivation

QUICK REVIEW QUESTION

7. What symptoms should the EMT expect to see in a patient who has overdosed on amphetamines?

OPIOID OVERDOSE

Pathophysiology

Opioids depress the CNS and lower the perception of pain by stimulating dopamine release. Opioid overdose depresses respiration and can be fatal.

What to Look For

- opioid overdose triad: pinpoint pupils, respiratory depression, decreased LOC
- hypotension
- wheezing or dyspnea
- nausea or vomiting
- seizure

HELPFUL HINT
Common opioids include codeine, fentanyl, heroin, hydrocodone, morphine, and oxycodone.

Care and Transport

- Priority is airway management and supplemental oxygen.
- Narcan (**naloxone**) is an opioid antagonist administered via IV, IM, or intranasally.
    - Naloxone is indicated for patients with agonal breathing or apnea to restore respiratory status.
    - Naloxone is not intended to restore consciousness or cardiac activity, although patients may regain consciousness after administration.
    - Place a nasopharyngeal airway and adequately ventilate patient with BVM before and after administration.
    - Initial IM dose is 0.4 mg; initial intranasal dose is 2 mg.
    - Closely monitor patients who respond to naloxone. The effects of naloxone may wear off while opioids remain in the patient's system, resulting in the reappearance of overdose symptoms.
    - A side effect of Narcan is vomiting. An oropharyngeal airway may also induce vomiting when the patient's gag reflex returns.
- If the patient is pulseless, follow BLS protocols for patients in cardiac arrest.

HELPFUL HINT
Do not delay BLS measures to administer naloxone.

QUICK REVIEW QUESTION

8. A patient has overdosed on fentanyl. He has pinpoint pupils, has a respiratory rate of 20, and is alert to painful stimuli. What should the EMT do?

Other Drug Overdoses

- **Alcohol** is a central nervous system (CNS) depressant.
  - Overconsumption of alcohol can lead to respiratory depression and excessive vomiting.
  - Alcohol interacts with many prescription and OTC medications, particularly other drugs that also suppress the CNS (e.g., benzodiazepines, antihistamines).
  - Alcohol use can mask other health conditions, such as TBI and hypoglycemia. Patients who appear intoxicated should be thoroughly evaluated for other conditions.
  - Patients who are intoxicated by alcohol are not considered competent and cannot refuse care.
- **Benzodiazepines** are CNS depressants. Overdose depresses respiratory and cardiac activity. The care priority is to provide oxygen and ventilations as needed and transport promptly.
- During **acetaminophen (Tylenol)** overdose, toxic metabolites accumulate in the liver causing hepatotoxicity.
  - Acetaminophen toxicity occurs at single doses higher than 250 mg/kg. (A single OTC Tylenol tablet is 500 mg).
  - Gastritis symptoms usually appear within hours; symptoms of hepatotoxicity do not appear until 24 – 72 hours after ingestion.
  - The antidote for acetaminophen overdose (N-acetylcysteine [Mucomyst]) is most effective when delivered within 8 hours, so patients with suspected acetaminophen overdose should always be transported promptly.
- **Inhalant abuse** (huffing) is the process of inhaling substances to experience a short high.
  - Many common household products release gases that can be inhaled, including freon, gasoline, paint, glue, and cleaning products.
  - Propellants in aerosols, such as **nitrous oxide**, can also be inhaled.
  - Inhalant abuse is most common in children and young adults because inhalants are cheap and easily accessible.
  - Overuse of inhalants can lead to respiratory distress, altered LOC, and cardiac dysrhythmias. Inhaled aerosols can also cause burns in or around the mouth.
- An overdose of cardiac medications, including beta blockers, calcium channel blockers, and digitalis, can cause hemodynamic instability and cardiac dysrhythmias.
  - These overdoses are most common with elderly patients who have mistakenly taken too much of a prescribed medication. Cardiac medications are also taken during suicide attempts by young people with access to these drugs in their households.

- Care includes management of ABCs and prompt transport. ALS intercept may be required for patients with severe symptoms.

QUICK REVIEW QUESTION

9. EMTs respond to a call for a 19-year-old female who took a large dose of acetaminophen 6 hours previously. The patient reports abdominal pain and vomiting earlier in the day but says she feels fine now. Why should the EMTs still transport her promptly?

Substance Withdrawal

- Chronic **alcohol abuse** alters the sensitivity of CNS receptors, and cessation of drinking causes hyperactivity in the CNS.
  - Alcohol withdrawal can be fatal and requires hospitalization for treatment.
  - Symptoms develop 6 to 24 hours after last consuming alcohol.
  - Symptoms of alcohol withdrawal: tachycardia, hypertension, agitation and restlessness, nausea and vomiting, sweating, seizures
  - **Delirium tremens (DTs)** is a type of severe alcohol withdrawal characterized by hallucinations and hyperthermia. Symptoms occur 2 to 4 days after stopping alcohol intake.
- Chronic use of **opioids** increases excitability of CNS neurons, and withdrawal leads to hypersensitivity of the CNS.
  - Symptoms of opioid withdrawal: drug craving, tachycardia, tachypnea, hypertension, GI upset, anxiety, yawning, rhinorrhea and lacrimation, pupil dilation, piloerection, sweating, muscle pain and twitching
  - The onset, length, and severity of symptoms will depend on the type of drug used. Withdrawal symptoms make take several weeks to completely resolve.
  - Opioid withdrawal is rarely fatal, but death can occur, usually as a result of hemodynamic instability or electrolyte imbalances.
- Care and transport for patients in alcohol and opioid withdrawal:
  - Manage patient ABCs.
  - Patients with dyspnea may require oxygen.
  - Be prepared to suction the airway if vomiting occurs.
  - Manage related medical conditions, including seizures, hallucinations, and hypovolemic shock (secondary to vomiting).

QUICK REVIEW QUESTION

10. A patient going through alcohol withdrawal is agitated and experiencing hallucinations. What condition does the patient have and how should the EMT care for him?

Carbon Monoxide and Cyanide Poisoning

Pathophysiology

Carbon monoxide (CO) displaces oxygen from hemoglobin, which prevents the transport and utilization of oxygen throughout the body. Mild CO poisoning can be resolved with oxygen; severe CO poisoning can lead to myocardial ischemia, dysrhythmias, pulmonary edema, and coma. Sources of CO include smoke from fires, malfunctioning heaters and generators, and motor vehicle exhaust.

<Helpful Hint: CO poisoning and cyanide poisoning often occur together.>

Cyanide interferes with the production of ATP in mitochondria. Cyanide poisoning is rare, but it is usually fatal without medical intervention. Sources of cyanide include smoke from fires, medications (e.g., sodium nitroprusside), and pits/seeds from the family *Rosaceae* (which includes bitter almonds, apricots, peaches, and apples).

HELPFUL HINT
Pulse oximeters should be used cautiously on patients with suspected carbon monoxide poisoning. They cannot differentiate between oxygen and carbon monoxide on hemoglobin, so they will show a high SpO_2 even if the patient's oxygen levels are actually low.

What to Look For

Table 10.4. Signs and Symptoms of CO and Cyanide Poisoning

Carbon Monoxide Poisoning	Cyanide Poisoning
headache	bitter almond smell on breath
altered LOC or confusion	anxiety, agitation, or confusion
dizziness	headache
visual disturbances	hematemesis
dyspnea on exertion	diarrhea
vomiting	flushed, red skin
muscle weakness and cramps	tachycardia and tachypnea
syncope	hypertension
	seizure

Care and Treatment

- Ensure scene safety before entering.
- Remove patient from the source of poisoning.
- For mild symptoms, provide high-flow oxygen through a non-rebreathing mask.
- For unconscious patients, insert airway adjunct and provide ventilations.
- Transport promptly.

QUICK REVIEW QUESTION

11. A patient's carbon monoxide detector went off, and the fire department was called to the scene. EMTs arrive to find the patient alert and sitting outside the home. They report a headache earlier in the day that has resolved. How should the EMTs treat the patient?

ANSWER KEY

1. Naloxone binds to opioid receptors and prevents opioid agonists (such as morphine and oxycodone) from binding to those sites.
2. Excessive bleeding may occur.
3. Augmented (A): Dizziness and weakness are predictable reactions arising from the pharmacological effects of the lisinopril, which lowers blood pressure.
4. MAOIs have a high risk for potential drug-drug interactions.
5. SL is the abbreviation for sublingual, meaning "under the tongue."
6. The EMT should request a HazMat team and move to a safe area.
7. Symptoms of amphetamine overdose include increased blood pressure and respiratory rate; hypertension; dilated pupils; moist, hot skin; agitation; and delirium.
8. The EMT should monitor the patient. (Naloxone should not be used unless there is respiratory depression.)
9. Acetaminophen is hepatotoxic, but symptoms of liver failure will not appear for 24 to 72 hours; the patient should be transported promptly so she can receive an antidote.
10. The patient is showing signs of delirium tremens (DTs). The patient should be transported immediately to the hospital because DTs can be life-threatening.
11. The CO poisoning is not severe: the EMTs should provide oxygen to the patient and encourage the patient to go to the hospital for further evaluation.

ELEVEN: SPECIAL POPULATIONS

Geriatric Patients

- **Geriatric** patients are those 65 years of age or older.
- Currently more than 40 million Americans are 65 or older, and 5.5 million people are 85 or older.
- The geriatric population is more than twice as likely to use EMS than other age groups and make up a significant percentage of call volume.
  - Geriatric patients are more likely to have chronic diseases that require complex care.
  - They may require emergency care due to poor management of chronic conditions or acute exacerbations of chronic conditions.
  - Due to underlying physiology, geriatric patients may experience more severe symptoms of common acute illnesses.
- Every physical system is affected by the aging process, though the degree of diminishment depends on the individual.

Table 11.1. Physiological Effects of Aging

System	Physiological Changes	Outcome of Physiological Changes
Cardiovascular	degeneration of valves, muscle, and conduction system; systemic thickening and narrowing of arteries; decreased cardiac output and stroke volume	high risk for MI, CVA, aneurysm, PAD, and DVT; cardiac dysrhythmias; orthostatic hypotension; decreased cerebral perfusion; lowered tolerance for physical activity
Respiratory	diminished lung volume, elasticity, and cilia activity; decreased cough and gag reflex	increased risk of pneumonia; lowered ability to increase oxygen intake as needed; increased choking and aspiration risk

Table 11.1. Physiological Effects of Aging (continued)

System	Physiological Changes	Outcome of Physiological Changes
Gastrointestinal	decreased GI motility; decreased production of stomach acid; decreased sense of taste; decreased ability to chew and swallow; degrading of GI lining and sphincters	constipation; bowel obstruction; malnutrition; dehydration; incontinence; high risk of GI bleeding, GERD, and GI cancers
Liver and kidneys	decreased ability to process and clear medications; decrease in clotting factor production	significantly higher risk of medication toxicity and negative interactions; higher risk of edema and bleeding disorders
Endocrine	gradual loss of thyroid and pancreatic function	lowered energy and metabolism; poor body temperature regulation; higher risk for type 2 diabetes
Musculoskeletal	decreases in mass and strength	general weakness; decreased mobility and ability to care for self; more prone to falling, often unable to pick themselves up; higher probability of fractures, even from minimal impact; development of arthritis and spinal curvatures
Nervous	decrease in number of neurons	decreased pain sensation; increased reaction time; decreased visual acuity and hearing; dementia and depression; sleep disorders
Integumentary	loss of subcutaneous fat	thin and frail skin; susceptible to burns, bruising, and skin tears; chilled very easily

- Treat geriatric patients with respect and dignity.
    - Do not assume that the patient cannot hear or understand you.
    - Speak slowly, clearly, and with adequate volume for the patient to understand.

- Give patients enough time to respond to questions.
- Begin by speaking directly to the patient, not to caretakers or bystanders.
- Take care when determining LOC and alertness.
    - Geriatric patients are more likely to have dementia or delirium.
    - If the patient seems to have altered mental status, attempt to determine the baseline from a caretaker or family member. (Confusion may be normal for a dementia patient.)
    - Geriatric patients often have less need to track the days of the week as closely as other demographics. A broader question such as, "What year is it?" or "What season is it?" may be more appropriate.
- Considerations for taking a SAMPLE history from geriatric patients:
    - Geriatric patients often have their medical history and medication lists in writing. Confirm whether the information is up to date or has been adjusted.
    - Determining degree of compliance with dosing schedule is critical: symptoms may be related to missing or extra doses of medications.
    - Dehydration is a very common cause of illness in geriatrics, so get an estimated amount of daily water consumption.
    - Gather and examine legal documents such as a DNR or living will during the SAMPLE history.
- Considerations during the physical examination of geriatric patients:
    - Keep the patient as warm as possible during the examination, both for patient comfort and to get the most accurate readings from your instruments.
    - Handle the patient carefully to avoid injuring the patient and minimize the pain of existing injuries, such as arthritic joints or bruised extremities.
    - Inform the patient of what you are doing as you are doing it to minimize fear or panic.
    - Maintain a high level of suspicion of any injury, even if the mechanism of injury would be less concerning for a younger patient.
- Considerations for the transport of geriatric patients:
    - Pressure ulcers and other injuries can develop quickly in geriatric patients, so take care when positioning the patient.
    - When a geriatric patient is immobilized, pad the void spaces and provide cushioning.
    - Drive as gently as possible to avoid further injury to the patient and to reduce panic.
- Use the acronym GEMS to remember special considerations for geriatric patients.
    - **Geriatric** patients present atypically.
    - Assess the **Environment** to look for signs of neglect or inadequate medical care.

HELPFUL HINT
UTIs are a common cause of delirium in geriatrics.

DID YOU KNOW?
Geriatric patients tend to have higher blood pressure and are more prone to postural blood pressure changes.

SPECIAL POPULATIONS

- Perform a thorough **Medical** assessment regardless of the chief complaint.
- Perform a **Social** assessment to determine if the patient's needs related to activities of daily living (ADLs) are being met.

- Be aware of the signs of **elder abuse**. These should be documented and handled per local protocols.
    - frequent visits to ED or urgent care
    - apathy or aggression from the caregiver
    - vague or inconsistent explanations for injuries or poor medical management
    - psychosocial issues such as depression, sleep disorders, or eating disorders

PRACTICE QUESTION

1. An EMT is dispatched to an assisted living facility for a 74-year-old female who had a ground-level fall (GLF) after standing up to walk to the restroom. She was assisted back into her bed by the staff members and is now complaining of left hip pain. Why is a full medical and trauma assessment necessary for this patient?

Pediatric Patients

- **Pediatrics** refers to the care of young children and adolescents.
- The parent must provide consent for any interventions performed on pediatric patients, with very few exceptions.
    - Necessary emergency care can be given if the legally responsible parent cannot be reached.
    - **Emancipated minors**, who are not legally bound to a caregiver, may make their own medical decisions.
    - Teachers or other professional caregivers may act *in loco parentis* when parents are not available.
- Significant variation can be seen in the growth and development of children, but they can be put into six general age groups.
    - **Newborns** (neonates) are in their first month of life. They may sleep up to 18 hours a day and must eat every 2 to 3 hours. They communicate through crying; a newborn that cries inconsolably should be transported immediately for further assessment.
    - **Infants** are between 1 month and 1 year old. During this stage, children grow rapidly. They develop social skills, including smiling, laughing, and making eye contact. Physically, they will learn to lift their heads, use their hands, sit up, and crawl. Infants older than 6 months may show anxiety when separated from their caregivers.
    - **Toddlers** are between 1 and 3 years old. Most children will learn to walk around the age of 1 and will begin exploring their environment. Common calls for toddlers include environmental injuries such as falls, poisonings, and airway obstruction. Children will begin to talk around age 2 and may

be able to communicate basic ideas to their caregiver or the EMT. However, they will not have developed the language to communicate precisely.

- ○ **Preschool** children are between 3 and 5 years old. They will be able to perform complex physical tasks such as running, jumping, and kicking. Preschool children will also have a large vocabulary and can communicate effectively. However, they will not understand medical terms and have vivid imaginations, so information should still be gathered from caregivers or bystanders when possible.
- ○ **School-aged** children are between 6 and 12 years old. They will be able to communicate effectively with the EMT and will have an understanding of basic medical terms and procedures. Children in this age group will have a basic understanding of concepts such as privacy, pain, and death. Explain procedures to them in plain language and respect their autonomy.
- ○ **Adolescents** are between 13 and 18 years old. They will be able to think abstractly and understand complex concepts. Adolescents should be actively involved in their care. Puberty begins in adolescence, and many adolescents will be involved in behaviors that put them at risk of injury.

- The younger the patient, the more dissimilar the normal vital signs will be compared to the average adult vital signs.
  - ○ For patients younger than 3 years old, **NIBP** (non-invasive blood pressure) is rarely taken. **Capillary refill time (CRT)** is the primary method of determining adequate perfusion.
  - ○ The following chart demonstrates the range of normal vital signs for pediatrics based on age grouping.

Table 11.2. Normal Pediatric Vital Signs (Ranges)

Age Range	Pulse Range	Respiratory Range	Systolic BP Range	Diastolic BP Average
Newborn	120 – 160	30 – 50	N/A	N/A
0 – 5 months	90 – 140	25 – 40	N/A	N/A
6 – 12 months	80 – 140	20 – 30	N/A	N/A
1 – 3 years	80 – 130	20 – 30	N/A	N/A
3 – 5 years	80 – 120	20 – 30	78 – 104	65
6 – 12 years	70 – 110	15 – 30	80 – 122	69
13 – 18 years	60 – 105	12 – 20	88 – 140	76

DID YOU KNOW?
Capillary refill time (CRT) is determined by pressing the nail bed, or the top of the hand or foot, until it turns white and then releasing. If circulation is adequate, normal color should return in less than 2 seconds.

- The anatomical differences between pediatrics and adults are naturally most profound in the earliest years of life. The EMT should be aware of how these differences may impact care, expressed in Table 11.3.
- How a pediatric patient is assessed will depend on the age of the child.
  - ○ For very young patients, the EMT will need to get a history and MOI/NOI from the caregivers or bystanders.
  - ○ School-aged children may be able to provide critical information to the EMT.

- Adolescents may be assessed much like adult patients. However, the EMT should be aware that adolescents may be less likely to share some information in the presence of caregivers or peers.
- Use visual cues, such as pointing or the Wong-Baker faces pain scale, for patients too young to effectively communicate verbally.

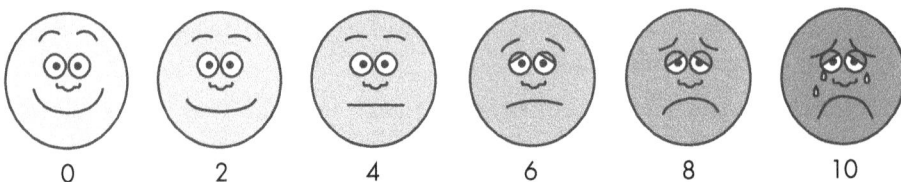

Figure 11.1. Wong-Baker Faces Pain Scale

Table 11.3. Important Anatomical Features of Pediatrics

Region	Description
Head	The head is disproportionally larger and heavier than the rest of their body until roughly age 4, causing children to often fall headfirst.
	Fontanelles, or soft spots, occur in infants due to the incomplete fusing of the skull plates until after birth. A bulging fontanelle may indicate increased intracranial pressure, and a sunken fontanelle may indicate dehydration.
Airway and upper body	The mouth and nose are smaller and the tongue is proportionally larger, causing a higher risk of airway obstruction.
	The trachea is narrower, softer, and more flexible, increasing the risk of obstruction due to inflammation or foreign bodies.
	Hyperextending the neck or allowing the head to fall forward can obstruct the airway in small children. Padding the shoulders of a pediatric patient helps maintain an inline neutral position.
	The thorax and chest wall are shorter and softer, forcing the patient to rely on the diaphragm for deeper breathing. This makes the use of accessory muscles very apparent.
Body surface area (BSA)	BSA is disproportionally larger than the body mass, making temperature regulation more difficult.
Blood	Children have a lower blood volume than adults. They will show signs of dehydration and hypovolemic shock after losing a smaller proportion of blood or fluids than adults.

- Use the **Pediatric Assessment Triangle (PAT)** to rapidly assess pediatric patients. The PAT can be done within the first 30 seconds of meeting the patient.
  - appearance: tone, interactiveness, consolability, look/gaze, speech/cry **(TICLS)**
  - work of breathing: airway noises, accessory muscle use, head bobbing, nasal flares

- circulation to skin: pallor, mottling, cyanosis
- Show care and consideration when interacting with pediatric patients and their families.
  - Children will be less likely to become anxious or scared if their caregivers are allowed to remain present and involved in their care.
  - Allow parents to hold young children until it is time for transport.
  - Unless it is going to interfere with patient care or the caregiver is a safety risk, have the caregiver ride in the back with the patient.
  - Always explain to the child and the parent what you are doing and why.
  - Use a calm, gentle voice, and attempt to communicate on their visual level.
  - Adolescents often wish to be treated as an adult and respond poorly to being patronized. However, they may revert to more child-like behaviors when injured or ill.

DID YOU KNOW?
Cardiac arrest in pediatrics is almost always due to respiratory arrest and hypoxia. Aggressive respiratory intervention is the key to a positive outcome.

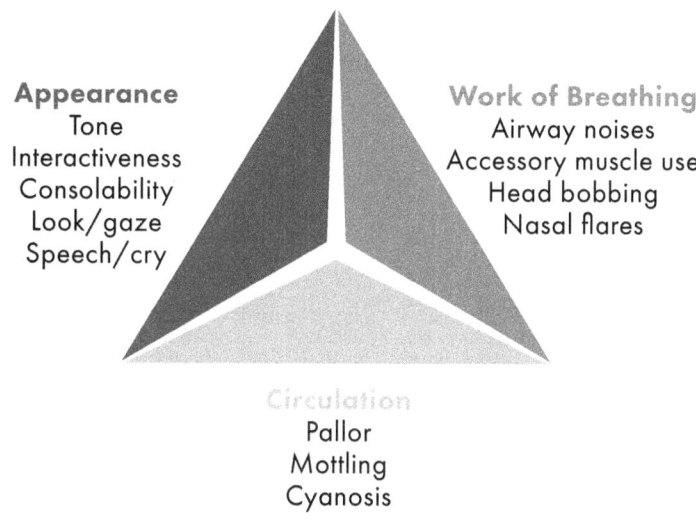

Figure 11.2. Pediatric Assessment Triangle (PAT)

- Below is a list of the most common injuries and medical conditions seen on pediatric calls.
  - trauma (MVC is most common)
  - foreign body airway obstruction
  - poisonings (usually from medications or household chemicals)
  - infections (e.g., pneumonia, croup)
  - anaphylaxis
  - dehydration

PRACTICE QUESTION

2. An EMT is dispatched to a single-family dwelling for a 6-month-old infant male who has been ill for two days. The patient is in his mother's arms in the living room, and the EMT can see and hear obvious signs of respiratory distress as she approaches them. What should be the EMT's priority?

SPECIAL POPULATIONS

ANSWER KEY

1. A full head-to-toe examination is imperative in geriatric patients, even on a simple GLF. The patient may have injured her upper extremities attempting to catch herself, hit her head, or injured her neck. The EMT should also perform a full medical assessment to look for underlying medical conditions that may have caused the fall.

2. The EMT's priority should be a rapid assessment and a decision to transport or upgrade to ALS. If an ALS intercept is called, the EMT may administer oxygen or ventilation while waiting and take a history. If the decision is made to transport, oxygen delivery and history should be done en route.

TWELVE: EMS OPERATIONS

EMT Scope of Practice

- EMTs are governed by protocols and legal guidelines created by the state, county, city, and local medical director.
- The National Highway Traffic Safety Administration (NHTSA) Office of EMS developed a **scope of practice** for EMTs that is followed nationwide.
    - The EMT provides basic acute care and transportation for critical and emergent patients.
    - The EMT provides only non-invasive care.
    - The EMT may assist patients with taking prescribed medications or provide patients with oral glucose, aspirin, or nitroglycerin (per local protocols). They do not provide any other pharmacological interventions.
    - The EMT must consult medical control when making decisions about patient disposition.
- The **standard of care** describes the type of care that a trained EMT should be expected to provide.
- EMTs can lose their certification/licensure or face legal consequences for working outside their scope of practice or not meeting the standard of care.
- The care provided by EMTs is guided by **medical control**, which is run by a **medical director**.
    - **Online medical control** (or direct medical control) is the direct communication between on-site EMTs and physicians via phone or radio. These physicians are usually on duty in emergency departments, but they may also be specialized personnel within larger EMS systems.
    - **Offline medical control** (or indirect medical control) includes guidelines and protocols written by the medical director who oversees EMS operations.
- **Protocols** are parameters written by medical control to guide EMTs. In some cases, the department that oversees EMS operations within a state writes the protocols.

HELPFUL HINT
Scope of practice describes what the EMT is allowed to do. Standard of care describes what the EMT should do.

HELPFUL HINT
State laws regulate what specific procedures EMTs can perform. The medical director can limit that scope, but they cannot expand it.

- Protocols provide detailed guidance for EMTs on the duties they perform and describe permissions given to them by medical control.
- Violation of standard protocols can lead to termination and possible legal liability.

PRACTICE QUESTION

1. EMTs are caring for a 37-year-old patient with a closed humerus fracture. The patient is agitated and asks the EMTs for something to help with the pain. What medications can the EMT administer?

Patient Communication

- Communication with the patient is a critical component of effective medical care and allows the EMT to identify the patient's complaint.
- Communication should be direct, non-threatening, and calm.
- EMTs should be aware of their tone and address patients properly. There are situations that require an EMT to be forceful or direct, while other situations may require the EMT to be supportive and nurturing.
- The EMT should be aware of their body language; negative body language can lead to patient mistrust and can affect care.
  - Work on the same level as the patient (e.g., crouch to speak to a seated patient).
  - Do not make facial expressions that suggest frustration, anger, confusion, or fear.
  - Face the patient when communicating with them.

Table 12.1. Dos and Don'ts of Patient Communication

Do	Don't
- Make eye contact with the patient - Introduce yourself and use the patient's name - Speak directly to the patient when possible - Ask open-ended questions - Speak slowly and clearly - Show empathy for the patient - Be silent when appropriate to allow patients time to think and process emotions	- Use medical jargon - Threaten or intimidate the patient - Lie or provide false hope - Interrupt the patient - Show frustration or anger - Make judgmental statements

- When treating a young patient:
  - Crouch or lie down at the patient's level.
  - Be honest and direct when speaking with them.
  - Ask parents for permission to communicate directly with the patient.

- When treating patients who are blind or have low vision, describe what actions are being taken throughout assessment, treatment, and transport so that the client understands what is occurring.
- EMTs should be prepared to communicate with patients who do not speak English or who have language impairments.
    - Address patients using short, simple sentences to gauge their level of English.
    - Learn basic medical terms in languages commonly used in the service area.
    - Carry tools such as communication boards and translation apps on phones or tablets.
    - Use family members as translators when necessary.

PRACTICE QUESTION

2. An EMT is caring for a 6-year-old patient with acute abdomen and vomiting. The patient's mother is aggressively questioning the child about what he recently ate and when he started feeling sick. The patient is withdrawn and is not speaking to his parents or the EMT. What techniques can the EMT use to communicate with this patient?

Professional Communication and Documentation

- EMS systems use a combination of radios and cell phones for communication.
    - EMTs usually communicate with dispatch using **mobile radios** located in the ambulance or **hand-held radios** that can be carried to the site of care.
    - EMTs usually communicate with receiving facilities via cell phone.
- An EMS call starts with a call to an **EMS dispatcher**. These calls usually come through 911 but may also come from automated systems (e.g., OnStar).
    - The 911 operator questions the caller to collect as much information as possible and may give directions of care including bystander CPR.
    - The EMS dispatcher dispatches the appropriate personnel and help (e.g., fire apparatus, rescue teams).
- The EMS dispatcher communicates with the EMS unit assigned to the call.
    - The EMS unit should report to dispatch when they arrive at the scene, leave the scene, and arrive at the point of transfer.
    - The dispatcher must give the crew the address of the call and the complaint of the patient.
    - The dispatcher may also give directions or follow-up information to the crew as the call continues.
    - The crew should always repeat information back to the dispatcher for confirmation and should ask for clarification if they are unsure.

DID YOU KNOW?

Cell phones and tablets are used to communicate with medical control and to pass images for notification. EMS-issued phones or tablets may have apps or programs that allow the EMT to communicate directly with the emergency department.

- The EMS unit should communicate with the receiving facility before their arrival to provide a **prehospital radio report**. The report should include:
    - unit ID and level of service
    - estimated time of arrival (ETA)
    - patient's age and gender
    - chief complaint and relevant history
    - mechanism of injury
    - patient's mental status
    - relevant physical findings and vital signs
    - treatment and patient response to treatment
- All aspects of patient care—from dispatch to transfer of care—should be documented in the **patient care report** (**PCR**).
    - The PCR may be used in legal proceedings, billing, research, or as a reference for further medical care.
    - Errors committed by the EMT should be carefully documented in the PCR.
    - Mistakes in the PCR should be crossed out and amended; content should never be erased from a PCR.

PRACTICE QUESTION

3. An EMT calls in the following report to the receiving hospital.

    Ambulance 714-BLS to the hospital: we are inbound with a 76-year-old male with chest pain radiating to jaw beginning at approximately 1:30 a.m. He has a history of stable angina. Patient is alert and oriented. Treatment was 325 mg aspirin and one sublingual nitroglycerin. ETA 6 minutes.

    What information is missing from the report?

Maintaining the Truck

- EMS crews use vehicles to get to the scene and transport the crew and their patient to their destination.
- It is vital that all parts of the vehicle are in good working order.
    - At the beginning of each shift, check and top off fluids to the level set by the vehicle manufacturer. Fluids include motor oil, steering fluid, transmission fluid, and radiator fluid.
    - Check vehicle tires to ensure they have proper tread, there is no unusual wear or damage, and they are at the proper pressure.
    - Ensure that the vehicle has a full tank of fuel at the beginning of the shift so that the crew can make calls without running out of fuel.
    - Check that all lights are properly working.
    - Check that windows are clear and clean to ensure that the crew has an unobstructed view.

- If there are any issues that may affect safety, the vehicle should be placed out of service.
- Maintenance also includes ensuring that the EMS crew has the proper equipment to do their job.
  - Before each shift, check the truck to ensure it is stocked with the proper type and amount of supplies and equipment.
  - Check equipment to make sure it has not expired, is operational, and is fully charged.
  - Replace all equipment and supplies as used or at the end of the shift to ensure the next crew is ready for their shift.
- Every EMT truck should include in stock:
  - oxygen masks and airway adjuncts
  - bandaging materials
  - blood pressure cuffs
  - AED
  - thermal blankets
  - thermometers
  - personal protective and safety equipment (e.g., gloves, sharps container)
  - pharmaceuticals as allowed by protocols
  - stabilization devices (e.g., C-collars)
  - other supplies specified by local requirements
- Maintenance of the vehicle and the requirements for supplies and their amounts may be set by the governing body within the jurisdiction or state where the vehicle is operated.

PRACTICE QUESTION

4. Why is it important to ensure all vehicle fluids are topped off at the start of every shift?

Driving to the Scene and Receiving Facility

- Driving the emergency vehicle in a safe manner ensures the safety of the crew, the passengers, and the public.
- When transporting a patient, one member of the unit is the driver and the other will attend to the patient.
- Protect crew and passengers by correctly using seat belts and restraints.
  - EMT personnel should wear seat belts at all times unless providing emergency care.
  - Patients should be appropriately restrained.
  - Equipment should be stowed properly.

- The operation of emergency vehicles, such as ambulances and fire apparatus, differs greatly from driving a personal vehicle.
  - EMS vehicles are usually much larger and heavier than personal vehicles. Their size means they require greater stopping distances and more space to turn corners.
  - EMS vehicles usually have larger blind spots that can make some driving maneuvers, such as backing up, more difficult.
- When operating the EMS vehicle in a **nonemergency**, the driver must adhere to all applicable motor vehicle laws where the vehicle is driven. This includes speed limits, direction of travel, and passing rules.
- During **emergency operation**, the driver uses the lights and siren and may be exempt from some traffic laws (per local regulations).
  - During emergency operation, turn on all lights and use the siren. (In some states, the law requires the use of the siren while the emergency lights are on.)
  - Use of the lights and siren give the vehicle right of way over other drivers on the road.
  - During emergency operation, the driver may proceed through red lights or stop signs, exceed the posted speed limits, drive against traffic, or drive against posted travel directions.
  - Some areas use traffic preemption devices to change traffic signals and give clear passage to emergency vehicles.
- Research has consistently shown that driving with lights and sirens is more dangerous than normal driving. Thus, driving during emergency operations should always be **defensive**.
  - Some drivers may panic or not know what to do when an emergency vehicle with lights and siren approaches. Be prepared for other drivers to behave in unexpected ways, such as stopping quickly, changing lanes, or speeding up.
  - Other drivers may not notice the approaching emergency vehicle, even if the lights and siren are on, and thus may not clear intersections or move to the side of the road.
- When arriving at a scene, the driver should park the vehicle such that it can exit the scene quickly and is not a threat to patients, bystanders, or emergency personnel.

PRACTICE QUESTION

5. The driver of an EMS vehicle is driving with lights and siren on. She approaches a red light at an intersection and cannot see cross-traffic. What should the driver do?

Postrun

- After the call is over, the crew should plan to clean up, restock, and report.

- When the call is done, clean and disinfect the stretcher and any equipment that was used.
- Restock as necessary any supplies that were used.
- Verbally give a report to the receiving facility and then follow up with a paper or electronic report as required by the jurisdiction in which the call was done.
- After the run is complete, the crew should discuss what happened and address any issues that occurred during the operation.
    - If a member of the crew is having trouble physically or mentally due to the call, contact a supervisor or chief officer to ensure the member gets the proper treatment and care for their issue.
- If necessary and appropriate, the crew should obtain insurance information from the patient, their family, or the facility to assist in the billing process.

PRACTICE QUESTION

6. Cleaning the ambulance attendant area and equipment after a call is routine. Why must this area and the equipment be cleaned after a call?

Legal and Ethical Considerations
LEGAL LIABILITY

- **Legal liability** means that a person has a legal obligation and is subject to criminal and civil penalties if they do not meet those obligations.
- EMTs have varying levels of legal liability during a run.
    - When an EMS crew has been dispatched, the driver is legally liable for their actions and must follow all federal, state, and local driving laws. However, the crew has no legal liability for the patient.
    - Liability to the patient starts when the crew makes contact with the patient.
    - Failure to use the proper equipment and follow protocols while rendering care may lead to legal action against the EMT.
    - If a dispatcher has sent out a crew and then cancels the call, the EMS crew has no liability to the patient.
    - For a canceled call, the EMT may be legally liable if the EMT should have been able to assess that the patient did not have the capacity to refuse treatment (e.g., unconscious, altered mental state). For this reason, EMS protocols often do not allow a call to be canceled unless the patient has been seen by the EMT.
    - The EMS crew is also liable for the maintenance and safety of their equipment. If it is determined that an injury was the result of faulty equipment, the EMS crew and their company may be held liable.
- **Negligence** is a type of tort (a wrongful civil act) defined as failure to offer an acceptable standard of care. There are four types of negligence:
    - Nonfeasance is a willful failure to act when required.

- ○ Misfeasance is the incorrect or improper performance of a lawful action.
- ○ Malfeasance is a willful and intentional action that causes harm.
- ○ Malpractice occurs when a professional fails to properly execute their duties.
- **Malpractice** is the most common type of legal claim against EMTs. For malpractice to occur, four things must happen:
  - ○ The patient-EMT relationship was established (duty).
  - ○ The EMT neglected to act or acted improperly (dereliction).
  - ○ A negative outcome occurred from an action or lack of an action (direct cause).
  - ○ The patient sustained harm (damages).
- **Gross negligence** describes an especially reckless action that the provider should have known would result in injury.
- **Abandonment** occurs when an EMT terminates care without the patient's consent or without transferring the patient to an equal or higher level of care.
- When EMTs are legally liable and the patient sustains injury, the EMT and their employer may be sued in civil court.
  - ○ Successful malpractice suits against EMS personnel are relatively rare.
  - ○ The most common sources of legal liability for EMTs are vehicle accidents, patient consent or refusal of care, and poorly restrained patients.

PRACTICE QUESTION

7. An EMS crew is dispatched to a patient who has been found lying on a sidewalk in an altered mental state. On arrival, the crew determines that the patient is under the influence of alcohol. His vital signs are within normal range, and he demands to be left alone because he has a terrible headache. The EMT believes the patient is drunk and does not require treatment or transport. Later that night, the patient is admitted to the ED with a subdural hematoma and dies shortly thereafter. Is the EMT legally liable for damages to the patient?

DUTY TO ACT AND GOOD SAMARITAN LAWS

- A **duty to act** is a legal term that describes the actions a person or an organization must take, by law, to respond to and prevent harm to a person or a community as a whole.
  - ○ An on-duty EMT has a duty to act in their jurisdiction: they are legally required to respond to dispatcher calls, assess patients, and provide treatment within their scope of practice.
  - ○ EMTs may have a duty to act when not on a call or not on duty depending on local regulations.
- A **Good Samaritan law** provides legal protection for people who give reasonable care to those who need assistance.

DID YOU KNOW?

States with duty-to-act laws for off-duty EMS include Ohio, Massachusetts, Vermont, Hawaii, California, Florida, Rhode Island, Minnesota, Wisconsin, and Washington.

- All states and the District of Columbia have some version of a Good Samaritan law. These laws vary, but most protect people who act rationally to provide aid but do not protect people from gross negligence.
- The laws in some states cover EMS personnel who render care while off duty. The EMT must do their best to help the injured individual and must not do anything outside their scope of practice.
- Good Samaritans may be on the scene when an EMT arrives.
  - Accept any information the Good Samaritan provides, and ask the Good Samaritan to step back so you can render care.
  - In some cases, a doctor or fellow rescuer may be on the scene and try to take over care. Thank them for their service, and ask them to step back so you can continue your care. Contact medical control if they request to continue their involvement in care.
  - If a Good Samaritan refuses to back away, ask the police to remove the person from the scene.

PRACTICE QUESTION

8. An off-duty EMT is eating dinner in a restaurant when a man at a nearby table collapses. The EMT assesses the man and finds he has no pulse and is not breathing. The EMT begins compressions and rescue breathing. The man survives but is left incapacitated due to anoxic brain injury. The family sues the EMT, claiming he did not do enough to provide treatment for the man. Will the EMT be protected under Good Samaritan laws?

PATIENT CONSENT

- Patient **consent** is required before any care is rendered.
  - Permission is obtained by asking if the patient would like help and if it is okay to touch the person.
  - **Expressed consent** is an affirmative verbal or nonverbal agreement to care.
  - **Implied consent** allows the EMT to provide care to unconscious or incapacitated patients if it can be assumed that any reasonable patient would consent to care under the circumstances.
  - A patient's consent can be withdrawn at any time. If a patient withdraws their consent, then an EMT must stop treatment.
- Patients may lack **competency** or **capacity** to make medical decisions.
  - There are many reasons a person may have an altered mental state, including organic conditions (e.g., Alzheimer's disease), mood-altering substances, and medical conditions (e.g., concussion, lack of oxygen, stroke).
  - Patients with dementia or mental illness may have a designated guardian who can consent to treatment.
  - When the EMT determines that a patient does not have the capacity to make medical decisions, they should render care to the patient under implied consent.

HELPFUL HINT
Treating a patient without their consent can result in civil lawsuits or criminal charges against the EMT for assault and battery.

- Local protocols will regulate if and when law enforcement can give consent for people who have been arrested or who are not competent to give consent.
- Care may be stopped if the patient returns to normal and declines care or if a person who has legal responsibility for the patient asks the EMT to stop care.

- For minor patients, the patient's guardian must provide consent.
  - In most cases, the legal age of consent to treat is 18 years old.
  - An **emancipated minor** has petitioned the court to be legally separated from their parents. They should be treated as an adult and asked for consent (if they can show the card verifying their emancipation).
  - When a minor has a child, the minor is the guardian of that child and can make decisions about treatment for that child. However, the minor cannot make decisions about their own treatment.

- Patients who are competent may deny consent for treatment.
  - The EMT may not force the patient to be treated or transported, even if their life is in danger.
  - Every effort must be made to convince an individual to go to the hospital if the EMT believes that it is the right course of action for the patient.
  - Law enforcement may be able to invoke their right to force a patient to seek help. However, this power usually only applies to people with mental illness or who are threatening self-harm.
  - The EMT may contact medical control and discuss the situation with them. The patient may also talk directly to medical control.

- If a patient refuses care, the EMT should document the refusal.
  - The EMT must have the patient (or guardian) sign a refusal-of-treatment form.
  - The EMT should also thoroughly document the patient's mental status and the EMT's attempt to explain the need for care to the patient.

- An **advance directive** is a legal document that describes the medical treatment a person has consented to if they become unconscious.
  - A **do-not-resuscitate (DNR)** order is written for patients who do not wish to be resuscitated in the event of cardiac or respiratory failure.
  - EMTs should carefully examine advance directives to ensure they are valid (e.g., has patient and physician signatures).

- Some patients may have **health care proxies** who hold **durable power of attorney** and can make medical decisions on behalf of the patient.

HELPFUL HINT
If a patient is alert and competent, their medical decisions cannot be overridden by their health care proxy.

PRACTICE QUESTION

9. A call comes in for a sick child. Upon arrival, the EMT is met by a 16-year-old girl who says her child is sick and she wants him taken to the hospital. Another woman steps in and identifies herself as the mother of the 16-year-old. She says she will not allow the child to be taken to the hospital as he is not that sick. How should the EMT respond?

CONFIDENTIALITY

- In 1996, the United States federal government enacted the **Health Insurance Portability and Accountability Act (HIPAA)**. This act details how private health information (PHI) and electronic medical records (EMR) can be shared.
- All efforts must be taken to ensure the **confidentiality** of the patient's PHI.
  - Information describing who they are, where they live, their social security number, and their diagnosis must not be shared with anyone other than personnel involved in treating the patient.
  - Any paperwork that has the patient's information shall be secured at all times.
  - In most cases, an authorization form signed by the patient is required before releasing any PHI to anyone other than personnel directly involved in the patient's care.
  - The passing of information between dispatchers, field crews, medical control, and emergency departments must be HIPAA compliant to ensure the privacy of patients (e.g., never use the patient's name over the air waves).
- Violating HIPAA by sharing PHI can result in job loss or civil liability.
- Confidentiality also covers conversations between the EMT and patients or bystanders.
  - EMTs should not disclose information shared by patients to anyone other than relevant medical personnel.
  - During calls, EMTs should work to ensure that patients can share information with the EMT without being overheard by bystanders.
- EMTs should not discuss calls (personally or professionally) such that listeners can determine the patient's identity.
- EMTs may not access information about patients they did not directly care for. This is a violation of patient privacy and can lead to legal action and job loss.

PRACTICE QUESTION

10. An EMS crew recently transported a celebrity from their home to a hospital. The EMT who provided care later recounts to a coworker the reason for the treatment but does not mention the celebrity by name. Did the EMT commit a HIPAA violation?

ANSWER KEY

1. EMTs cannot provide any medications for pain. They are only able to administer aspirin and nitroglycerin for possible ischemic chest pain and oral glucose.

2. The EMT should start by asking the parent if she can speak directly with the child. She should then crouch down to the patient's level, introduce herself, and explain that she is there to help the child. Because the child is frightened, she should use a non-threatening tone and not pressure the child to speak until he is ready.

3. The EMT has not included the patient's vital signs or any information about his response to treatment.

4. Vehicles can be driven for large amounts of time and long distances during a shift. Making sure fluids are topped off ensures that the vehicle can operate properly and safely and decreases the likelihood of a component failure at a critical time.

5. The driver should come to a stop at the intersection to make sure no traffic will be in the intersection when she passes through. Even though she has the right of way, drivers with a green light may not see her or stop in time. Going through the red light without stopping puts other drivers at risk.

6. Cleaning reduces the spread of disease and germs that might be present after a call.

7. The EMT may be legally liable. The EMT should have known that an altered mental state and a headache are symptoms of intracranial hemorrhage. He should have transported the patient to the ED for a full assessment or contacted medical control before releasing him.

8. Yes, the EMT will be protected under Good Samaritan laws. The EMT provided treatment within the scope of his training and committed no acts of negligence, so he is not liable for any injury the man suffered.

9. The 16-year-old mother is the guardian of the child and has the legal right to make decisions about her child's care. The grandmother has no legal right to determine the boy's care, so the EMT should prepare to transport the child.

10. Yes, the EMT most likely committed a HIPAA violation. The coworker may be able to identify the patient through gossip or news reports, meaning the EMT has now shared a patient's PHI and will be legally liable if the patient sues.

THIRTEEN: THE PSYCHOMOTOR EXAM

What is the Psychomotor Exam?

- The psychomotor examination is a standardized, hands-on test in which the EMT candidate must perform specific emergency medical skills.
    - The psychomotor exam is conducted in a proctored environment in which the EMT candidate may not reference notes or course material.
    - The examiners are typically EMT instructors and are not allowed to assist the EMT candidate.
    - The EMT candidate is graded using standard **NREMT performance checklists**, often referred to as "skill sheets."
- The psychomotor exam consists of seven skills:
    - Patient Assessment/Management – Trauma
    - Patient Assessment/Management – Medical
    - Bag-Valve Mask (BVM) Ventilation of an Apneic Adult Patient
    - Oxygen Administration by Non-Rebreather Mask
    - Cardiac Arrest Management/AED
    - Spinal Immobilization (Supine Patient)
    - Random EMT Skill
- The random EMT skill will consist of one of the following:
    - Spinal Immobilization (Seated Patient)
    - Bleeding Control/Shock Management
    - Long Bone Immobilization
    - Joint Immobilization
- All skills are scenario based, with the examiner relaying a synopsis of the simulated emergency after reading the instructions.
    - Scenario-based skills will require the EMT candidate to maintain dialogue with the examiner. For example, "I am palpating all four abdominal

HELPFUL HINT
The information in this chapter is meant to supplement the skill sheets, not replace them. You should reference the NREMT checklists as you read. They can be found at https://www.nremt.org/rwd/public/document/emt.

HELPFUL HINT
You will not be informed what the random skill is until that section of the test is about to begin.

quadrants for distension and tenderness" or "Your patient states he is prescribed nitroglycerine for chest pain."

- Each skill has **critical criteria**, which is a list of items that will lead to automatic failure.
    - In this chapter, critical criteria are shown in **bold**.
    - Although not listed under critical criteria, inability to complete an examination within the set time limit will also result in failure.
- This chapter will focus only on the NREMT-recommended psychomotor examination criteria. Some states or individual agencies may deviate from or modify the NREMT curriculum.

Patient Assessment/Management – Trauma

- This skill is designed to evaluate the EMT candidate's ability to effectively assess and treat an adult patient with multi-system trauma.
    - The simulated patient will have moulage (makeup or prosthetics imitating injuries), some of which may not be immediately visible during scene size-up.
    - The patient's injuries will vary in severity.
    - There will be two EMT assistants available.
    - **This skill must be completed within 10 minutes.**
- The NREMT checklist for this skill is divided into five areas: scene size-up, primary survey/resuscitation, history taking, secondary assessment, and reassessment.

Scene Size-Up

- **Use appropriate PPE or verbalize use of PPE to examiner.**
- **Determine if the scene is safe.**
    - During the exam, the EMT candidate determines scene safety by asking the examiner, "Is the scene safe?"
- Determine mechanism of injury. (The mechanism of injury will be inferred by the scenario description as read by the examiner but will still need to be verbalized by the EMT candidate.)
- Request additional resources if the patient could benefit from advanced life support (ALS) care.
- **Assess whether spinal immobilization would be performed based on mechanism of injury.**

Primary Survey/Resuscitation

- Verbalize a general impression (a brief statement of the patient's stability based upon the size-up and mechanism of injury).

HELPFUL HINT
During this skill, an EMT assistant can be used to hold manual in-line stabilization.

- Determine level of consciousness and expose patient (remove clothing) to determine chief complaint or life threats.
- **Manage airway, breathing, and circulation (ABCs), including hemorrhage and shock.**
    - **Provide high concentration oxygen and adequate ventilation.**
    - **Assess and treat ABCs before addressing other injuries.**
- **Determine patient priority and make a transport decision within 10 minutes of the start of the scenario.**

History Taking

- Gather vital signs.
    - Baseline vital signs are given verbally by the examiner once asked.
    - Each vital sign must be asked for individually.
    - The EMT candidate should be prepared to explain how he or she would obtain each vital sign (e.g., "I will obtain a heart rate by palpating the carotid artery with my index and middle fingers.")
    - Some examiners may require the EMT candidate to take actual vital signs.
    - If allowed by the examiner, obtaining vital signs may be delegated to an EMT assistant earlier in the scenario.
- Obtain SAMPLE history.
    - If a SAMPLE history cannot be obtained due to the patient's level of consciousness, the EMT candidate should verbalize this.

Secondary Assessment

- Inspect, palpate, and assess the patient head-to-toe for injury and function.
- Use the mnemonic DCAP-BTLS. (See chapter 2 for detailed information on secondary assessment of trauma patients.)
- The most successful method for completing the secondary assessment is to integrate portions of it into the Primary Survey/Resuscitation during ABCs (check the mouth and nose when checking the airway, or the chest when checking breathing).
    - If this method is used, it must be communicated to the examiner (e.g., "As I open the airway using the jaw thrust maneuver, I am performing an assessment of the mouth and nose.")
- Verbalize treatment for any injuries encountered during the secondary assessment.

Reassessment

- Reassess the patient every 5 or 15 minutes based on the patient's condition.

HELPFUL HINT

Not all items on the performance checklists have to be conducted in the order they are listed.

- If the patient's vital signs trend negatively, this is an indication the EMT candidate improperly performed an intervention or missed an injury.

PRACTICE QUESTION

1. How long does the EMT have to make a transport decision for the patient during the Patient Assessment/Management – Trauma skills exam?

Patient Assessment/Management – Medical

- This skill will measure the EMT candidate's ability to manage and treat an adult patient with a medical-related chief complaint.
  - The patient may ultimately be suffering from multiple illnesses of varying severity.
  - The examiner will verbally role-play most or all of the patient's responses.
  - There will be two EMT assistants (real or imaginary) to help as needed.
  - The time limit for this skill is 15 minutes.
- The NREMT checklist for this skill is divided into six areas: scene size-up, primary survey/resuscitation, history taking, secondary assessment, vital signs, and reassessment.

Scene Size-Up

- The same scene size-up procedures can be used for Patient Assessment/Management – Trauma and Medical skills exams.

Primary Survey/Resuscitation

- Verbalize a general impression (a brief statement of the patient's stability based upon the size-up and nature of illness).
  - The medical patient will often state their own chief complaint. However, there may be other life threats besides the chief complaint.
- Assess responsiveness and level of consciousness using the acronym AVPU. (See chapter 2 for detailed information on assessment of medical patients.)
- **Manage airway, breathing, and circulation (ABCs), including hemorrhage and shock.**
  - **Provide high concentration oxygen and adequate ventilation.**
  - **Assess and treat ABCs before performing secondary assessment.**
- **Determine patient priority and make a transport decision within 15 minutes of the start of the scenario.**

History Taking

- Take patient's history using the acronyms OPQRST and SAMPLE. (See chapter 2 for detailed information on assessment of medical patients.)

- OPQRST and SAMPLE do not have to be performed in order.
- The EMT candidate is encouraged to ask any necessary clarifying questions in addition to OPQRST and SAMPLE.

Secondary Assessment

- Perform a physical examination of the affected area and ask further clarifying questions specific to the body part or system involved.
- The secondary assessment does not need to be completed prior to patient transport.

HELPFUL HINT
Unacceptable affect with patients or personnel (e.g., aggression, impatience) is critical criteria that will result in failure.

Vital Signs

- Physically obtain vital signs from the simulated patient.
  - The examiner will compare the vital signs obtained by the EMT candidate with their own findings. The EMT must be within 10 mm Hg (BP), 10 beats per minute (HR), and 5 breaths per minute (RR) of the examiner.
  - After the actual vital signs are obtained, the examiner may adjust the figures to more accurately represent the scenario.
- The field impression of the patient is the EMT candidate's verbal opinion of what the patient's illnesses are.
- Verbalize treatment and interventions to the examiner.
  - If online medical direction is required, the examiner will play the role of the physician.
  - Explain the dosage, route, indications, and contraindications of any medications that are to be given.

Reassessment

- Reassess patient every 5 or 15 minutes based on the patient's condition.
  - If the patient's vital signs trend negatively, this is an indication the EMT candidate improperly performed an intervention or missed an illness.
- **Give accurate verbal transfer-of-care report.**
  - The transfer-of-care report is typically a brief statement of the patient's age, sex, chief complaint, illnesses/injuries, pertinent medical history, interventions, and vital sign trends.

PRACTICE QUESTION

2. The EMT candidate has completed the primary survey during the Assessment/Management – Medical skills exam and determined the patient does not require immediate transport. What should the EMT do next?

BVM Ventilation of an Apneic Adult Patient

HELPFUL HINT

The BVM Ventilation skill exam is often done in conjunction with the Oxygen Administration by Non-Rebreather Mask examination.

- This skill is designed to measure the EMT candidate's ability to successfully provide artificial ventilations to an adult patient who has a pulse but is not breathing.
  - The EMT candidate will be required to use a bag-valve mask, supplemental oxygen, suction device, and an oropharyngeal airway adjunct.
  - The EMT candidate will need to assemble the bag-valve mask, oxygen components, and suction device during the examination.
- **Verbalize PPE precautions.**
- **Assess responsiveness.**
- **Assess pulse and breathing simultaneously for no more than 10 seconds.**
- **Open airway and suction the mouth and oropharynx.**
  - **Suction for no more than 15 seconds.**
- Insert oropharyngeal airway and begin BVM ventilation.
  - **After suctioning is complete, artificial ventilations must begin within 30 seconds.**
  - **Maintain appropriate ventilation rate (10 – 12 breaths per minute) and volume.**
  - **Do not stop ventilations for more than 30 seconds.**
- **Attach BVM to oxygen.**
  - Supplemental oxygen can be used immediately, or the oxygen can be postponed until after the first pulse check (about 2 minutes).
  - If the EMT candidate elects to wait until after the first pulse check to connect supplemental oxygen to the BVM, the examiner or an assistant will take over ventilations while the EMT candidate prepares the oxygen delivery system.

PRACTICE QUESTION

3. What is the maximum length of time the EMT candidate should spend suctioning an adult patient?

Oxygen Administration by Non-Rebreather Mask

- This skill is designed to measure the EMT candidate's ability to assemble the components of a supplemental oxygen system and provide oxygen therapy to a patient using a non-rebreather mask.
  - The patient will have no other injuries or illnesses.
  - The regulator and mask will be disconnected from the oxygen cylinder when the examination begins.
- **Verbalize PPE precautions.**

- Gather appropriate equipment.
  - Check to ensure the proper washer or O-ring is present on the regulator to prevent leaks.
- "Crack" the valve on the oxygen cylinder by opening it slightly for a brief moment to clear out any dust or debris in the port.
- Line up the pins on the regulator to the holes on the oxygen cylinder for proper assembly.
- After opening the cylinder valve, check the gauge and verbally state the pressure.
  - The pressure is measured in pounds per square inch, or psi (e.g., "The gauge reads approximately 2100 psi.").
- **After looking, listening, and feeling, verbalize the absence of leaks.**
- **Set flow rate to at least 10 liters per minute after the non-rebreather mask is attached.**
- **Prefill the reservoir bag on the non-rebreather mask.**
  - To prefill the reservoir bag, place a finger over the exhaust port on the inside of the mask.
- **Ensure the mask has a tight seal on the patient's face.**

PRACTICE QUESTION

4. Oxygen should be given at what flow rate during the Oxygen Administration by Non-Rebreather Mask skill exam?

Cardiac Arrest Management/AED

- This skill measures the EMT candidate's ability to use CPR and an AED to manage an adult patient in cardiac arrest. (See chapter 4, "Cardiovascular Emergencies," for detailed information on how to perform CPR and use the AED.)
  - No bystanders will be present.
  - After 2 minutes (5 cycles) of CPR, a second rescuer will arrive with an AED.
  - The EMT candidate will then use the AED while the second rescuer continues CPR.
  - The maximum time for this skill is 10 minutes.
  - Use the time allotted before the beginning of the examination to become familiar with the AED trainer and ensure all components are present and ready for use.
- **Take or verbalize appropriate PPE precautions and evaluate the scene for safety.**
- Upon determining the patient is unresponsive, request an AED and additional EMS assistance.

- **Check for pulse and breathing simultaneously for no more than 10 seconds.**
- **Immediately begin 1-rescuer CPR when the examiner states that the patient is apneic and pulseless.**
- After 2 minutes (5 cycles) of CPR, simultaneously reassess pulse and breathing for no longer than 10 seconds.
  - During reassessment, the examiner will state that the patient is still apneic and pulseless, and a second rescuer has arrived with an AED.
- After directing the second rescuer to take over CPR (with less than 10 seconds of interruption), turn on the AED and follow the prompts.
- Expose the patient's chest and apply AED pads while CPR is still in progress.
- Direct the second rescuer to stop CPR and stay clear of the patient as the AED analyzes the heart rhythm.
- **Once shock is advised by the AED, direct all individuals not to touch the patient; announce "All clear" before delivering shock.**
- **Resume CPR immediately after delivery of the shock.**

> **HELPFUL HINT**
> Interrupting CPR for more than 10 seconds is a critical criteria and will result in failure.

> **HELPFUL HINT**
> Inform the second rescuer not to stop compression as you expose the chest and apply AED pads.

PRACTICE QUESTION

5. An EMT candidate is taking the Cardiac Arrest Management/AED skill exam. She approaches the patient to perform a primary survey. The examiner tells her that the patient is unresponsive. The EMT candidate then simultaneously assesses airway and breathing, and the examiner then tells her the patient is apneic and pulseless. The EMT candidate immediately begins chest compressions.

   What step did the EMT candidate not perform?

Spinal Immobilization (Supine Patient)

- The Supine Patient Spinal Immobilization exercise will test the EMT candidate's ability to secure a supine (lying flat on the back) patient to a long spine board.
  - The patient will not have any illnesses or injuries apart from a suspected unstable cervical spine.
  - Any approved spine board, straps, and padding may be used.
  - The EMT candidate will be allowed one trained assistant to maintain manual in-line stabilization as directed.
  - The EMT assistant and skill examiner will assist with moving the patient from the ground onto the spine board at the candidate's direction.
  - The examination must be completed in 10 minutes or less.
- **Take or verbalize PPE precautions.**
- **Direct the EMT assistant to apply and maintain in-line spinal immobilization.**

> **HELPFUL HINT**
> The spinal immobilization (supine) examination is often combined with the random skill.

- **Apply properly sized cervical collar.**
  - Check pulse, motor function, and sensory perception in all four extremities prior to applying cervical collar.
  - **Ensure EMT assistant does not release manual stabilization after collar is applied.**
- Move patient onto long spine board.
  - Provide instructions to the EMT assistant and skill examiner for their assistance in moving the patient onto the spine board.
  - The EMT assistant maintaining manual stabilization of the head is responsible for initiating movement of the patient.

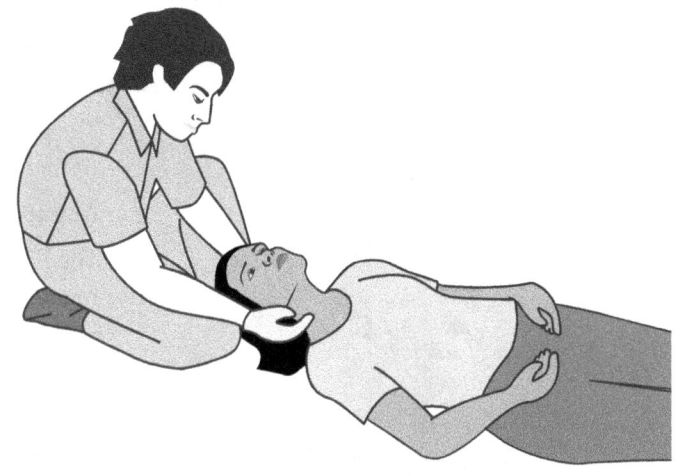

Figure 12.1. In-Line Spinal Immobilization (Supine)

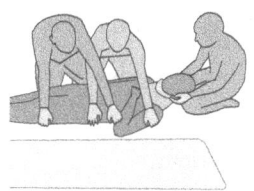 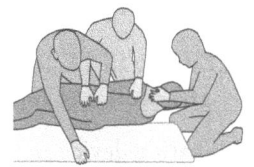 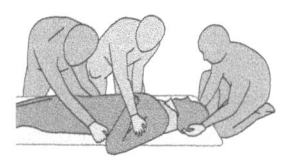

1. Maintain in-line stabilization with patient in supine position.
2. Grasp patient on far side and roll patient onto their side. Slide spine board under patient.
3. Roll patient onto the spine board.

Figure 12.2. Moving Patient to Long Spine Board

- Pad the voids between the patient and spine board as needed using appropriate padding.
  - Padding any voids behind the patient's head can be completed here or immediately prior to securing the patient's head to the board.
  - If padding voids is unnecessary due to the patient's body type, verbalize this to the examiner.
- **Secure patient's torso to spine board prior to securing the head.**
  - **Secure patient's head in a neutral position.**
  - **Prevent excessive movement of the patient or patient's head.**
- Secure the patient's legs and then the arms.
- **Reassess pulse, motor function, and sensory perception in all four extremities after securing the patient to the spine board.**

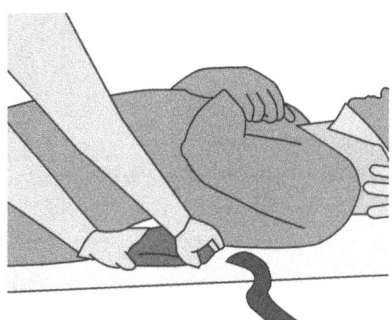

Figure 12.3. Padding Voids on Long Spine Board

PRACTICE QUESTION

6. The EMT candidate, the EMT assistant, and the examiner are in position to move the patient onto a spine board. Which person should initiate movement of the patient?

Spinal Immobilization (Seated Patient)

- The Seated Patient Spinal Immobilization tests the EMT candidate's ability to provide spinal immobilization of a seated patient to a long spine board.
  - The patient will be stable in a seated position with no illnesses or injuries apart from a suspected unstable cervical spine.
  - Any approved half-spine immobilization device may be used.
  - The EMT candidate will be allowed one trained assistant to maintain manual in-line stabilization as directed.
  - The examination must be completed in 10 minutes or less.
- **Take or verbalize PPE precautions.**
- **Direct the EMT assistant to apply and maintain in-line spinal immobilization.**
- **Apply properly sized cervical collar.**
  - Check pulse, motor function, and sensory perception in all four extremities prior to applying cervical collar.
  - **Ensure EMT assistant does not release manual stabilization after collar is applied.**
- Position immobilization device and secure patient.
  - **Secure the patient's torso before securing the head.**
  - **Secure patient's head in a neutral position.**
  - **Prevent excessive movement of patient or patient's head.**
  - **Do not tighten the device to the torso such that it inhibits adequate chest rise and fall.**

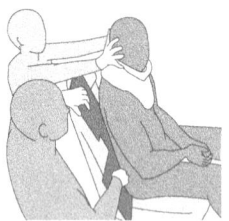
1. Slide half spine board behind patient.

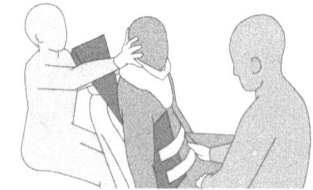
2. Secure patient torso to board.

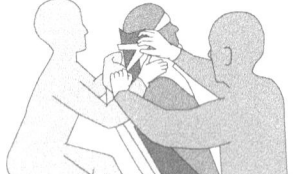
3. Secure patient head to board.

Figure 12.5. Securing Patient to Half-Spine Immobilization Device

- Verbalize the process of transitioning the patient from a seated position to a long backboard.
- **Check pulse, motor function, and sensory perception after verbalizing the process of securing the patient to a long backboard.**

Figure 12.4. In-Line Spinal Immobilization (Seated)

PRACTICE QUESTION

7. Which part of the body is attached first to the half-spine board?

Bleeding Control/Shock Management

- The Bleeding Control/Shock Management exercise tests the EMT candidate's ability to effectively treat an adult patient with arterial hemorrhage and hypoperfusion (shock).
  - The bleeding site will be at one of the four extremities.
  - Available equipment will include bandages, dressings, a tourniquet, a blanket, and a system for delivering supplemental oxygen.
  - The maximum time limit for this skill is 10 minutes.
  - Before the exercise begins, use the available time to become familiar with the equipment, particularly the tourniquet and oxygen delivery system, to avoid time delays later.
- **Take or verbalize PPE precautions.**
- Apply direct pressure to the wound using the available dressings and bandages.
  - The examiner will inform the EMT candidate that the wound continues to bleed.
- Immediately apply tourniquet proximal (closer to the torso) to the wound.
  - **Do not attempt other interventions (such as elevating the extremity or applying additional dressings) before applying the tourniquet.**

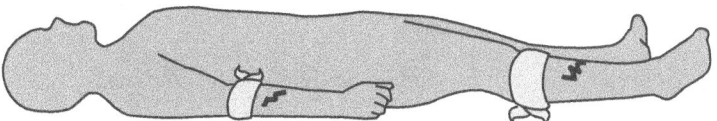

Figure 12.6. Tourniquet Placement for Arterial Bleeding in Extremities

  - The examiner will inform the EMT candidate that the patient is now exhibiting signs of hypoperfusion.
- Reposition the patient to a supine position if they will tolerate it, or place in a position of comfort.
- **Administer supplemental oxygen.**
- Prevent heat loss by covering the patient with a blanket.
- **Declare to the examiner that this is a priority patient requiring immediate transport.**

HELPFUL HINT

Placing the patient in the Trendelenburg position (legs elevated 8 – 12 inches above the level of the head) is no longer recommended.

PRACTICE QUESTION

8. An EMT candidate is performing the Bleeding Control/Shock Management skill exam. At what point should she expect to apply the tourniquet?

Long Bone Immobilization

- The Long Bone Immobilization exercise measures the EMT candidate's ability to effectively splint one of the following long bones in an adult patient: radius, ulna, tibia, or fibula.
  - This examination will not require the EMT candidate to perform a primary assessment or monitor the patient's ABCs.
  - There will be one EMT assistant available.
  - The use of traction, pneumatic, and vacuum splints is not allowed.
  - This skill must be completed within 5 minutes.
- **Take or verbalize PPE precautions.**
- **Direct the EMT assistant to apply manual stabilization of the injury by supporting the proximal and distal joints.**
- **Check pulse, motor function, and sensory perception distal to the injury.**
- Measure and apply the splint.
  - **Immobilize the joints above and below the injury.**
  - Methods for measuring and applying the splint will vary based on the devices available.
- Secure splinted extremity to the patient's body to restrict unnecessary movement.
  - Upper extremities can be secured to the torso using a swathe.
  - Lower extremities can be secured to each other with a rigid splint between, or to a long backboard.
- **Secure the hand or foot in a position of function.**
  - Extend the wrist slightly upward and allow the fingers to be flexed in a comfortable position. Do not extend the palm or fingers into a flat position.
  - The foot should be in a naturally upright position with no forced flexion.

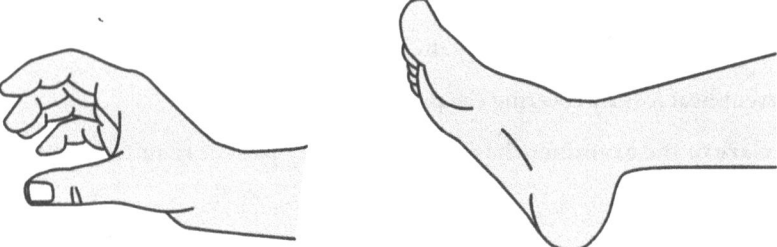

Figure 12.7. Position of Function for Hand and Foot

- Reassess pulse, motor function, and sensory perception distal to the injury.

> PRACTICE QUESTION
>
> 9. After immobilizing a fractured tibia, how should the entire extremity be secured?

Joint Immobilization

- The NREMT Joint Immobilization exercise tests the EMT candidate's ability to effectively splint a shoulder injury using a sling and swathe on an adult patient.
    - The EMT candidate will not be required to perform a primary survey or monitor the patient's ABCs.
    - One EMT assistant will be provided.
    - This skill must be completed within 5 minutes.
- **Take or verbalize PPE precautions.**
- **Direct the EMT assistant to apply manual stabilization of the injury by restricting movement of the entire arm and providing support to the elbow and forearm area.**
- **Check pulse, motor function, and sensory perception distal to the injury.**
- Use a large triangle bandage (cravat) to apply the sling to the injured arm.
    - If available, use padding (such as additional bandages) between the knot and the neck.
    - Avoid tying the knot directly over the spine or carotid artery.
    - Form a pocket using the extra bandage material at the elbow to prevent the arm from slipping out of the sling. (The pocket can be formed by folding and pinning the excess material or tying a knot.)
- Apply the swathe over the injured arm and the torso, but do not include the uninjured arm.
    - A swathe is like a strap or belt and is used to restrict movement of the injured extremity.
    - A swathe is typically made by folding a triangle bandage into a strip approximately 2 inches wide, which is then wrapped over the injured arm and tied around the torso.
- **Reassess pulse, motor function, and sensory perception distal to the injury.**
    - Some states or agencies require distal circulation, motor function, and sensory perception to be checked after application of the sling and again after application of the swathe.

HELPFUL HINT
The certifying state or testing agency may elect to have the EMT candidate immobilize a joint other than the shoulder.

HELPFUL HINT
The most appropriate distal pulse to check for an adult patient with a shoulder injury is the radial artery.

HELPFUL HINT
The only equipment available for immobilization during this skill exam will be large triangle bandages.

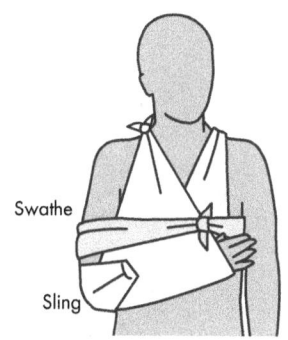

Figure 12.8. Sling and Swathe

> PRACTICE QUESTION
>
> 10. What is the difference between a sling and swathe?

ANSWER KEY

1. Transport must be initiated or called for within 10 minutes.

2. The EMT candidate should tell the examiner that he has determined immediate transport is not necessary and that he will continue assessment and treatment on the scene. He may then begin the patient history and secondary assessment.

3. An adult patient should not be suctioned for more than 15 seconds at a time. Prolonged suction is a critical failure point.

4. The oxygen flow rate should be at least 10 L/min.

5. After determining that the patient was unresponsive, the EMT candidate should have sent the assistant to get the AED and requested additional EMS assistance.

6. Movement must only be initiated by the person holding manual in-line stabilization of the head (in this case, the EMT assistant). The EMT candidate should provide instructions to the EMT assistant and skill examiner for moving the patient and direct the EMT assistant to initiate movement.

7. The patient's torso should be secured first. Failing to secure the torso before the head will result in failure of the examination.

8. A tourniquet should be applied immediately after the examiner notifies the EMT candidate that the wound continues to bleed after direct pressure application. Additional bandages, elevation of the extremity, and using pressure points are not required before tourniquet application and could result in critical failure.

9. To entirely secure an injured lower extremity, the legs can be secured together with a rigid splint in between or the legs can be secured to a long spine board.

10. A sling is designed to support the weight of the injured extremity. A swathe is a narrow strap or bandage intended to keep the injured appendage from excessively moving.

FOURTEEN: PRACTICE TEST

DIRECTIONS: READ THE QUESTION, AND THEN CHOOSE THE MOST CORRECT ANSWER.

1. To select the proper size nasopharyngeal airway, measure
   A. from the nostril opening to the earlobe.
   B. the diameter of the selected nostril.
   C. the circumference of the cranium.
   D. from the corner of the mouth to the earlobe.

2. You are treating a 73-year-old patient complaining of chest pain. Which of the following vital signs is a contraindication for nitroglycerin administration?
   A. respiratory rate of 22 breaths per minute
   B. blood pressure of 90/50 mm Hg
   C. resting heart rate of 130 bpm
   D. skin that is hot and dry

3. You are called to a 61-year-old unconscious female. Upon arrival, you find her lying motionless in bed. After opening the airway and observing no pulse or breathing, your next step is to
   A. immediately begin CPR.
   B. check for signs of trauma.
   C. move the patient to the floor or other hard surface.
   D. insert a nasopharyngeal airway.

4. An 84-year-old woman called 911 after accidentally setting her hand down on her stovetop. Upon arrival, you note an obvious burn injury to her entire palm. You should describe the burn as covering what percent of her body surface area?
   A. 1%
   B. 5%
   C. 9%
   D. 18%

5. A patient was struck in the upper right abdomen with a baseball and has substantial bruising. The patient may have injured his
   A. spleen.
   B. appendix.
   C. urinary bladder.
   D. liver.

6. A patient who responds to a physical stimulation but not to EMTs calling their name would be considered
   A. unresponsive.
   B. alert.
   C. responsive to verbal stimuli.
   D. responsive to painful stimuli.

7. A 45-year-old male with a history of diabetes is complaining of abdominal pain and nausea. The assessment reveals a blood sugar of 385. The patient's symptoms are MOST likely being caused by

   A. hypoglycemia.
   B. alcohol withdrawal.
   C. diabetic ketoacidosis.
   D. pancreatitis.

8. A 75-year-old male has left-sided weakness and slurred speech that resolves while you are evaluating him. This patient MOST likely had a

   A. myocardial infarction.
   B. transient ischemic attack.
   C. hemorrhagic stroke.
   D. migraine headache.

9. A patient with cardiogenic shock is expected to have

   A. hypertension and trouble breathing.
   B. decreased urine output and warm, pink skin.
   C. increased urine output and cool, clammy skin.
   D. hypotension, weak pulse, and cool, clammy skin.

10. The incident commander at a motor vehicle collision assigns you to treat a motorcyclist who was hit by a moving car. The patient is awake and talking with a chief complaint of severe pain to the waist and leg. You find an obvious deformity to the right femur, and his pelvis is unstable. While your EMT partner holds manual traction, your next step is to

    A. secure the patient to a long spine board.
    B. tightly wrap the pelvis with bandages.
    C. elevate the injured leg above the head.
    D. apply a traction splint.

11. You are assessing a 6-year-old child with an acute asthma attack. You find a pulse oximetry reading of 91%. You should first

    A. request an ALS intercept.
    B. provide supplemental oxygen.
    C. begin rescue breathing.
    D. administer a nebulized albuterol treatment.

12. You are providing CPR to a 54-year-old male in cardiac arrest as your EMT partner assembles and operates the AED. You stop compressions, and your partner delivers a shock from the AED. Your next step is to

    A. immediately resume chest compressions.
    B. wait for the AED to provide instructions.
    C. check pulse and breathing for no longer than 10 seconds.
    D. place the patient in recovery position.

13. Which of the following terms defines chest pain resulting from the coronary arteries being unable to supply an appropriate amount of oxygenated blood to meet the needs of the heart?

    A. angina pectoris
    B. congestive heart failure
    C. cerebrovascular accident
    D. coronary vein distension

14. A 73-year-old female with a history of smoking and chronic cough is complaining of shortness of breath after a recent lung infection. Knowing these symptoms, you suspect that she has

    A. sepsis.
    B. valley fever.
    C. tuberculosis.
    D. COPD.

15. You are treating a patient who accidentally amputated his finger while attempting to clean a large packaging machine. Suddenly, the patient's coworker yells that she found the finger in a puddle of blood on the factory floor. Your next step is to

    A. leave the finger in place and call the police.
    B. photograph the finger as evidence.
    C. place the finger in a clean bag in the freezer.
    D. wrap the finger in moist, sterile gauze.

16. You locate an adult patient who has a penetrative neck wound from sharp-force trauma. You notice bubbles forming at the site of the wound. Law enforcement has already secured the scene. Your priority treatment should include

    A. applying a C-collar.
    B. palpating the cervical spine.
    C. applying an occlusive dressing.
    D. checking the pupils for size and reactivity.

17. You arrive on scene and are about to enter a house when you hear gunshots from inside. You should

    A. enter the home to investigate.
    B. sound the siren to alert bystanders.
    C. leave the home and contact law enforcement.
    D. remain in front of the home and wait for someone to come out.

18. For a patient to successfully sue an EMT for malpractice, they must prove that the EMT

    A. purposefully caused the injury.
    B. was the cause of the injury.
    C. knew the injury occurred.
    D. felt no remorse for the injury.

19. A 19-year-old male is complaining of abdominal pain in the right lower quadrant. Detailed examination reveals rebound tenderness and fever. The patient MOST likely has

    A. pancreatitis.
    B. endometriosis.
    C. kidney stones.
    D. appendicitis.

20. You are called to care for a patient who was floating for 30 minutes in water at a temperature of 39.9°F (4.4°C) after his boat capsized. The patient is alert but confused. What should you do first?

    A. administer 100% oxygen
    B. move the patient to a warm area and then remove his clothing
    C. apply an AED
    D. apply heat packs to the patient's hands

21. You are evaluating an infant immediately after birth and find a pulse of 40 bpm. You stimulate the infant and provide oxygen with a non-rebreathing mask. You should next

    A. start compressions.
    B. attach the infant to an AED.
    C. administer epinephrine.
    D. allow the mother to hold the infant.

22. When communicating with a patient you should

    A. use medical terms to demonstrate competence.
    B. always remove bystanders to make the patient more comfortable.
    C. speak loudly to establish authority.
    D. ask open-ended questions to gather as much information as possible.

23. A patient found unconscious outside a bar wakes during assessment and states that he does not want to be transported. He knows the month and year, but he does not know where he is or how he got there. You may provide care for the patient because

    A. he is intoxicated.
    B. implied consent was given while he was unconscious.
    C. he is not competent.
    D. you cannot cease care once you have contact with the patient.

24. You are assessing a 72-year-old male patient with trouble breathing and pink, frothy sputum. The patient reports that he was treated for a myocardial infarction 2 weeks earlier. You should suspect the patient has developed

    A. pneumonia.
    B. pulmonary embolism.
    C. pulmonary edema.
    D. hemorrhagic stroke.

25. A patient with upper GI bleeding should be expected to have

    A. increased heart rate.
    B. decreased heart rate.
    C. warm, dry skin.
    D. bounding peripheral pulses.

26. After receiving online instruction from medical direction to help your asthmatic patient with their metered-dose inhaler, you should prepare the device by

    A. warming it for 10 seconds in the microwave.
    B. holding it upright and flicking the canister.
    C. shaking it vigorously.
    D. cooling it for 5 minutes in the refrigerator.

27. Online medical direction authorizes you to administer up to 3 doses of nitroglycerin to your patient, who has a chief complaint of chest pain. You know that you must wait at least how long between doses?

    A. 30 seconds
    B. 5 minutes
    C. 30 minutes
    D. 1 hour

28. Which of the following is NOT a reason to terminate CPR?

    A. The patient regains a pulse.
    B. Patient care is transferred to ALS providers.
    C. The patient is transported to a hospital.
    D. The patient's spouse asks you to stop.

29. During your secondary assessment of a 12-year-old boy who fell off his bike, you find an abrasion on his knee with slow and oozing bleeding that seems to be clotting itself. This bleeding would be categorized as

    A. venous.
    B. severe.
    C. capillary.
    D. profuse.

30. Your ambulance is dispatched to a middle school for a seventh-grade student who tripped and fell with a pencil in her hand. Upon arrival to the health office, you observe the patient in severe pain with the pencil impaled in her eye. Your intervention primarily consists of

    A. quickly removing the object.
    B. surrounding the object with gauze and stabilizing with a cup.
    C. irrigating the eye with saline solution.
    D. securing the patient to a long spine board.

31. After applying water-based lubricant to a nasopharyngeal airway, insert it
    A. as quickly as possible.
    B. by placing the bevel toward the septum.
    C. into one nostril while plugging the other.
    D. by placing the bevel toward the cheek.

32. A patient with partial thickness burns on 30 percent of his body is at risk for complications related to
    A. rhabdomyolysis.
    B. hyperglycemia.
    C. hypothermia.
    D. hemorrhagic stroke.

33. You arrive on a scene and discover an overturned semi hauling hazardous materials. Where should you park the ambulance?
    A. downwind from the accident
    B. as close to the semi as possible
    C. uphill from the accident
    D. on the road to block traffic

34. A 15-year-old female developed hives, difficulty breathing, and stridor after eating a peanut butter cookie. The definitive treatment for this patient is
    A. epinephrine.
    B. beta agonist.
    C. nitroglycerin.
    D. oxygen.

35. An abdominal stab wound to which organ is MOST likely to result in acute hemorrhage?
    A. stomach
    B. liver
    C. small intestine
    D. colon

36. A patient has pain and redness on her left forearm right after swimming in the ocean. She says that she saw a jellyfish and then her arm began to hurt. Her vital signs are stable, and she is not having any respiratory problems. You should
    A. wash with salt water and bandage the wound.
    B. remove the stinger with a credit card.
    C. immediately give the patient epinephrine.
    D. evacuate all swimmers from the beach and call animal control.

37. You apply a splint too tightly on a patient's lower leg and cut off circulation to the patient's foot. You do not notice and transport the patient to the hospital. You have most likely committed
    A. abandonment.
    B. assault and battery.
    C. negligence.
    D. false imprisonment.

38. To relieve chest discomfort in a patient with pericarditis, you should
    A. apply a heating pad to the patient's chest.
    B. apply cool compresses to the patient's chest.
    C. have the patient sit up and lean forward.
    D. administer sublingual nitroglycerin.

39. A contraindication for the insertion of an oropharyngeal airway is
    A. blockage from the tongue.
    B. bleeding within the mouth.
    C. an intact gag reflex.
    D. jugular vein distention.

40. What is the proper method for opening the airway of an unconscious patient who fell from the top of a 16-foot ladder?

  A. jaw-thrust maneuver
  B. head tilt–chin lift maneuver
  C. Heimlich maneuver
  D. Sellick maneuver

41. You respond to assist ocean lifeguards with an 18-year-old female who dove into a shallow sandbar and is now complaining of severe neck pain. Your assessment reveals a blood pressure of 88/66 mm Hg and a heart rate of 48 bpm. You believe this patient is exhibiting signs of

  A. concussion.
  B. neurogenic shock.
  C. hypothermia.
  D. septic shock.

42. You and your EMT partner are performing two-rescuer CPR on a pulseless and apneic adult patient. You are currently providing compressions and your partner is providing ventilation. You should plan to switch roles

  A. every 2 minutes.
  B. once the EMT performing compressions is too tired to continue.
  C. never, as this will waste critical time.
  D. after 2 cycles.

43. After being unable to rouse a 4-month-old child from an unresponsive state, you listen and feel for breathing while simultaneously palpating which pulse for 10 seconds?

  A. femoral
  B. vena cava
  C. ankle
  D. brachial

44. Aspirin is given to patients with chest pain because it

  A. dilates blood vessels
  B. slows blood clot formation
  C. relieves pain
  D. fights infections

45. You are treating a patient with a penetrating wound just above the clavicle. After applying a pressure dressing to the wound, you notice the blood begins to soak through the bandages. Your next step is to

  A. apply additional dressing.
  B. instruct the patient to lean back and let gravity control the bleeding.
  C. use a liquid bandage or glue to seal the wound.
  D. remove the dressing and apply a new one.

46. You arrive at a scene to find an adult male home alone with an open fracture of the ulna. The patient is speaking to you in a language you do not understand. You should

  A. use gestures to get nonverbal consent for treatment.
  B. not treat the patient until a translator can be found.
  C. ask the patient in loud, clear English if he consents to treatment.
  D. wait for the patient to lose consciousness and treat under implied consent.

47. A sunken fontanel on an infant is associated with

  A. dehydration.
  B. traumatic brain injury.
  C. hypotension.
  D. congenital defects.

48. You respond to a nursing home for a patient in cardiac arrest. The staff produces a do-not-resuscitate (DNR) order for the patient stating that the patient does not want medication during cardiac arrest. You should

- **A.** start CPR immediately.
- **B.** contact medical direction for pronouncement of death per protocols.
- **C.** call for ALS intercept to administer epinephrine.
- **D.** contact the patient's family and ask if they want CPR started.

49. What vital sign is taken to assess perfusion in patients under 3 years old?

- **A.** systolic blood pressure
- **B.** capillary refill
- **C.** brachial pulse
- **D.** rectal temperature

50. You are assessing a patient with chest pain who begins to act violently and throw items at you. What should you do?

- **A.** ask bystanders for help restraining the patient
- **B.** grab the patient and subdue him
- **C.** leave the scene
- **D.** retreat and call for law enforcement assistance

51. You are called to a high school for a 16-year-old football player who experienced a hard collision to the body. His chief complaint is difficulty breathing accompanied by one-sided chest pain. You palpate a deformity of the rib cage. This patient is likely experiencing

- **A.** traumatic pneumothorax.
- **B.** diaphragm spasm.
- **C.** renal failure.
- **D.** pulmonary edema.

52. Which of the following is NOT an indication for supplemental oxygen administration?

- **A.** altered level of consciousness
- **B.** abdominal pain
- **C.** shock
- **D.** cardiac arrest

53. A psychological emergency patient being transported to the hospital points at the back door of the ambulance and states she sees spiders. You should

- **A.** call for a different ambulance to transport the patient.
- **B.** tell her the spiders are real but are not dangerous.
- **C.** tell her there are no spiders.
- **D.** change the topic to distract the patient.

54. Which of the following can be applied to counteract neck flexion when opening the airway of a supine pediatric patient?

- **A.** manual in-line stabilization
- **B.** cervical collar
- **C.** padding under the shoulders
- **D.** pressure to the forehead

55. Many patients experiencing an aortic aneurysm present with

- **A.** jugular vein distention.
- **B.** low blood sugar.
- **C.** no symptoms.
- **D.** swelling in the lower extremities.

56. A fracture located at the base of the skull is known as which kind of fracture?

- **A.** linear
- **B.** crown
- **C.** basilar
- **D.** cervical

57. Upon your arrival for a patient complaining of intense shoulder pain after falling down a flight of stairs, you notice an obvious deformity at the joint, and you cannot palpate a distal pulse. You suspect this patient has experienced

   A. a compound fracture.
   B. a dislocation.
   C. sciatica.
   D. hyperextension.

58. You are preparing to take over chest compressions on a 44-year-old apneic patient in cardiac arrest. The depth of your compressions should be

   A. 1 – 6 inches.
   B. 2.0 – 2.4 inches.
   C. 25% of the depth of the chest.
   D. as deep as you can go.

59. During an initial assessment, you discover that the patient is not breathing. You should first

   A. check a pedal pulse.
   B. provide rescue breaths.
   C. request an ALS intercept.
   D. get the AED from the vehicle.

60. Blood pooling within the brain tissue is known as

   A. intracerebral hemorrhage.
   B. epidural hematoma.
   C. Battle's sign.
   D. compartment syndrome.

61. A 44-year-old male was involved in a motor vehicle crash (MVC), and you have determined the patient is unstable. You should immediately

   A. request police assistance.
   B. take the patient's vital signs.
   C. immediately splint any broken bones.
   D. perform a rapid head-to-toe assessment.

62. You are assessing an 11-month-old infant with a barking cough, a respiratory rate of 66, and a very runny nose. To help the patient's breathing, you should place the child

   A. sitting upright in a parent's lap.
   B. on a stretcher in a prone position.
   C. in reverse Trendelenburg.
   D. in semi-Fowler's.

63. A 35-year-old woman is confused and acting irrationally according to her friends. Her skin is cool and clammy, and her blood glucose level is 32. You should

   A. provide 100% oxygen via a non-rebreathing mask.
   B. provide the patient with oral glucose or sugar.
   C. provide immediate transport in left lateral recumbent position.
   D. restrain the patient and request an ALS unit.

64. A 17-year-old male presents with sudden-onset sharp chest pain. You note that he is tall and thin and that the pain is worse on deep inspiration. You should suspect

   A. spontaneous pneumothorax.
   B. esophageal rupture.
   C. diabetic ketoacidosis.
   D. ascending aortic rupture.

65. An electrician was wiring a circuit panel when he was shocked. He fell away from the panel, and another electrician shut off the power. You find the patient to be pulseless and apneic. You should

   A. treat the electrical burns and transport.
   B. begin CPR and apply the AED.
   C. move the patient away from the scene.
   D. provide rescue breathing and AED without compressions.

66. You arrive at the home of a patient who is suicidal. She is on a couch in the middle of a large room and appears to be agitated. Police are on scene as well. You should

  A. remain in the doorway.
  B. kneel in front of the patient.
  C. stand directly over the patient.
  D. make sure she has access to an exit.

67. A 25-year-old pregnant female calls 911 because she has started to have contractions. You evaluate the patient and find the infant is crowning and the mother is feeling the urge to push. You should

  A. immediately load-and-go to the hospital.
  B. instruct the mother not to push and prepare for transport.
  C. instruct the mother not to push until an ALS unit arrives.
  D. call for ALS and prepare to deliver the infant.

68. An 84-year-old male patient was found lying in a back bedroom. He is wearing a soiled diaper, and you observe animal feces in the room. The caregiver on scene is a 15-year-old girl who states that the man does not need any care. What should you do?

  A. assess the patient and allow the 15-year-old to sign a refusal form
  B. contact social services and file an adult neglect report
  C. move the patient to the shower and clean him before transport
  D. call for an ALS intercept to assist with care

69. Which of the following is NOT a symptom of hypertensive crisis?

  A. blurred vision
  B. ear ringing
  C. flushed skin
  D. nausea and vomiting

70. An 83-year-old male has a sudden onset of right-sided weakness with a splitting headache and slurred speech. The patient's symptoms are MOST likely being caused by

  A. stroke.
  B. myocardial infarction.
  C. diabetic ketoacidosis.
  D. hypoglycemia.

71. As you prepare to administer nitroglycerin to a patient experiencing chest pain, you must verify

  A. the expiration date of the medication.
  B. the patient's blood type.
  C. that you have the antidote to the nitroglycerin.
  D. that the patient has food to eat with it.

72. Cardiac arrest in children and infants is MOST often caused by

  A. respiratory arrest.
  B. accidental overdose.
  C. electrocution.
  D. acute coronary syndrome.

73. The AED pad placement for a 4-month-old patient is

  A. only one pad on the center of the chest.
  B. one pad directly on top of the other.
  C. one pad on the center of the chest and one on the center of the back.
  D. one pad on the upper right and one on the lower left chest.

74. Which of the following is NOT a common symptom of myocardial infarction?

  A. chest pressure or tightness
  B. diaphoresis
  C. nausea or vomiting
  D. wheezing or crackles

75. A hiker fell through ice while crossing a river and then hiked 2 hours to a vehicle access trail. At the trail, you note that the patient's feet are white, waxy, and hard to the touch. You should

- **A.** rub both feet to warm them.
- **B.** immerse both feet in warm water.
- **C.** splint both feet and give the patient oxygen.
- **D.** apply pressure dressing to both feet.

76. You are called to care for a roofer who has passed out on a hot day. The patient was acting confused before he passed out. He is now unconscious, hot, and dry. He MOST likely has

- **A.** heat cramps.
- **B.** heat exhaustion.
- **C.** heat stroke.
- **D.** heat rash.

77. During one-rescuer BVM ventilation, which technique is preferred to maintain a patent airway and proper mask seal?

- **A.** cricoid pressure
- **B.** vagal maneuvers
- **C.** "EC" clamp
- **D.** palm wrap

78. You receive a call for a 3-year-old who is having difficulty breathing. On assessment, you find the patient is in tripod position, wheezing on exhalation, and using accessory muscles. You should suspect

- **A.** pneumonia.
- **B.** pulmonary embolism.
- **C.** foreign body aspiration.
- **D.** asthma.

79. Your unconscious patient has excess secretions, including vomitus, in his mouth. After attaching the rigid catheter to the suction unit, your next step is to

- **A.** begin suctioning while inserting the catheter into the patient's oral airway.
- **B.** blindly swab the patient's mouth while applying suction.
- **C.** insert an airway adjunct and begin suctioning around it.
- **D.** position the tip of the catheter where it can be seen prior to applying suction.

80. Inadequate blood flow to the tissues and organs as the result of problems with the circulatory system is known as

- **A.** shock.
- **B.** hemorrhage.
- **C.** dyspnea.
- **D.** hypotension.

81. You respond to an adult patient bleeding significantly from blunt-force trauma to the head. The patient's heart rate is 130 bpm with a blood pressure of 102/68 mm Hg. The patient's skin is cool, pale, and diaphoretic. You suspect this patient is experiencing which of the following conditions secondary to the head trauma?

- **A.** neuropathy
- **B.** hemorrhagic shock
- **C.** anemia
- **D.** gastroenteritis

82. An EMS unit is dispatched to a residential address for a 58-year-old male with chest pain. You should report to dispatch when you

- **A.** arrive at the scene.
- **B.** enter the patient's home.
- **C.** begin assessing the patient.
- **D.** determine the nature of illness.

83. A 95-year-old woman is having severe abdominal pain and has been vomiting blood. The patient is confused and does not want to go to the hospital. Her son tells you that he wants her transported. You must transport the patient if

    A. the son has durable power of attorney.
    B. the son gives informed consent.
    C. the patient has a do-not-resuscitate order.
    D. the patient is competent.

84. You are caring for an 85-year-old man who has fallen down the stairs. When placing the patient on a backboard, what precaution should be implemented due to the patient's age?

    A. insert an airway adjunct after the patient has been secured on the backboard
    B. ensure the voids between the patient and backboard are padded
    C. check carotid pulse every 5 minutes
    D. restrain the patient before placing him on the backboard

85. You are preparing to deliver an infant. You notice that when the water breaks the fluid is light green. You know that the fluid is

    A. a normal color.
    B. stained with meconium.
    C. mixed with blood.
    D. infected with bacteria.

86. A 17-year-old patient has explained to you that she does not want to be transported. Her parents are not on scene. The patient can refuse care if she is

    A. competent.
    B. an emancipated minor.
    C. pregnant.
    D. accompanied by a grandparent.

87. A college student dove into a shallow lake and struck his head on the bottom, hyperextending his neck. He is floating facedown in 2 feet of water. You should

    A. pull the patient from the water by his arms.
    B. slide a backboard under the patient and pull him out prone.
    C. lift the patient's head out of the water and check for breathing.
    D. move the patient's arms above his head and grasp his biceps while rotating him face up.

88. While the AED is analyzing the patient's heart rhythm, the EMT should

    A. briefly discontinue CPR.
    B. check pulse and breathing for no longer than 10 seconds.
    C. insert an airway adjunct.
    D. raise the patient's legs above heart level.

89. A patient has just delivered an infant. You should first

    A. check the infant for a brachial pulse.
    B. suction the infant's mouth and nose.
    C. lift the infant and slap its feet.
    D. rub the infant vigorously.

90. Which of the following is a life-threatening source of chest pain?

    A. indigestion
    B. rib fracture
    C. pneumothorax
    D. sternum contusion

91. You are assessing an infant immediately after birth. Findings are as follows:

pink trunk with blue extremities

pulse of 120 bpm

strong vigorous cry

moving spontaneously

breathing well

What is the infant's APGAR score?

A. 7

B. 8

C. 9

D. 10

92. You respond to a 6-month-old patient with a weak brachial pulse and no respirations. After opening the airway, you provide artificial ventilation at a rate of

A. 1 – 6 breaths per minute.

B. 10 breaths per minute.

C. 12 – 20 breaths per minute.

D. 60 breaths per minute.

93. Which of the following is true for the mouth-to-mouth form of artificial ventilation?

A. It should never be used.

B. It is recommended only for patients whose medical history is known.

C. It should be used only on immediate family members.

D. It is not recommended unless no other methods are available.

94. You are triaging patients at the scene of a multi-car motor vehicle crash. Which patient is at highest risk for a crush injury?

A. an unrestrained passenger

B. one who was ambulatory at the scene

C. one who was ejected from the vehicle

D. one with a prolonged extraction

95. Which dressing would be MOST appropriate for a patient with a partial thickness wound to the epidermis?

A. transparent dressing

B. occlusive dressing

C. nonstick adherent dressing

D. bulky dressing

96. You are assessing a 14-year-old patient with delirium, respiratory distress, and headache. Upon examination of the airway, you note a burn to the roof of the patient's mouth. You should suspect

A. ingestion of a hot beverage.

B. inhalation of chemicals from a compressed gas can.

C. ingestion of dry ice.

D. marijuana use.

97. Which appearance is MOST consistent with an avulsion?

A. open wound with presence of sloughing and eschar tissue

B. skin tear with approximated edges

C. shearing of the top epidermal layers

D. separation of skin from the underlying structures that cannot be approximated

98. Approximately 90 minutes after a catastrophic earthquake, you are dispatched to the treatment area of a partial building collapse. Rescue workers bring you a 34-year-old female with an obvious and significant leg deformity who has just been extricated from underneath the rubble. You suspect your patient has

A. syncope.

B. deviated septum.

C. rhabdomyolysis.

D. hemorrhagic stroke.

99. A patient with emphysema tells you that he feels like he can't breathe. You should help the patient so he is

- A. lying flat on his back.
- B. in a prone position.
- C. sitting up and leaning forward.
- D. lying on his side with feet elevated.

100. A patient with a history of deep vein thrombosis who is complaining of sudden difficulty breathing along with chest pain that worsens with deep breaths is possibly experiencing

- A. appendicitis.
- B. kidney stones.
- C. pulmonary embolism.
- D. congestive heart failure.

101. Which of the following is NOT a symptom included in Cushing's triad?

- A. altered respiratory pattern
- B. pinpoint pupils
- C. hypertension
- D. bradycardia

102. Hyperventilation syndrome is MOST often caused by

- A. air pollution.
- B. allergic reaction.
- C. psychological reasons.
- D. painful stimuli.

103. An unresponsive patient in ventricular fibrillation requires

- A. epinephrine.
- B. nitroglycerin
- C. low-flow oxygen.
- D. defibrillation.

104. As an EMT in a mountainous region, you come across a patient from out of town who recently hiked quickly to the top of a tall peak and is now experiencing dyspnea, fatigue, and a worsening cough. You suspect this patient has

- A. high-altitude pulmonary edema.
- B. decompression sickness.
- C. respiratory failure
- D. pneumonia.

105. The hardening and narrowing of the arteries due to plaque buildup is known as

- A. aneurysm.
- B. atherosclerosis.
- C. thrombosis.
- D. melanoma.

106. While completing the SAMPLE history of your hypertensive patient, she tells you her ears are ringing. Which of the following terms do you use to note this symptom in your patient care report?

- A. photophobia
- B. tinnitus
- C. audiography
- D. migraine

107. You respond to the laboratory of a local university for a 19-year-old research assistant who inadvertently spilled a chemical on her torso. After treating the patient, your EMT partner is preparing to load her in the ambulance. Before leaving the scene, you should

- A. attempt to neutralize the residual chemical.
- B. obtain a sample of the chemical and bring it to the hospital.
- C. test the chemical for acidity.
- D. document the chemical name and its properties.

108. A patient with an oxygen saturation of 84% would be considered

- A. normal.
- B. mildly hypoxic.
- C. moderately hypoxic.
- D. severely hypoxic.

109. Which of the following is a psychological disorder characterized by severe mood swings between mania and depression?

- A. anxiety
- B. bipolar disorder
- C. schizophrenia
- D. clinical depression

110. During a history, a patient states that they have recently started taking Adderall for attention-deficit/hyperactivity disorder. The EMT knows that this drug places the patient at a higher risk for

- A. seizures
- B. renal failure
- C. stroke
- D. bradycardia

111. You arrive at a scene to find a woman clutching her throat. When you ask if she is choking, she is unable to speak but nods yes. You should first

- A. establish an airway by tilting the chin back
- B. administer five quick chest compressions
- C. administer two rescue breaths
- D. perform the abdominal-thrust maneuver

112. Oxygen cylinders should always be stored

- A. in a heated room.
- B. in an approved flammable gas cabinet.
- C. on their side.
- D. upright.

113. The use of standard precautions is required for contact with all of the following EXCEPT

- A. blood
- B. urine
- C. sweat
- D. vomit

114. Which of the following medications is prescribed to patients at high risk for deep vein thrombosis?

- A. Celebrex (celecoxib)
- B. Ambien (zolpidem)
- C. Topamax (topiramate)
- D. Xarelto (rivaroxaban)

115. Breathing that does not support life due to insufficient oxygen intake is known as

- A. asystole.
- B. respiratory arrest.
- C. respiratory failure.
- D. pulmonary shock.

116. You are treating an apneic patient with a tracheostomy. What are the proper steps for ventilation?

- A. wait for ALS to intubate the patient
- B. cover the tracheal opening and ventilate through the mouth and nose
- C. provide high-flow supplemental oxygen blow-by
- D. attach the one-way valve of a pocket mask or BVM directly to the trach tube

117. Septic shock results from

- A. head trauma.
- B. significant infection.
- C. traumatic blood loss.
- D. prolonged exposure to cold temperatures.

118. Your 12-year-old female patient plays multiple types of contact sports. After a sporting event, she complains of chest pain at the point where her ribs meet her breastbone. While palpating this area you notice it is inflamed. You suspect she most likely has

   A. costochondritis.
   B. flail segment.
   C. heartburn.
   D. floating ribs.

119. Which of the following types of blast injuries is caused by the human body being thrown against a hard surface after an explosion?

   A. secondary
   B. shockwave
   C. tertiary
   D. ferrous

120. A patient has acknowledged your arrival on scene and is asking for help. The patient has given

   A. direct consent.
   B. written consent.
   C. implied consent.
   D. expressed consent.

ANSWER KEY

1. A.
For nasopharyngeal airway placement, measure from the opening of the nostril to the tip of the earlobe.

2. B.
Nitroglycerin is contraindicated in the presence of a systolic blood pressure of less than 100 mm Hg.

3. C.
Patients requiring CPR must be moved onto a hard surface before starting compressions.

4. A.
Using the rule of palm, also known as the rule of one, the size of the patient's palm is approximately 1% of their body surface area.

5. D.
The right upper quadrant contains the liver, pancreas, gallbladder, small intestine, and colon. The liver is a vascular organ, and significant bruising may result if it is injured.

6. D.
When checking a patient's level of consciousness, use the acronym AVPU (Alert, Verbal, Pain, Unresponsive). An **A**lert patient answers questions. In response to **V**erbal prompting, the patient moans or moves when being called. In this scenario, the patient responds to a physical or **P**ainful stimulus. An **U**nresponsive patient does not respond at all.

7. C.
This patient is experiencing diabetic ketoacidosis, which is determined by the blood glucose reading. A blood glucose of less than 70 is hypoglycemia, above 200 is hyperglycemia, from 350 to 800 is diabetic ketoacidosis, and above 800 is hyperglycemic hyperosmolar syndrome.

8. B.
The patient had a transient ischemic attack (TIA). The symptoms of TIA resolve themselves with no permanent effects.

9. D.
Classic signs of cardiogenic shock include hypotension; a rapid pulse that weakens; cool, clammy skin; and decreased urine output.

10. A.
Since a traction splint cannot be applied due to a suspected pelvic fracture, the next best choice is to secure the patient to a long spine board.

11. B.
The priority intervention for a patient with SpO_2 below 94% is supplemental oxygen. If the patient has an albuterol nebulizer, it may be administered after supplemental oxygen has been started.

12. A.
CPR should resume immediately after delivering a shock from an AED.

13. A.
Angina pectoris, or simply angina, is the term describing chest pain resulting from poor blood flow to the heart.

14. D.
COPD (chronic obstructive pulmonary disease) is most commonly caused by smoking. The chronic cough associated with COPD is often exacerbated by lung infection.

15. D.
Amputated appendages should be wrapped in sterile gauze moistened with saline before being placed on ice. They should never be frozen.

16. C.
An occlusive dressing should be applied to any open neck wound to prevent an air embolus from entering the blood vessels.

17. C.
If the scene is not safe, you should not enter the scene. You should contact the appropriate agency to mitigate the hazard (in this case, the police).

18. **B.**

To sue for malpractice the patient needs to prove four things: the EMT had a duty to act; the EMT acted improperly; the EMT was the cause of the injury; and there was an injury or harm caused by the action.

19. **D.**

Appendicitis typically presents with a fever, right lower quadrant pain, and rebound tenderness. Occasionally the patient will have referred pain around the umbilicus.

20. **B.**

Move the patient to a warm area like the back of the ambulance or a building. Remove wet clothes to facilitate rewarming.

21. **A.**

You should start CPR if the pulse of a newborn infant is less than 60 bpm. You should also request ALS intercept.

22. **D.**

Asking patients open-ended questions (as opposed to yes/no questions) will help you gather more information about the patient and scene.

23. **C.**

This patient would not be considered competent to deny care because he is unable to demonstrate that he knows where he is or the history of present illness.

24. **C.**

The patient is experiencing symptoms of pulmonary edema, a complication of left-sided heart failure.

25. **A.**

Upper GI bleeding causes signs and symptoms of hypovolemia, including tachycardia; cold, clammy skin; and weak peripheral pulses.

26. **C.**

Inhalers contain a propellant in addition to medication. Shaking the inhaler prior to administration ensures a proper mixture of medication and propellant.

27. **B.**

Multiple doses of nitroglycerin should be separated by at least 5 minutes.

28. **D.**

CPR should continue unless the patient regains a pulse or patient care is transferred to someone of equal or higher training, such as an ALS provider or emergency room physician.

29. **C.**

Capillary bleeding is slow and oozing. It is usually a result of minor abrasions and can sometimes clot itself.

30. **B.**

Objects impaled in the eye should first be stabilized with soft material such as folded or rolled gauze, then protected with rigid stabilization such as a paper cup.

31. **B.**

To insert a nasopharyngeal airway, place the bevel (angled portion) toward the septum and smoothly slide it in.

32. **C.**

Damage to the skin caused by burns with large body surface area affects the body's ability to thermoregulate and puts patients at risk for hypothermia.

33. **C.**

As part of scene size-up, you should determine the best location to park the ambulance. At a HazMat incident, be sure to park uphill, upwind, and upstream to prevent the hazardous materials from contaminating the ambulance.

34. **A.**

The symptoms described indicate anaphylactic shock. The definitive treatment for this is epinephrine (often in the form of an EpiPen).

35. **B.**

Solid organ (e.g., liver) injury usually results in hemorrhage, while hollow organ (e.g., stomach, small intestine, colon) injuries lead to spillage of gastrointestinal contents.

36. **A.**

As with other animal bites or insect stings, if there is no concern of an anaphylactic reaction, you should clean and bandage the wound. Jellyfish stings should be washed with salt water.

37. C.

Providing improper care for a patient may be negligence.

38. C.

Sitting up and leaning forward will pull the inflamed cardiac sac away from the muscle and relieve the chest discomfort.

39. C.

An oropharyngeal airway should not be inserted when the patient has an intact gag reflex, as this may cause vomiting and aspiration.

40. A.

The jaw-thrust maneuver is used to open the airway of trauma patients with suspected head, neck, or back injury.

41. B.

Key findings for neurogenic shock include spinal trauma combined with significantly low blood pressure and bradycardia.

42. A.

When two EMTs are performing CPR, they should switch roles every 5 cycles to avoid fatigue. Five cycles should take approximately 2 minutes.

43. D.

The brachial artery of the upper arm is used to check the pulse of infants.

44. B.

The mechanism of action of aspirin includes antiplatelet properties that reduce the likelihood of blood clots forming.

45. A.

If the wound continues to bleed through and a tourniquet is not an option, apply additional dressing. Never remove a pressure dressing once it has been applied.

46. A.

When a patient does not speak English, you may use gestures to get implied consent (e.g., you may gesture at the patient's arm, and the patient may nod or lift the arm in response).

47. A.

If the fontanel is sunken the infant could be dehydrated.

48. A.

DNR orders may indicate specific treatments that should be withheld. You should read the DNR order and follow the patient's wishes documented on it. Because the DNR only addresses medication, you should initiate CPR.

49. B.

Capillary refill is used to assess perfusion in children less than 3 years old.

50. D.

When faced with a patient who suddenly becomes violent, retreat from the scene and call for help to protect the safety of the patient, bystanders, and yourself.

51. A.

Traumatic pneumothorax is the result of thoracic trauma and often presents with unilateral chest pain and dyspnea.

52. B.

Altered level of consciousness, shock, and cardiac arrest are all indications for prehospital supplemental oxygen.

53. D.

When caring for a patient having delusions, do not confirm or deny the delusion. Confirming plays into the delusion, and denying may cause an altercation. Change the subject or distract the patient by reassessing vital signs or with conversation.

54. C.

Placing padding under the shoulders of a pediatric patient can counter neck flexion and reduce the risk of injury while opening the airway.

55. C.

Aortic aneurysms can develop slowly over time, with no obvious symptoms among many patients.

56. C.

Basilar fractures are those that occur at the base of the skull.

57. B.

Dislocations occur at the joint and are caused by sudden significant force, such as falls. The shoulder is a common joint for dislocation, and the symptoms will likely include a deformity along with intense, localized pain. Severe dislocations can cause vascular disruption.

58. B.

Current guidelines for adult CPR indicate a chest compression depth of 2.0 – 2.4 inches.

59. B.

When you find a problem during the initial assessment, correct the problem before moving to the next step. Here, the EMT finds during the initial assessment that the patient is not breathing, so the EMT should provide rescue breaths immediately.

60. A.

Intracerebral hemorrhage is the pooling of blood within the brain tissue.

61. D.

In trauma situations, perform a rapid head-to-toe assessment in unstable patients. You should also transport immediately.

62. A.

The child should remain with the parent in an upright position. Taking the child from the parent could cause anxiety and crying and worsen the respiratory distress.

63. B.

This patient has hypoglycemia. She should be given sugar orally if she is conscious.

64. A.

Tall, thin teenage males are the most likely population to experience a spontaneous pneumothorax. Symptoms typically arise suddenly with pain worsening on inspiration.

65. B.

Pulseless patients who have been electrocuted respond well to CPR and AED use.

66. D.

The patient is agitated. Do not put yourself in a position where you could be injured if the patient becomes combative. Always look for an exit route before needing it.

67. D.

If birth is imminent, call for ALS and prepare to deliver the infant on scene. Signs of imminent birth include contractions less than 2 minutes apart, crowning, and feeling the urge to push. If the mother has had multiple births and says she is about to give birth, that is also a sign of imminent birth.

68. B.

EMTs who observe adult abuse or neglect have a responsibility to file a complaint with the appropriate social service government agency.

69. C.

Flushed skin is not a symptom of hypertensive crisis.

70. A.

The patient is most likely having a stroke. Strokes can present with one-sided weakness or numbness, facial droop, headache, slurred speech, confusion, or altered mental status.

71. A.

The expiration date of medication should always be verified early to ensure it can be used.

72. A.

Respiratory arrest is the most common cause of cardiac arrest in infants and children.

73. C.

For infants and small children, it will likely be necessary to apply one pad to the center of the chest and the second pad to the center of the back.

74. D.

Wheezing and crackles are not symptoms of myocardial infarction.

75. C.

The patient has frostbite. Handle the feet gently and splint them. Administer oxygen to the patient.

76. C.

A patient with heat stroke may be found unconscious; confused; and with hot, dry skin. The patient will no longer be sweating.

77. C.

The "EC" clamp, achieved by placing the fingers in the shape of an "E" and "C," is the preferred method for achieving an effective face seal during one-rescuer BVM ventilation.

78. D.

The child is presenting with signs of asthma exacerbation, including trouble breathing, tripod positioning, wheezing on exhalation, and use of accessory muscles.

79. D.

The tip of the catheter should be positioned before applying suction and only in places where it can be seen.

80. A.

Shock, or hypoperfusion, is a state of inadequate blood flow to the tissues and organs.

81. B.

Tachycardia and hypotension are symptoms of hemorrhagic shock along with cool, pale, and moist skin. Hemorrhagic shock, a form of hypovolemic shock, is most often caused by trauma.

82. A.

The EMS unit should report to the dispatcher when they have arrived at the scene.

83. A.

Durable power of attorney gives an individual the power to make medical decisions for another person.

84. B.

Patients over 65 have a loss in fatty tissue and joints that do not move as well as those of a younger patient. Padding the voids will make the backboard much more comfortable for the patient.

85. B.

The fluid is stained with meconium (the infant's feces).

86. B.

An emancipated minor can make choices regarding their medical care as long as they are competent.

87. D.

Use care in removing the patient from the water due to the likelihood of a spinal cord injury. Maintain in-line stabilization and rotate the patient face up to clear the airway.

88. A.

CPR should be momentarily halted, and nobody should touch the patient while the AED is analyzing the patient's heart rhythm.

89. B.

To stimulate breathing after the infant is born, suction the mouth and nose.

90. C.

Pneumothorax is a life-threatening source of chest pain.

91. C.

The APGAR score is 9.

pink trunk with blue extremities: 1

pulse of 120 bpm: 2

strong vigorous cry: 2

moving spontaneously: 2

breathing well: 2

92. C.

The rate of artificial ventilations for infants and children is 12 – 20 breaths per minute.

93. D.

Mouth-to-mouth is recommended only if there are no other means available for artificial ventilation.

94. D.

A patient in a motor vehicle crash with a prolonged extraction will likely have sustained compressing or crushing force or pressure damaging underlying vascular and musculoskeletal structures.

95. C.

Nonstick adherent dressing such as a Telfa pad is the appropriate choice.

96. B.

Adolescent patients presenting with frostbite burns to the roof of the mouth are most likely abusing inhalants, typically in the form of aerosols, glues, paints, and solvents.

97. D.

An avulsion is characterized by the separation of skin from the underlying structures that cannot be approximated.

98. C.

Crush pressure that is sustained for a long period (> 60 minutes) can lead to a rapid breakdown of muscle tissue known as rhabdomyolysis. Sometimes shortened to "rhabdo," this condition is the second leading cause of death following earthquakes.

99. C.

A patient with emphysema can improve their breathing by sitting up and leaning forward.

100. C.

The most common form of pulmonary embolism (PE) is a blood clot due to deep vein thrombosis. A key symptom of PE is pleuritic chest pain that worsens upon inhalation and exhalation.

101. B.

Cushing's triad, a sign of increased intracranial pressure and/or herniation syndrome, does not include pinpoint pupils.

102. C.

While hyperventilation can be caused by an underlying medical condition, it is most often a result of a psychological concern.

103. D.

Ventricular fibrillation is a shockable dysrhythmia that requires defibrillation to return the heart to a sinus rhythm.

104. A.

High-altitude pulmonary edema occurs after a rapid ascent to altitudes greater than 8,200 feet.

105. B.

Atherosclerosis occurs when arteries are hardened and/or narrowed due to the deposition of fatty plaques on the inner walls.

106. B.

Tinnitus is the medical term for the perception of ringing in the ears.

107. D.

If possible, you should document the chemical name and its properties and provide this information to the receiving hospital. Never bring chemicals into the ambulance or hospital.

108. D.

A patient with a pulse oxygenation of less than 85% is considered severely hypoxic.

109. B.

Bipolar disorder is characterized by extreme shifts between mania and depression.

110. A.

Seizures are a serious, adverse drug effect that may occur when taking Adderall.

111. D.

In responsive patients with airway obstruction, the first intervention should be the abdominal-thrust (Heimlich) maneuver.

112. C.

To prevent damage to the regulator and valve, oxygen cylinders should be stored on their side so they cannot fall or be knocked over.

113. C.

Standard precautions are recommended whenever the nurse comes in contact with blood or body fluids that could transmit blood-borne pathogens.

114. D.

Xarelto (rivaroxaban) is an anticoagulant that helps prevent clots and DVT.

115. C.

A patient in respiratory failure is still breathing, but the breaths are not sufficient to support life.

116. D.

The universal fitting on the one-way valve of pocket masks and BVMs will attach directly to a tracheostomy tube.

117. B.

Septic shock is the result of a massive infection, typically of the urinary or respiratory tract, damaging the blood vessels.

118. A.
Costochondritis is an inflammation of the junction where the ribs and sternum meet. This condition can be caused by repeated minor chest trauma.

119. C.
Tertiary blast injuries are those caused by the human body being thrown into a hard surface, such as a wall, by the blast force of the explosion.

120. D.
A patient verbally asking for help is giving expressed consent.

Follow the link for your second EMT practice test: **ascenciatestprep.com/emt-online-resources**

www.ingramcontent.com/pod-product-compliance
Lightning Source LLC
Chambersburg PA
CBHW080334170426
43194CB00014B/2562